The Production, Distribution and
Readership of a Conservative Journal
of the Early French Revolution:

The *Ami du Roi*
of the
Abbé Royou

L'AMI DU ROI,

PAR L'OMBRE

DE L'ABBÉ ROYOU.

Le ciel est pour les Dieux, la terre pour les Rois.

Il siége enfin sur le trône de Saint-Louis, notre roi débonnaire. L'ivresse est générale ; les patriotes sont dans le deuil ; nous espérons bientôt les rappeler à leur serment *vivre libre ou mourir !* et le miasme de la royauté, comme disoient leurs écrivains, leur doit être mortel. Qu'ils se pendent tous, je leur conseille, pour nous épargner les frais d'exécution : le trésor royal auroit besoin de cette petite économie ; j'en connois plusieurs qui sont décidés à prendre ce parti. Ah ! mes chers conventionnels ! et vous tous, rogneux Rhadamantes des administrations républicaines, qui faisiez de si longues listes d'émigrés, dépêchez-vous, l'exé-

First page of Royou's journal

The Production, Distribution and
Readership of a Conservative Journal
of the Early French Revolution:

The *Ami du Roi*
of the
Abbé Royou

Harvey Chisick

American Philosophical Society
Independence Square ● Philadelphia
1992

MEMOIRS OF THE
AMERICAN PHILOSOPHICAL SOCIETY
Held at Philadelphia
For Promoting Useful Knowledge
Volume 198

Library of Congress Catalog Card Number 91-57945
International Standard Book Number 0-87169-198-1
US ISSN 0065-9738

For my Parents
with Affection and Respect

CONTENTS

NOTE ON CITATIONS FROM
EIGHTEENTH-CENTURY SOURCES

I have translated almost all citations from French into
English. In doing so I have preserved the irregularities of
the originals. Passages cited in French retain original spelling
and punctuation.

Preface

This is a book that I never intended to write, but which, over the last years, more or less imposed itself on me. I came across the documents that form the heart of this study, the subscription lists to the *Ami du Roi*, by mistake. For more than ten years now I have been working on a comparative study of the *Année Littéraire* and *Journal Encyclopédique*. The study of these two journals, as I conceived it, would have three parts. The first would treat the sociology of the journals, the second would be a quantitative analysis of content along the lines laid down by Ehrard and Roger in their pioneering study of the *Journal des Savants* and the *Mémoires de Trévoux*, and the third would proceed in the manner of traditional textual analysis. I had reduced the periods I wished to study to manageable dimensions by concentrating on the years 1762/63, 1773/74 and 1783/84, and had made an analysis of the text of the journals for these years, so that I was ready to write the second and third parts of the study, but I lacked materials for the first part, particularly on readership.

Correspondence with M. de Weissenbruch, who maintains the archives of the *Journal Encyclopédique*, indicated that no subscription lists to that journal have survived. My attempts to discover the same kind of source for the *Année Littéraire* appeared to have ended more happily when I found a reference to several registers of subscribers to Fréron's journal in an inventory of sources for literary history in the Archives Nationales. Though one of the registers did in fact contain a short list of subscribers to the *Année Littéraire*, it soon became clear that the large registers, the most extensive of which did not carry the name of a paper at all, could not belong to the *Année Littéraire*. Two of the registers bore the name of the *Ami du Roi*, and the third, it became apparent, was for the same paper. On the one hand I was distressed that I had made little progress in my attempt to discover who bought

Fréron's journal during the old regime, but on the other, I was now aware how rare documents of this kind were, and I could not help but be impressed by their extent. It seemed worthwhile to leave my pursuit of the publics of the *Année Littéraire* and *Journal Encyclopédique* for what I expected would be a short while, and work through the subscription lists of the *Ami du Roi*. More easily thought than done.

The three registers in the Archives Nationales series T*546 contained a total of roughly 7,000 names with information on geographical distribution, gender, status and occupations of subscribers, as well as on how subscriptions were made. Moreover, full as these lists were, they were heavily weighted toward the provinces. Writing about the *Ami du Roi* in the first volume of the *Histoire générale de la presse française*, Jacques Godechot asserted that, "It has not been possible to discover the list of provincial subscribers . . ." (p. 485). This led me to believe that he or his source had discovered the lists of Parisian subscribers. I therefore planned a trip to Paris to find and use these lists, and so complete my study of the subscribers to the *Ami du Roi*. After several days examining the series C, D and F in the Archives Nationales I concluded that if the lists in question indeed existed, it would take a more resourceful researcher than I to uncover them. Unexpectedly finding myself with several weeks to use in the archives, I began examining the contents of carton T546 for what it might be able to tell me about the public of the *Ami du Roi*.

The initial result was disappointing. The documents in the carton added little if anything to what could be learned from the registers about subscribers to the paper. Once they were classified and organized, however, they threw a good deal of light on the way the paper was produced, managed and organized. Thus instead of completing my study of the readership of the *Ami du Roi*, I found myself drawn into another area of press history. It soon became obvious that one or two articles could not be made to contain the information on the *Ami du Roi* and its subscribers that by virtue of its intrinsic value I thought deserved to be made public. There was nothing for it but to do the reading and supplementary research necessary to integrate the *Ami du Roi* into the history of the press and of the Revolution, and then to try to write a monograph that would do justice to a subject that I had not chosen, but that had slowly grown, as if by a logic and will of its own.

In the course of preparing this study I have incurred debts of various sorts that I wish to acknowledge here. The Research Committee of the Faculty of Humanities of the University of Haifa provided a grant which made it possible to hire an assistant to help with the coding of information on subscribers to the *Ami du Roi* and the clerical staff that transcribed this material to machine-readable form. The Research Authority of the university has since generously provided the support services necessary for producing a study of this kind. While this book was begun at Haifa and received its final form here, the second half of it was written and many revisions were carried out during a sabbatical leave in Vancouver, Canada. I wish to express my appreciation to the Department of History of the University of British Columbia for hosting me and making available the resources I needed during the academic years 1986/87 and 1987/88. I would particularly like to thank Al Tully, Dick Unger, Peter Ward, Ed Hundert and Harvey Mitchell for their help and hospitality during this time.

In working on this book I have benefited from the generous and able help of a large number of people. I would like first to acknowledge the assistance of the archivists, librarians and personnel of the Archives Nationales, Bibliothèque Nationale, Minutier Central and the Archives de la Préfecture de Police of Paris where most of the research on which this study is based was carried out. Without their help and cooperation my work would have proceeded more slowly and painfully than it in fact did.

The task of coding the roughly seven thousand cases of

subscribers to the *Ami du Roi* for eleven variables was shared by Yossi Trilnik in the formal capacity of research assistant. In practice, Mr. Trilnik worked with me as a colleague. The curiosity, critical intelligence and capacity for detailed analysis that he brought to our shared task led me to believe that he was capable of carrying out his own projects of comparable scope. His consistent good humor and willingness to help further increased my appreciation of his collaboration.

Having embarked on a project to which computer analysis of quantitative data was essential, but lacking experience with statistical programs, I drew heavily on the abilities and good will of a series of consultants at the Haifa University computer facility. I would particularly like to thank my friend and colleague, Dr. Udi Makov of the Department of Statistics at Haifa University, for having taken the time to write programs and to solve problems that were beyond my limited abilities. The incisiveness and elegance of his solutions were as impressive as they were humbling.

Before the advent of word processing, the preparation of a typescript was arduous, but straightforward. With computers this task should in theory be easier, but in practice often is not. And where mainframes use different languages and are not always compatible with personal computers, the task becomes significantly more complicated. At different stages Heather Kernoff, Angela Greenson and Danielle Friedlander all worked on the manuscript. The final draft was produced efficiently and with inexhaustible good humor by Heather Kernoff. Her willingness to make yet another set of alterations and corrections went well beyond her formal obligations and calls for a special expression of thanks.

The final versions of the graphs and maps were drawn with care and accuracy by Aliza Stokelman of the Geography Laboratory at the University of Haifa. Yossi Trilnik drew the map on which Figure 5.1 is based.

The final form this study has taken owes much to the close and constructive criticisms of John Gilchrist and Peter Paret.

I wish to thank both scholars for the exceptional care they took in reading the manuscript and for the constructive nature of their comments. At the American Philosophical Society, Associate Editor Carole N. Le Faivre guided the manuscript through the process of publication in an admirably efficient and helpful manner. I am also indebted to the copy editor of this book, Tamara Stech, for catching many more errors than I thought it possible to have survived so many revisions and for making innumerable improvements in style.

I would also like to acknowledge the patience and help of friends and colleagues who contributed to the elaboration of this study. Menahem Kellner and Peter Sorek listened with apparent good cheer to more talk about journalism and the readers of newspapers during the French Revolution than nonspecialists should decently be subjected to. Robert Forster, Harvey Mitchell, Mary Lynn Stewart and Jack Censer read the entire manuscript and offered many valuable criticisms and suggestions. In return I wish to express my gratitude, and to accept responsibility for any errors of fact or interpretation that remain.

The editors of *French Historical Studies* have kindly permitted me to use in Chapter IV material that has already appeared in an article published in that journal in 1988. I wish to express my appreciation for their having done so.

Finally, I would like to thank my family for their support and toleration while I was researching and writing this book. My daughters, Rachel and Michelle, in their frequent and noisy trips into my study introduced an atmosphere of spontaneity, enthusiasm (unrelated to the eighteenth century) and disorder not inappropriate to the period I was writing about. My wife, Tammy, who wondered that my penchant for lost causes should extend to the conservative press in a time of revolution, offered a combination of moral and practical support and ironic toleration. For all of which I am most grateful.

Harvey Chisick
Haifa, September 1989

ABBEVIATIONS
AN	Archives Nationales
APP	Archives de la Préfecture de Police
AR	*Ami du Roi*
BN	Bibliothèque Nationale
FHS	*French Historical Studies*
MC	Minutier Central
P&P	*Past & Present*
RH	*Revue Historique*
RHMC	*Revue d'Histoire Moderne et Contemporaine*
VS	*Studies on Voltaire and the Eighteenth Century*

INTRODUCTION*

What follows is the history of a newspaper with scant reference to its text. Rather, emphasis is placed on the production, distribution and readership of the paper. There are a number of reasons I have chosen this course. First, the content of the *Ami du Roi* has recently received close attention from two competent scholars.[1] Since the writing of history ought to be cumulative, I have refrained from saying again what has recently been well said. Where I differ in interpretation from Bertaud and Murray, I indicate this. For the most part, I find little to quarrel with in their analyses of the content of the *Ami du Roi*. This study is devoted to other issues.

The second reason I have chosen to treat the content of the *Ami du Roi* cursorily is that I believe a journal is more than its text. How a newspaper, or any other genre of literature, is produced and distributed, whom it is intended for and who reads it are integral parts of the history of any kind of writing. Historians primarily interested in ideas and their development need not, it is true, concern themselves with these questions. But historians of the press interested in these and related issues often find themselves at a loss for sources, for the techniques of production and the business practices involved in producing, distributing and managing a paper seldom leave the records we would like to have of them. Yet these questions significantly influence a paper's success or failure.

Whether, for example, a paper produced in Paris was granted a preferential postal tariff determined, to a considerable degree, whether or not it could expect to have a large provincial readership. So too could a paper's relations with

---

* For full references to footnotes, see the Bibliography.
[1] See J.-P. Bertaud, *Les Amis du Roi: Journaux et journalistes royalistes en France de 1789 à 1792*, and W.J. Murray, *The Right-Wing Press in the French Revolution: 1789–1792*.

local booksellers. Similarly, in evaluating a paper's influence, historians want to know not only what a paper said, but also how it was distributed. Was the size of the press run determined by the number of subscribers, or were copies printed for casual sale by booksellers or street vendors? And whatever a newspaper's political orientation, did it reach its readers soon enough after the events it described so that the information it contained still seemed fresh? Who bought and read newspapers? The approach and methods of the *histoire du livre* can answer, more or less fully, questions such as these which traditional textual analysis tends to leave aside.

Thanks to chance, and to the revolutionary police, the records of the *Ami du Roi* contain the information necessary for answering the kinds of questions just raised.[2] This information is seldom as full as we would like, but it does allow systematic analysis. That is to say, much of this material is serial in nature, and lends itself to quantification. To be sure, these data are far from complete, so that tables derived from them cannot reflect the full contemporary reality. But they do represent more than impressions or isolated instances. The years covered by these records—September 1790 to May 1792—were as exceptional for publishing as they were for much else. It was a time during which the government allowed almost unlimited freedom of the press and during which a vastly increased demand for the printed word, especially for news, resulted in a flowering of periodicals and newspapers. For publishers this meant both exceptional opportunity and the challenge of finding enough paper, related materials and workers, then organizing and managing these effectively. The records of the *Ami du Roi* reveal how one publishing enterprise met this challenge. But they also reflect the conditions in which all Parisian publishers worked.

Nor are questions of the production and distribution of a newspaper altogether without ideological implications. Ide-

---

[2] Archives Nationales (henceforth AN) T546 and T*546.

ology and the expression of ideas and opinion are central in times of revolution. But ideas can only be given broad expression by the intermediary of material means. Behind every ideologist in a print culture stands a businessman or manager. The reconciliation of business and ideology, which the *Ami du Roi* seems to have achieved with great success and without the support of subsidies, was another aspect of publishing that affected all those engaged in the management of print culture. I maintain, therefore, that consideration of the production, distribution and managerial techniques involved in producing newspapers will enhance our understanding of the revolutionary press, and of conditions under which ideas circulated at this time.

The second main question this study seeks to address is the readership of the periodical press. With rare exceptions,[3] this is a subject about which little is known, and for which sources are lacking. Yet there is little doubt that the subject is important. Literature is seldom if ever produced without an audience in mind. And if public opinion is ascribed a role in politics, then surely it is desirable to know something of the composition of the public. The extent and richness of the subscription lists of the *Ami du Roi* make them a unique source for the study of the reading public.

Strictly speaking, this study presents an analysis not of the readership, but of the subscribers to the *Ami du Roi*. The distinction is important. The subscribers to a paper are those who buy it for an extended period and pay for it in advance. The readership includes not only family and friends of whoever actually paid for the paper, but servants who might peruse an abandoned copy, clients of a café or members of a club which took a paper, and indeed anyone else who read it. And if we think in terms of audiences rather than readership, it would be fitting to include those who heard a paper read out loud.

---

[3] See below, Chap. VII.

That all newspapers have a readership in the sense just
described is certain. That historians are, and are likely to
remain, unable precisely to reconstruct this aspect of social
reality, seems equally clear. There are, to my knowledge, no
sources that tell us just whose hands and eyes any copy of a
paper reached. No less interesting than the broad readership
of a paper is how any individual reader may have been stim-
ulated, inspired or annoyed by it. But this, again, is an issue
for which sources are hard to find, and in the case of the
Ami du Roi, altogether lacking.[4] A broader readership of the
paper surely existed, and it probably centered on informal
institutions such as cafés and reading rooms, and on the
overlapping circles of family, friends, acquaintances and
household. One wonders, for example, how often such figures as mayors, *curés* and other local notables were offered
newspapers they had not subscribed to by generous or offi-
cious members of their communities who did take them. To
this, and many similar questions, we lack sources that might
provide answers. On the basis of subscription lists alone we
are unable to gauge with precision either the broader readership of a paper or the responses of individual readers. On
the other hand, these lists do provide information that allows
us to draw a detailed professional and sociological profile of
the immediate public of the paper.

Determining the social basis of the readership of an important right-wing newspaper also raises broader questions.
A comparison of subscribers to the *Ami du Roi* and to other
periodicals of the old regime and Revolution brings attention
to the relationship between social groups that tended to support the Revolution, others that opposed it, and the relation
of both to the Enlightenment. It is, of course, possible to

---

[4] For attempts to handle this issue see, for example, Robert Darnton, "Readers
Respond to Rousseau," in *The Great Cat Massacre and Other Episodes in French
Cultural History*, Roger Chartier and Daniel Roche, "Les Pratiques urbaines de
l'imprimé," and Françoise Parent, "De Nouvelles pratiques de lecture," in H.-J.
Martin and R. Chartier, eds., *Histoire de l'édition française*.

approach the question of the relationship between the Enlightenment and the Revolution on the level of the broad sweep of ideas. But it is also possible to do so from the ground up, and to ask how certain books and periodicals were produced, how they were distributed and who bought and read them. This second approach is the one adopted here.

In examining the history of the *Ami du Roi,* I found it difficult to fit the role of the paper and its managers into accounts of the Revolution offered in general histories. On reflection, I found that there were a number of reasons for this. First, Royou and his circle belonged to a losing side, and historians generally do not spend much time or effort in describing and analyzing failure. Second, most general histories tend to look on the period 1792 to 1794 as the heart of the Revolution, so that earlier phases come to be relegated to subordinate status and interpreted accordingly. More than this, most historians, whether of the right or of the left, tend to assume the essential unity of "the" Revolution, so that the events of 1792 to 1794 cast a long and sinister shadow back to earlier periods. It is this shadow, which heightens polarities and emphasizes extremism, and the assumption of the unity of the Revolution that casts it, that I found interfered more than anything else with a proper understanding of the *Ami du Roi* and its career. Neither Madame Fréron nor the abbé Royou knew in 1790 what would happen in the next few years. They accordingly related to the issues they faced without the benefit of the knowledge of subsequent events that often color our view of the Revolution. To understand properly the *Ami du Roi* and those who produced it, we must, I think, make an effort to see the paper in the context of the time in which it functioned, and accord to the period 1790 to early 1792 a specificity that it is generally denied. This perspective makes it possible to pay more attention to the changes that occurred in France during the period under consideration, and to the way the *Ami du Roi* evolved during its relatively short duration. It also makes it possible, as I argue below, to see the *Ami du Roi* as less extreme and more open than it has sometimes been portrayed.

The first chapter of this study treats a number of issues relating to the publication and distribution of periodical literature during the old regime and the impact that the early phases of the Revolution had on the regulation and business conditions pertaining to journalism. Specifically, it seeks to summarize existing knowledge on the readership of the periodical press, to determine the minimal level of economic viability for periodicals and to examine the relationship between the businessmen who owned the privileges for periodicals and the editors and writers who worked for them. These are issues that provide the context necessary for understanding the difficulties the *Ami du Roi* faced and how it overcame them.

Chapter II follows the brief but stormy history of a number of newspapers called the *Ami du Roi*. Emphasis has been placed on the paper founded by Madame Fréron and subsequently edited by her brother, the abbé Royou. But since the history of this paper is inextricably bound up with those of Montjoie and the publishers Briand and Crapart, the relations between the papers are also examined. It appears that differences concerning the allocation of profits of a surprisingly successful publishing venture, not ideology, lay at the heart of the disputes among the writers and publishers of the group of papers that went by the name of the *Ami du Roi*. In this chapter I also follow the career of the *Ami du Roi* from its foundation to its closure, and examine how it responded to the events and legislation of the Revolution. The paper's initial openness to reform and the way it changed during its relatively short existence suggest that right-wing opinion was less narrow and dogmatic in the early stages of the Revolution than has often been thought.

The third chapter examines the organization and business practices of the *Ami du Roi*. The questions raised here concern the printing of the paper, how it was prepared for distribution, how distribution was carried out, the relations of the offices of the paper with the postal system and with booksellers, and conditions and patterns of subscription. The records of the paper make it possible, for example, to determine what periods of subscription were preferred by the public, and what proportion of subscribers ordered their papers through local booksellers rather than directly from the offices of the *Ami du Roi*. The richness of the records of the *Ami du Roi* makes it possible to provide answers to these questions on the basis of reasonably large numbers of cases, so that we are not restricted to the announced policy of the paper, or to a few instances that may or may not be representative. Correspondence with booksellers also allows us a glimpse of the level of efficiency at which Royou's paper ran.

Chapter IV treats the production and distribution of pamphlets by the offices of the *Ami du Roi*, and compares the costs and profitability of pamphlets with those of the newspaper. The findings of this chapter indicate that pamphlets were an important supplement to the newspaper in the battle for opinion, that pamphlets were printed in press runs far exceeding those of the daily and, moreover, that they were highly profitable. It is not possible to say whether the importance of pamphlets in the operations of the *Ami du Roi* was typical, but the existence of one case in which pamphlets were massively used to supplement a daily paper raises questions about the use and importance of pamphlets during the Revolution. It may be that the lack of archival sources and the difficulty of establishing a corpus of pamphlets have resulted in our having underestimated the importance of this medium of communication during the Revolution.

Chapters V and VI present an analysis of the subscription lists of the *Ami du Roi*. Containing more than 7,000 names with addresses, indications of gender and often of status and occupation, these lists are the most extensive yet discovered for any periodical of either the old regime or Revolution. More than this, they are unique in having been drawn up in that short period during which new social and institutional categories were being introduced into general usage, but before the categories of the old regime had been eliminated. As a result, the subscription lists of the *Ami du Roi* contain both the richness and variety of old-regime social, occupational and institutional categories, and the corresponding new categories introduced by the Constituent Assembly. The resulting documents are especially revealing. They have been analyzed according to geography, gender, status and occupation, and special attention has been paid to collective subscriptions.

The seventh chapter seeks to place the findings of the previous two in a broader historiographical context. It does so, first, by comparing the social composition of the subscribers to the *Ami du Roi* to subscribers of other periodicals of the old regime and Revolution, and then by raising the question of the relationship between the Enlightenment and the Counter-Revolution. I suggest that a common social basis of the two movements provides grounds for entertaining the hypothesis that the Enlightenment may have informed the vision of many of the men identified with the Counter-Revolution, and that recent work on the social thought of the Enlightenment lends support to this view. It is, I think, fitting that a study devoted for the most part to the history of a single newspaper, and specifically to the mechanics of the production and distribution of this paper, and to its readership, culminates in a question of broad significance. Neither the Enlightenment nor the Revolution existed on the level of ideas alone, and both can be approached by working from the ground up.

I.
The Periodical Press
in the Eighteenth Century

A. Censorship and Freedom of the Press

At the beginning of 1789 about 60 periodicals circulated in France. At about the same time England, with a third the population, had approximately two and a half times as many newspapers and magazines.[1] There are a number of reasons for this discrepancy. Literacy levels were significantly higher in Great Britain than in France.[2] It would appear, too, that a larger proportion of the population of England lived in something approaching economic ease, or at least economic independence, than was the case in France. Most French periodicals, especially those aspiring to a national readership, modeled themselves on serious literary or scientific reviews. English papers, on the other hand, were more often geared to the practical and commercial interests of the man in the street, and so appealed to a broader readership.[3] Finally, the French government exercised a close and systematic censorship of the press, while the British did not.[4]

By 1789 the system of licensing works that could legally be printed or imported into France had been in place for

---

[1] C. Bellanger et al., *Histoire générale de la presse française*, I, 434-36. S. Botein, J.R. Censer and H. Ritvo, "The Periodical Press in Eighteenth-Century English and French Society: A Cross-Cultural Approach," 470-71.
[2] L. Stone, "Literacy and Education in England, 1640-1900," 120-21.
[3] Botein, Censer and Ritvo, "The Periodical Press," 471-73. French provincial papers, however, were more practical than journals of the capital. See Daniel Mornet, *Les Origines intellectuelles de la Révolution française*, 350 and Gilles Feyel, "La Presse provinciale au XVIIIe siècle: géographie d'un réseau."
[4] This is not to say that the British allowed complete freedom of the press. Rather, their controls were indirect. See F.S. Siebert, *Freedom of the Press in England 1476-1776: The Rise and Decline of Government Control.*

centuries, working effectively, if never with complete success, to control the spread of ideas and to protect the interests of certain publishers.[5] One should avoid portraying the system of censorship under the Bourbon monarchy as more sinister or rigorous than it really was. A recent account of this system for the last century of the old regime has found that between 70 percent and 90 percent of books presented for inspection were given permission to be published, and that between 1659 and 1789 an average of seven prisoners a year entered the Bastille for infractions of laws governing the production and distribution of printed matter.[6] These figures are taken as indicating a moderate administration of censorship by the government, this moderation being explained in terms of the economic interests of French publishers and a mutual accommodation between officers of the absolutist state and writers setting forth views and values of the Enlightenment.[7] Exceptional cases, such as Malesherbes's personal protection of the

---

[5] See Joseph Klaits, *Printed Propaganda Under Louis XIV: Absolute Monarchy and Public Opinion*, chap. 2; D.T. Pottinger, *The French Book Trade in the Ancien Régime, 1500-1791*, chap. 4; A. Bachman, *Censorship in France from 1715 to 1750: Voltaire's Opposition*, chaps. 1 and 2; J.P. Belin, *Le Commerce des livres prohibés à Paris de 1750 à 1789;* N. Hermann-Mascard, *La Censure des livres à Paris à la fin de l'ancien régime: 1750-1789;* M. Cerf, "La Censure royale à la fin du XVIIIe siècle," 2-28; and H.-J. Martin and R. Chartier, eds, *Histoire de l'édition*, II, 64-93.

[6] *Histoire de l'édition*, II, 63. John Lough, basing himself on Estivals, states that more than a third of the works proposed for privileges between 1715 and 1788 were refused them. See his *Writer and Public in France from the Middle Ages to the Present Day*, 175. Raymond Birn cites Isabelle Lehu's thesis "La Diffusion du livre clandestin à Paris de 1750 à 1789," which finds that during the 1750s and 1760s between 35 and 40 percent of imprisonments in the Bastille were related to infringements of regulations governing the book trade. "Malesherbes and the Call for a Free Press," in Robert Darnton and Daniel Roche, eds., *Revolution in Print: The Press in France, 1775-1800*, 51. Nor was the Bastille the only prison to intern those who ran afoul of state regulation of the book trade. Moreover, one's attitude to prison would have been influenced by whether one had spent any time there. See, for example, the case of Diderot as described by Arthur Wilson, *Diderot*, chap. 9.

[7] *Histoire de l'édition*, II, 63. If one bears in mind that among works receiving privileges and permissions to publish there would be a significant proportion of religious texts and Greco-Roman as well as seventeenth-century classics, and that obviously subversive or radical works would not have been submitted for examination at all, a figure of one in ten or three in ten works being refused permission to publish might also be taken as proof of fairly rigorous censorship.

Encyclopédie or a censor's reading Helvétius's *De l'Esprit,* probably one of the most radical works of the Enlightenment, at a level of abstraction at which all things appear harmless, then giving it a *privilège,* indicate that the system could be lax and even beneficent. The introduction over the century of categories of tolerated books, besides those that could receive official approval, shows that the bureaucracy tried to adapt to changing circumstances.[8] Censors, moreover, often came from the same backgrounds and moved in the same circles as the authors, or at least the more successful authors, whose works they examined.[9] There are also instances of censors working closely and amicably with authors or publications for which they were responsible. From 1774 to 1782, for example, Gadanne, the censor of the *Journal Encyclopédique,* was on good terms with the editors and sometimes contributed to the paper himself.[10] Nor were the efficiency and competence of the police so great as to prevent the existence and success of a large trade in clandestine books and of publishers whose businesses depended largely on smuggling.[11] Yet if the state and its agents found it impossible to control the production and distribution of books and pamphlets as closely as they would have liked, the same was not true of the periodical press. The open, public and continuing nature of periodicals made it virtually impossible for them to function without official sanction, one remarkable exception notwithstanding.[12]

---

[8] François Furet, "La 'Librairie' du royaume de France au 18e siècle," 6-9.

[9] *Histoire de l'édition,* II, 82. A rather extreme example of the overlap between writers and censors is the fact that in 1757 nine of the ten editors of the *Journal des Savants* were also royal censors. Ibid.

[10] Raymond Birn, *Pierre Rousseau and the Philosophes of Bouillon, Studies on Voltaire and the Eighteenth Century* (henceforth *VS*), 29, 145-47.

[11] See Ira O. Wade, *The Clandestine Organization and Diffusion of Philosophic Ideas in France from 1700 to 1750;* and Robert Darnton's collections of essays, *The Literary Underground of the Old Regime,* and his *The Great Cat Massacre* and *The Business of Enlightenment: A Publishing History of the Encyclopédie.*

[12] Mornet, *Les Origines intellectuelles,* 159. The exception was the Jansenist *Nouvelles Ecclésiastiques* which was published against the wishes of the government from 1728 to 1803. Cyril B. O'Keefe, *Contemporary Reactions to the Enlightenment (1728-*

In the early months of 1789 the censorship functioned as smoothly and as comprehensively as ever it had, its authority unquestioned by authors, publishers and readers. Works ranging from political tracts to textbooks were being submitted for approval, and approval, whether mitigated or entire, they normally received. In January a "Memoir on the Suppression of Privileges and the Establishment of a Tax on the Privileged" was given tacit permission to publish.[13] About the same time a teaching order that offered free education to the poor, the Frères des Ecoles Chrétiennes, applied to the chancellor's office for permission to print certain texts that they used routinely.[14] In May authorities in Lyon complained that the Kehl edition of Voltaire's works was circulating in the city, and that the police had been unable to seize a single copy. The Chancellor's office was not concerned, and responded that the edition might indeed be sold, provided it was not displayed publicly.[15] The distinction indicates something of the embarrassment of the censors as well as a penchant for practical, if inelegant, solutions. A few days later a work that the authorities could not shut their eyes to was seized. This was a play entitled "The Triumph of the Third Estate, or the Absurdities of the Nobility [les Ridicules de la Noblesse]."[16] On 26 June, a week after the Tennis Court Oath, of which he was to produce a memorable painting, David requested a privilege for a book of engravings to be entitled "The Estates General in 1789 Represented by Allegorical Figures."[17]

For the first half of 1789, it appears, the office of the chancellor sought to conduct the business of censorship as usual. Following the taking of the Bastille by the Parisian

---

1762): *A Study of Three Critical Journals: The Jesuit Journal de Trévoux, the Jansenist Nouvelles Ecclésiastiques and the Secular Journal des Savants*, 9-11.

[13] Archives Nationales (henceforth AN) V¹ 549⁷⁶⁵; 21 January 1789.

[14] AN V¹ 549⁵¹² to ⁵²³.

[15] AN V¹ 551; 4 May 1789.

[16] AN V¹ 551; 7 May 1789.

[17] AN V¹ 552.

crowd on 14 July, the municipal revolutions and the peasant risings that were often associated with the Great Fear, the authority of the royal administration was undermined, if not largely destroyed. After July, submitting manuscripts to the censor came to be seen as an unnecessary formality by many writers. Toward the end of August the National Assembly voted the Declaration of the Rights of Man and the Citizen, the eleventh article of which read: "The free communication of thought, and of opinion, is one of the precious rights of man. Every citizen, therefore, may freely speak, write and publish his sentiments; subject, however, to answer for the abuse of that liberty, in cases determined by the law."[18] The right to speak, write and publish freely one's sentiments implied the end of censorship, and was so understood by the authorities. Late in September a royal censor of twelve years standing, the Chevalier de Gaignes, wrote to the Keeper of the Seals to ask whether censorship was still in place, "despite the usurpation of the liberty of the press by a very large number of authors" and if so, whether he could expect to be sent more manuscripts.[19] In response the Keeper of the Seals replied that de Gaignes must know that "the national assembly has declared that the Liberty to print one's ideas belongs to the Rights of man," and assured him that "If in the Future The Rules Established Concerning the Freedom to Write allow writers to have recourse to censorship," he would certainly keep de Gaignes in mind.[20]

Among the liberating effects of the spring and summer of 1789, the sudden withering of the apparatus of state censorship was one of the more dramatic and more immediately felt. Some authors and publishers, it is true, continued to turn to the chancellor's office on matters concerning publi-

---

[18] As translated in the *Annual Register* for 1789.
[19] AN V¹ 552; 23 September, 1789.
[20] AN V¹ 552; undated. De Gaignes was a former army officer who had become disabled and had a family to support.

cation.[21] Most did not. And so France, which had about 60 periodicals at the beginning of 1789, had several hundred by the end of that year, and a far greater number of brochures and pamphlets.[22] The Declaration of the Rights of Man spoke of the liberation of thought, and made it possible for writers to publish their views without prior approval. At the same time the deputies of the National Assembly achieved the liberalization of enterprise in publishing. For the *privilèges* of the old regime were not merely permissions to publish, but a form of property, and in the case of periodicals, a form of property conferring a monopoly on the coverage of certain subjects and enforceable at law. With the elimination of *privilèges*, anyone who had the necessary backing and wished to start his own paper could do so. The ideas put forward, the information offered and the business acumen of the owners and editors would now determine the success of the paper without regard to a supervisory bureaucracy.

The measure that extended freedom of enterprise to publishers was intended primarily to guarantee freedom of expression to writers. It is true that even in the first flush of its liberating enthusiasm the National Assembly remained aware that freedom of the press might entail certain dangers, and expressed its intention to hold responsible those who abused this freedom "in cases determined by the law." Neither the Constituent nor the Legislative Assemblies put a comprehensive press law in place. The Thouret Law of 22 August 1791 was intended to set the limits of press freedom, but was loosely drafted, and failed to do so.[23] The Assemblies of the period of the constitutional monarchy contented themselves with ad hoc measures against specific papers as cir-

---

[21] These were for the most part well-established publishers who were integrated into the old system. Thus the publishers of the *Journal Encyclopédique* asked in September 1789 that the pensions the journal paid the crown be ended because of declining subscriptions. AN V¹ 552; 25 September 1789.

[22] Bellanger, *Histoire générale de la presse*, I, 436.

[23] Murray, *The Right-Wing Press*, 86.

cumstances seemed to demand. Indeed, regulation of the press did not fall exclusively within the jurisdiction of the national authorities. The Police Committee of the Municipality of Paris laid down and enforced guidelines on publishing, and so did other municipal authorities.[24] This fragmentation of authority made regulation of the press more difficult. The result was a period of virtually unlimited press freedom, unlike anything that preceded or followed it. This period may be said to have begun in July 1789 and to have ended after 10 August 1792, when the activists of what is often called the Second French Revolution moved to suppress papers of the right, many of which had been advocating counter-revolution and calling for foreign invasion.[25] Once war broke out and counter-revolution posed ever more serious threats to the new regime, freedoms of all kinds were curtailed. A law of 29 March 1793 subjected both authors and publishers to the death penalty and has been described as "effectively reestablishing a repressive press censorship."[26] After the fall of Robespierre there was a revival of relative press freedom, and royalists could publish again. The Constitution of 1795 reasserted the principle of freedom of the press and negated preliminary censorship, but itself temporarily restricted press freedom.[27] The press law of 22 Fructidor (8 September 1797) provided for the deportation of journalists, editors and owners of papers.[28] Napoleon did not have to destroy a free press when he came to power. But his treatment of journalists and their papers was heavy-handed. In 1800 he suppressed most of the newspapers appearing in the Département of the Seine, and five years later reestablished press censorship.[29] This new censorship authority was

---

[24] Gary Kates, *The Cercle Social, the Girondins and the French Revolution,* 31-33.
[25] Murray, *Right-Wing Press,* 182-86, and J.-P. Bertaud, *Les Amis du Roi,* 227-28 and 235-39.
[26] *Histoire de l'édition,* II, 527.
[27] Lough, J. *Writer and Public,* 190.
[28] Murray, *Right-Wing Press,* 208.
[29] Lough, *Writer and Public,* 191.

probably more stringent, as well as more effective, than that of Louis XVI.

Between July 1789 and August 1792, while one system of government was being dismantled and before another had replaced it, writers and journalists enjoyed the unwonted opportunity of publishing what they wanted, virtually without constraint. This period of unlimited press freedom coincided with a time of broad consensus during which the worst abuses of the old regime were abolished or modified, and the basis for a constitutional monarchy laid. After the attempt of the royal family to leave France secretly in June 1791, tensions increased, in effect destroying the consensus that had developed around the model of a reformed constitutional monarchy. As opinion polarized, freedom of the press came to seem less desirable and tolerable, and, as noted above, was brought to an end in August 1792.

Among the hundreds of often ephemeral papers published during the first years of the Revolution, most of the better known ones belong to the left. These include Marat's *Ami du Peuple*, Camille Desmoulins's *Révolutions de France et de Brabant*, Stanislas Fréron's *Orateur du Peuple* and Prudhomme's *Révolutions de Paris*.[30] Many of the journalists of the left during the early years of the Revolution went on to play dramatic or important roles during the critical years 1793 and 1794, the fame they achieved at a later period reflecting back on their earlier works. Having espoused a failed cause, most journalists of the right, as also most politicians of the right, have received less attention. Recently, however, right-wing papers such as de Rozoi's *Gazette de Paris*, Fontenai's *Journal Général*, Gautier's *Journal de la Cour et de la Ville*, also known as the *Petit Gautier*, the *Mercure de France*, edited by Mallet du Pan, the *Actes des Apôtres*, the *Rocambole*, the *Journal de M. Suleau* and Royou's *Ami du Roi* have been the subject of exten-

---

[30] On these papers see Jack R. Censer, *Prelude to Power: The Parisian Radical Press, 1789-1791*.

sive research.[31] It is to an investigation of the abbé Royou's important paper, the *Ami du Roi*, that this study is devoted. The aspects of the paper I wish to examine concern not its text, but the way it was produced and distributed, how it regularly published pamphlets while functioning as a daily and above all, who read it.

B. The Readership of the Periodical Press

In general terms Daniel Mornet put the potential readership of the periodical press in the eighteenth century at "a few tens of thousands," and he thought that this was a lot.[32] But determining the readership of any given journal is difficult, for it implies a knowledge not only of the size of press runs, but also of how copies of papers circulated once they had been delivered to subscribers or bought from vendors. With the exception of collective subscriptions, it is almost impossible to know how many and whose eyes a paper has passed before, or who might have heard it read out loud.[33] A well-informed contemporary has suggested that on the average each copy of a paper had ten readers.[34] If anything this estimate may be low.[35] It may well be, too, that papers

[31] See especially J.-P. Bertaud, *Les Amis du Roi* and W. J. Murray, *The Right-Wing Press*. Also relevant is Jeremy Popkin's fine study *The Right-Wing Press in France, 1792-1800*. A number of theses on the press, including the right-wing press during this period, were written at the Sorbonne during the 1950s and 1960s but are not readily accessible. See the bibliography of the *Histoire générale de la presse*, I.

[32] Mornet, *Les Origines intellectuelles*, 160-61.

[33] For a recent treatment of this problem focusing on street readings and the roles of clubs and the army, see Françoise Parent's contribution to the *Histoire de l'édition*, II, entitled "Nouvelles pratiques de lecture," especially 606-612.

[34] Delisle de Sales, *Essai sur le journalisme depuis 1735 jusqu' à l'an 1800*, 96-97.

[35] It is well known that *cabinets de lecture* and cafés normally made journals available to their patrons. With the formation of popular societies during the Revolution, newspapers became available to larger audiences. In the smaller clubs whole meetings were sometimes devoted to reading papers, while larger clubs opened reading rooms that were carefully regulated. Indeed, club sessions were sometimes timed to coincide with the arrival of mail coaches. The influence of the

such as the *Père Duchesne*, which were directed specifically at a popular readership, had a higher proportion of readers, or auditors, per copy than did more traditional papers. But on the more solid criterion of press runs, we find that the *Ami du Roi*, which at its peak printed 5,700 copies,[36] was among the most widely distributed papers of the old regime or Revolution.

Without being so full or so precise as might be wished, there is sufficient information on press runs to allow us to form a fairly accurate idea of the numbers of copies printed of different kinds of journals toward the end of the eighteenth century. During the reigns of Louis XV and his successor, books were normally published in press runs of between 500 and 3,000.[37] The figures for periodicals did not differ significantly from those for books.[38] For most of the old regime a paper with between one and two thousand copies would be considered successful. Papers printing fewer could still survive, while those printing more would have been highly profitable.[39] During the early 1760s the *Mercure de France* had

---

papers was also felt outside the clubs, for having subscribed to papers, the clubs sometimes saw to it that they reached a broader public by being posted at the town hall or read in public in the evenings. See Michael L. Kennedy, *The Jacobin Clubs in the French Revolution: The First Years*, chap. 3 and "The Jacobin Clubs and the Press: Phase Two," and Max Fajn, "La Diffusion de la presse révolutionnaire dans le Lot, le Tarn et l'Aveyron, sous la Convention et le Directoire," 300-303.

[36] See below, Graph 2.1.

[37] *Histoire de l'édition*, II, 29.

[38] Jean Sgard puts the press runs of successful periodicals in the second half of the eighteenth century at "several thousand." Ibid., II, 200.

[39] In 1774 the *Mercure*, with 12,000 subscribers, yielded Panckoucke an annual profit of 114,000 *livres*, while the *Gazette de France* with 6,250 yielded him 25,500. During the 1770s the *Journal de Genève* and the *Journal de Bruxelles* each on the average brought Panckoucke 25,000 and 28,000 *livres* a year (Suzanne Tucoo-Chala, *Charles-Joseph Panckoucke et la librairie française, 1736-1789*, 250-51). However, the figure for the *Gazette* must be treated with caution as it does not square with the averages for 1787 and 1788 (ibid., 250). At the height of its prosperity, the *Courrier d'Avignon* was making an annual profit of 15,000 to 20,000 *livres*,(René Moulinas, *L'Imprimerie, la librairie et la presse à Avignon au XVIIIe siècle*, 359). The budgets of the journal for 1785 and 1787 which Moulinas reproduces, however, show great differences in profit, though not in numbers of subscribers or production costs (ibid., 356-58). It has been calculated that Brissot's *Patriote français* would have made a profit of 30,000 *livres* with 3,000 subscribers, and above 100,000 with

a press run of about 1,600, but such important periodicals as the *Journal des Savants* and the *Journal de Trévoux* have been estimated as having no more than a thousand.[40] The mainstream Enlightenment *Journal Encyclopédique* seems to have published between 1,200 and 2,000 copies at different times, while the *Année Littéraire*, which probably exceeded 2,000 subscribers during the early 1760s, had fallen after Fréron's death to about 1,000 between 1778 and 1780.[41]

Undistinguished from a journalistic point of view, for it was merely a rehash of news printed in other, mostly Dutch, periodicals, the *Courrier d'Avignon* published 2,800 copies in 1748. Though this figure fell drastically to 800 during the next two years because of difficulties over postal rates, when these difficulties were overcome press runs again rose to 2,300 in 1755.[42] Under the combined stimuli of the Seven Years War and a preferential postal tariff the *Courrier d'Avignon* reached the remarkable number of "perhaps" more than 9,000 subscribers.[43]

The lower limit of economic viability for a periodical in the eighteenth century seems to have been a press run of about 300 copies. François Morénas, who had founded and been dispossessed of the *Courrier d'Avignon*, began another

---

5,000, while the more modest *Journal de Marseille* with only 400 subscribers would have made a profit of 2,500 livres. (Bellanger, *Histoire générale*, I, 439).

[40] Daniel Mornet, "L'Intérêt historique des journaux littéraires et la diffusion du *Mercure de France*," 119-22; Jean Ehrard and Jacques Roger, "Deux périodiques françaises du 18è siècle: le *Journal des Savants* et les *Mémoires de Trévoux:* Essai d'une étude quantitative," 37.

[41] The figures for the *Journal Encyclopédique* are from Bellanger, *Histoire générale*, I, 278, and Birn, *Pierre Rousseau*, 151. Fréron's *Lettres sur quelques écrits de ce temps* were published in press runs of 2,500 (Jean Balcou, *Fréron contre les philosophes*, 92), and it is virtually certain that the *Année Littéraire* was initially, at least, as widely distributed. The press run for this work in 1778 was 1,250, while the number of subscribers was 850 in 1779 and 960 in 1780 (AN T*546¹). The size of the press run need not, of course, be the same as the number of subscribers. Balcou also refers to a financial crisis at the *Année Littéraire* just before Fréron's death (Balcou, *Fréron*, 453).

[42] René Moulinas, "Les Journaux publiés à Avignon et leur diffusion en France jusqu'en 1768."

[43] Moulinas, *L'Imprimerie à Avignon*, 383.

paper, the *Entretiens historiques sur les affaires présentes de l'Europe*, which was printed in press runs of 300. Yet this paper suspended publication not because it proved unviable, but because its privilege was revoked.[44] The *Journal militaire et politique* of de Rosay had only 200 subscribers for 1778 and 1779, and ceased publication two years later. It did so, however, because of a surcharge placed on it, not because of the size of its subscription list.[45] The *Affiches de Reims*, which was founded in 1772, still did not have 250 subscribers four years later, but survived nonetheless.[46] Royou and Geoffroy bought the privilege to the *Journal de Monsieur* in 1781, when it had less than 100 subscribers. They had raised that number to 300 two years later when they were forced to abandon the journal, according to a contemporary, as a result of intrigue.[47] However, during the Revolution the *Journal du Tarn* closed because it could not find 300 subscribers.[48] The publisher of the *Journal Général de l'Orléanais*, on the other hand, put his break-even point at 250 subscribers.[49] In 1778 Panckoucke thought it worthwhile to buy the *Journal français*, even though it had only 261 subscribers.[50] But in touching on Charles-Joseph Panckoucke, probably the first press baron in history, we come to a man who changed the conditions of publishing in his time.

Panckoucke once observed that, "One sells ten times, twenty times more political journals than other kinds of journals."[51]

---

[44] Moulinas, "Les Journaux publiés à Avignon," 129.

[45] Denise Aimé-Azam, "Le Ministère des Affaires Etrangères à la fin de l'Ancien Régime," 435.

[46] Mornet, *Les Origines intellectuelles*, 356.

[47] E. Hatin, *Histoire politique et littéraire de la presse en France*, III, 209-11. Hatin's source here is Bachaumont. A bill from the printer Knapen for the *Journal de Monsieur* shows that from January to March 1782 the journal was being printed in press runs of between 470 and 750 copies. AN T546⁹⁵.

[48] Fajn, "La Diffusion de la presse révolutionnaire," 306.

[49] Hugh Gough, *The Newspaper Press in the French Revolution*, 29.

[50] Tucoo-Chala, *Panckoucke*, 197.

[51] Letter to Amelot, 13 May 1778. Cited in Aimé-Azam, "Le Ministère des Affaires Etrangères," 432. Mornet too observed that the only successful new journals in France after 1770 were those reporting news. *Les Origines intellectuelles*, 343.

He accordingly directed his remarkable business acumen to winning the privilege for political news, and he succeeded in doing so.[52] Armed with this privilege he was able to eliminate, buy out or in effect impose a tax on rivals, as he had done in the case of de Rosay. He soon brought the subscription levels of his papers to unprecedented levels for France. His *Journal de Genève* had more than 8,500 subscribers in 1783, while his *Journal de Bruxelles* was published in press runs of 6,000 in the mid-1770s, though neither paper enjoyed stable popularity.[53] Panckoucke's most striking success was the *Mercure*. Taking control of the paper in 1777, when it had less than 2,000 subscribers, he annexed the political section of the *Journal de Bruxelles* to it, and saw its press runs rise steeply until they peaked at 20,000 in 1783. Even after the decline in demand for the paper that came with the end of the war in America, the *Mercure* was not published in press runs of less than 10,000.[54] This was an achievement which no literary periodical of the old regime approached, and one that it is not clear was surpassed during the Revolution. It is also an achievement that fully justified Panckoucke's observation on the demand for political news, a demand which was to be renewed with increased intensity from 1789.

While the Revolution had a sudden and dramatic effect on the numbers of papers and periodicals published,[55] and while it also resulted in the eventual closure of most of the great independent literary journals of the old regime, it had little or no effect on methods of production or the size of press runs.[56] With few exceptions these did not exceed levels common before 1789.

One authority has asserted that most papers during the

---

[52] For an account of how he achieved this see Tucoo-Chala, *Panckoucke*, part III, chap. 2.

[53] Ibid., 207-208.

[54] Ibid., 220-21.

[55] For graphs showing the increase in the publication of periodicals from 1789 see Bellanger, *Histoire générale de la presse*, I, 436.

[56] Ibid., 435.

Revolution had press runs of between 300 and 500, while the largest printed about 12,000 copies.[57] Another puts the circulation "among the more influential papers" at between 2,000 and 5,000.[58] These figures show that by virtue of the number of copies printed the *Ami du Roi* was one of the more successful papers of the period. Few other papers had more subscribers. The republican *Journal des hommes libres* had 6,000 in 1794, though this number fell to between 2,200 and 2,500 in 1795 and 1796, when the republican press was largely eclipsed.[59] The moderate *Feuille villageoise* had, according to its editor, the abbé Cerutti, 14,000 subscribers, and there is archival evidence that it reached nearly 15,000.[60] For its duration of roughly a year and a half the Jacobin *Journal de la Montagne* had a total of just over 5,500 subscribers.[61] In examining Stamp Tax records for 1799 Jeremy Popkin has found estimates for the number of subscribers to five papers of varying outlooks. These are the conservative monarchist *Propagateur* with 4,000 subscribers; the neo-Jacobin *Journal des hommes libres* with 3,500; the royalist *Feuille du jour*, also known as the *Véridique*, with 3,000; the constitutional monarchist *Indispensable* with 2,800; and the royalist *Bulletin de l'Europe* or *Quotidienne* with 2,500.[62] Though the *Ami du Roi* compares favorably with these papers, conditions for the publication

---

[57] Ibid., 438.

[58] J. Gilchrist and W.J. Murray, *The Press in the French Revolution*, 9.

[59] Max Fajn, *The Journal des hommes libres de tous les pays, 1792-1800*, 29, 40 and 52.

[60] Melvin Edelstein, *La Feuille villageoise: Communication et modernisation dans les régions rurales pendant la Révolution*, 68. The existence of a subscriber number 14,900 is solid proof that this journal had at least that number of subscribers. But it is not certain that it had 14,900 subscribers at one time. We will see below (Chap. III) that the most common form of subscription was for a period of three months and that renewal was not automatic.

[61] Hugh Gough, "Les Jacobins et la presse: Le *Journal de la Montagne* (juin 1793–brumaire an II)," 288.

[62] Popkin, *The Right-Wing Press*, 80. The descriptions of the affiliations of the papers are Popkin's. Popkin regards these estimates as reliable, and his careful handling of the sources inclines one to accept his view. The total number of newspapers sold daily in 1797 seems to have been somewhere between 80,000 and 150,000. Ibid., 79.

of newspapers were far less auspicious in 1799 than they had been in the first years of the Revolution.

Of right-wing journals roughly contemporaneous with the *Ami du Roi*, the *Actes des Apôtres* (4,500 copies), the *Gazette de Paris* (2,300–4,000), the *Journal de M. Suleau* (estimated at between 2,000 and 4,000) and the *Spectateur national* (estimated at between 1,000 and 1,500) had smaller press runs than Royou's paper.[63] Fontenai's *Journal Général* plausibly claimed it was publishing in press runs of 7,000 in 1792, while Murray estimates the *Petit Gautier* to have had press runs of between 6,000 and 10,000.[64] The only paper which can be shown to have had larger press runs than Royou's *Ami du Roi* at this time was Panckoucke's *Mercure de France*, which was edited by Mallet du Pan. In 1790 it was publishing about 12,000 copies of each number, and though this figure fell substantially, it was still publishing in press runs of above 9,000 in 1792.[65] It is probably no coincidence that this success was achieved by an able businessman with extensive publishing experience.

Most of our figures on the circulation of papers during this period are reports by more or less well-informed contemporaries. Max Fajn, on the authority of Roederer, gives the press runs of the royalist *L'Accusateur publique* as 10,000 after Thermidor, and that of the anti-Jacobin *Orateur du Peuple* at 15,000.[66] He also asserts that the moderate *Journal de Perlet* in 1795–96 boasted 21,000 subscribers.[67] Jacques Godechot estimates Brissot's *Patriote Français* to have had 10,000 subscribers.[68] He further notes that "it seems" that the royalist *Journal Général* had 7,000 subscribers, and that "it is esti-

---

[63] See Murray, *The Right-Wing Press*, 306–307.
[64] Ibid.
[65] Ibid.
[66] Fajn, *Journal des hommes libres*, 40.
[67] Ibid., 52.
[68] Brissot maintained that he was read by (which does not imply that his paper was bought by) 50,000 to 100,000 people. Bellanger, *Histoire générale de la presse*, I, 445.

mated" that the similarly conservative *Journal de Paris* had 12,000.[69] However, he regards the claim that the royalist *Rocambole des journaux* had between 12,000 and 20,000 subscribers as implausible, and dismisses Camille Desmoulins' contention that the radical *Révolutions de Paris* had 200,000 subscribers in similar terms.[70] Gilchrist and Murray regard this last claim as possible, but while reporting that the *Père Duchesne* was said to have reached press runs of a million when it was subsidized and distributed to the army in 1793, they commit themselves only to commenting that "at the height of its fame it was the best known paper in France."[71] They further state that two Girondin papers, the *Gazette Universelle* and the *Journal du Soir*, had over 10,000 subscribers each.[72] The Girondin *Sentinelle*, which was conceived as an urban analogue of the *Feuille villageoise*, and which was normally posted on walls, was initially published in press runs of 1,500, but when a Girondin ministry was formed it benefited from a large subsidy and increased this figure to 10,000.[73]

If our information on press runs of periodicals is less substantial than we might wish, that on subscribers is sparser yet. For the old regime we have lists of 125 subscribers to the *Mercure de France* from Grenoble for the later seventeenth century, 300 subscribers to the *Année Littéraire* for the 1780s and another of 750 subscribers, again to the *Mercure de France*, together with 63 provincial booksellers and a number of street vendors who distributed nearly 700 copies more of the paper.[74] Examination of the correspondence of old-regime journals

[69] Ibid., 467 (Godechot here seems to be following the estimate of the editors of the *Journal Général* and 464.
[70] Ibid., 469 and 452.
[71] Gilchrist and Murray, *The Press in the French Revolution*, 9.
[72] Ibid., 30.
[73] Kates, *The Cercle Social*, 228 and 236. It does not seem, however, that right-wing papers received subsidies during the early Revolution. See Murray, *The Right-Wing Press*, 5 and 67.
[74] G. Feyel, "Réimpressions et diffusion de la *Gazette* dans les provinces: 1631-1752," 73; AN T*546[1]; Mornet, "L'Intérêt historique," passim.

has also added to our knowledge of their readership.[75] But on the whole uncovering sources for the readership of the periodical press under the old regime has proven an intractable problem.[76]

For the Revolution, especially its later phases, we are better informed, thanks largely to the revolutionary police. The subscription registers of the *Journal de la Montagne* were sequestered in the winter of 1794 and show a total of more than 5,500 subscribers.[77] Among the results of the suppression of Babeuf's conspiracy was the seizure of a list of 590 subscribers to the *Tribun du peuple* for 1796.[78] The same police force provided lists of 83 subscribers to the neo-Jacobin *Ami du Peuple*, seized in 1795, and of 50 subscribers to the royalist *Gazette Française*, seized in September 1797, following the coup of 18 Fructidor.[79] It is to police activity following the same coup that we owe lists of subscribers to three right-wing

---

[75] Birn, *Pierre Rousseau*, 151.

[76] Under the old regime the papers of a journalist would normally contain information on subscribers only if the editor was also the publisher, and this was rarely the case. Madame Fréron, for example, owned the privilege for the *Année Littéraire*, but had the paper produced and distributed by the booksellers and publishers Merigot le jeune (1777–89) and Crapart (1790). Similarly, Linguet had Lequesne, a friend who was also a cloth merchant, see to the distribution of his *Annales* in Paris. See Darlene Gay Levy, *The Ideas and Careers of Simon-Nicolas-Henri Linguet: A Study in Eighteenth-Century French Politics*, 190.

Probably the most likely source from which to derive precise information on subscribers to journals under the old regime is the records of the most important publisher of periodicals of the time. Unfortunately, having analyzed Panckoucke's papers as closely as anyone is likely to do, Mme. Tucoo-Chala was unable to find any (*Panckoucke*, 17-18). Another likely source of subscription lists is the archives of the *Journal Encyclopédique*, as the editing and publication of the journal were carried out by the same house. Responses to enquiries I have made of the keepers of the Archives Weissenbruch in Bouillon and Brussels indicate that such lists have not survived.

[77] Gough, "Les Jacobins et la presse," 288. It should be noted, however, that there are two separate sets of records. The first, which is complete, gives only the numbers of subscribers. The second, which contains about half the total, is a mailing list analogous to the records that have survived for the *Ami du Roi* and provide information on gender, occupation and the addresses.

[78] Albert Soboul, "Personnel sectionnaire et personnel babouviste."

[79] Max Fajn, "The Circulation of the Press during the Revolution." The author appears to have included only those subscribers for whom an occupation is indicated in his sources.

papers, 180 for the *Tribune Publique,* 864 for the *Gazette Fran-çaise* and 999 for a paper it has not been possible to identify with certainty.[80] Simply in terms of quantity, then, the subscription lists to the *Ami du Roi* are privileged documents.

For purposes of analysis the value of a subscription list depends largely on how often information on the socioeconomic standing of the subscribers is given, and this varies considerably. The list for the unknown paper analyzed by Popkin has such information for 56.65 percent of the subscribers, that for the *Gazette Française* for 25.23 percent. The occupations of only 12 percent of Parisian subscribers to the *Journal de la Montagne* are given, while in the provinces this figure rises to 22 percent.[81] The corresponding figure for the *Ami du Roi* is 60 percent. In Chapters V and VI, I will examine the composition of these lists, which will, I hope, throw new light on the readership of the periodical press during the last years of the old regime and the beginning of the Revolution.

C. Between the Authorities and the Public: Relations between Publishers and Editors

Our knowledge of financial arrangements between authors and publishers in eighteenth-century France is sketchy. This is so largely because contracts between writers and publishers were normally signed privately rather than before notaries, and in most cases have not found their way to the archives.[82] It is clear, however, that the normal practice was for an author

---

[80] Popkin, *Right-Wing Press,* Table 4, p. 65. Taking together Popkins's subscribers (2,043), Soboul's (690) and Fajn's (133), we have information on 2,866 subscribers to journals for the later phases of the Revolution. For the old regime we have information on 125 provincial subscribers to the *Mercure* for the seventeenth century, approximately 750 for the mid-eighteenth, and a further 300 for the *Année Littéraire.* The only known lists of subscribers that approach those of the *Ami du Roi* in extent are those of the *Journal de la Montagne.*
[81] Gough, "Les Jacobins et la presse," 291.
[82] Lough, *Writer and Public,* 199.

to sell his manuscript outright to a publisher for a lump sum which, if he did not enjoy a considerable reputation, was likely to be modest.[83] Instances of authors being granted royalties (that is, a share of profits) do exist, but they are rare.[84] Thus, even if a writer produced a book that proved popular, his reputation might benefit, but his income probably would not, at least directly. Rousseau, for example, received only 2,160 *livres* for his *Nouvelle Héloïse*, one of the most widely sold books of the century.[85]

Yet it would not be sound to conclude that Rousseau's Amsterdam publisher, Rey, made all the profits. Because there was no adequate system of copyright in France, successful books were universally pirated. Accepting this as part of normal practice, publishers calculated their profits only in terms of their first editions.[86] Authors therefore found their incomes depressed not only by the parsimony of publishers and booksellers—and one must bear in mind that publishing is a business in which the publisher, like any other businessman, buys his product as cheap, and sells it as dear, as he can—but also by the lack of an effective copyright, which opened the way to exploitation by publishers in Belgium, Holland and Switzerland, as well as others within the borders of France. In any case, few historians now believe that it was possible for more than a small number of authors to have lived from the sale of their writings in the second half of the eighteenth century, and none before.[87]

Though England also had a large number of Grub Street writers who eked out a living doing hack work, and sometimes

---

[83] Ibid., 201.
[84] Ibid., *Histoire de l'édition*, II, 25.
[85] Lough, *Writer and Public*, 210. On the purchasing power of the *livre* in the eighteenth century see below, Chap. II, n. 15.
[86] Lough, *Writer and Public*, 201.
[87] Ibid., 207. Robert Darnton has probably done more than any other scholar to revise the view that a growing market supported a new class of professional writers in the eighteenth century. See especially his articles "The High Enlightenment and the Low-Life of Literature," reprinted in *The Literary Underground*, and "A Police Inspector Sorts His Files" in *The Great Cat Massacre*.

failed to do even that, it also had a number of authors, such as Pope, Dr. Johnson, David Hume and William Robertson, who were able to achieve substantial wealth by their writings, and who spoke favorably of their publishers and of book-sellers in general.[88] The contrast in treatment of prominent authors in France and England was remarked on both sides of the channel in the eighteenth century,[89] but it probably had more to do with a better developed notion of copyright in England than with a greater sense of fairness.[90]

While it is not true to say that more than a few authors could live by selling their writings in the second half of the eighteenth century in France, this does not mean that the profession of letters was likewise closed to all but a few. Robert Darnton and John Lough have both recently brought attention to the degree to which a successful career in letters implied the pursuit and cumulation of places, pensions and sine-cures.[91] One source of pensions, as well as of positions carrying handsome salaries for relatively little effort, was the periodical press.[92] As a condition for being granted a privilege, most independent periodicals were required to pay the government an annual sum that was usually treated as a pension. For semi-official periodicals, such as the *Mercure* and the *Journal des Savants*, editorships were often treated as sine-

---

[88] One would have to look far in France for the equivalent of Dr. Johnson's comment, made in response to Boswell's observation that he had been paid less than he deserved for his *Dictionary*, that "The booksellers are generous, liberal-minded men" (Boswell, *Life of Johnson*, [Oxford Standard Authors, 1957], 217). For Robertson's views see ibid., 980. Hume speaks of the "noble encouragement . . . given to literature in England, without the intervention of the great, by means of the booksellers alone, that is, by the public." J.Y.T. Greig, ed., *The Letters of David Hume* (Oxford, 2 vols., 1932), vol. II, 203.

[89] Lough, *Writer and Public*, 199-200; Hume, *Letters*, I, 367.

[90] Dr. Johnson noted that while the law recognized a fourteen-year exclusive copyright, the "trade" in fact acted as if it was perpetual, and he approved of this. Boswell, *Life of Johnson*, 310.

[91] See Darnton, "The High Enlightenment" and Lough, *Writer and Public*, 225-33.

[92] Ibid., 232-33.

cures.[93] For the fashionable or prestigious men of letters who received these pensions or who were able to treat their editorships virtually as sinecures, this no doubt seemed an admirable arrangement. For the writers who actually did the work required to put out a periodical and who were subject to the economic imperatives of the literary marketplace, it must have seemed less so. The experience of these lesser writers brings us back to the relationship between those who published journals and those who edited them.

Most periodicals at this time were owned by printers or booksellers, that is, the printers or booksellers usually owned the privileges for the journals, which often represented a significant investment,[94] and assured both production and distribution of their periodicals, hiring editors and writers on terms determined by the literary marketplace. This system had two important consequences. First, it assured that subscription records remained in the hands of businessmen, who tended to be less troubled by the police than writers,[95] and who had no incentive to preserve such lists once they had lost their commercial value. Second, it made publishers the buyers of literary talent in a marketplace in which supply exceeded demand. The result was that printers and booksellers could and frequently did treat their editors and staff-writers as little more than clerks, and paid them accordingly.

While it is true that publishers normally put up the capital and assumed any risks involved, the lowness of many salaries and the disproportion between the editor's salary and the publisher's profits, especially when circulation was high, are so great as to seem like the grossest exploitation. To take an

---

[93] Darnton describes Suard's job editing the *Mercure* as bringing him "lodging, heating, lighting and 2,500 *livres* for half a day's work putting polish on the materials provided every week by the ministry of foreign affairs." "The High Enlightenment," 4.

[94] The privilege of the *Gazette de France*, for example, sold for 97,000 *livres* in 1749. Feyel, "Réimpressions de la Gazette," 70. Because of its official standing the *Gazette* cannot, of course, be regarded as typical.

[95] See the Table in the *Histoire de l'édition*, II, 86.

example, François Morénas founded the *Courrier d'Avignon* and, after seeing the privilege for the journal awarded to the publisher-bookseller Giroud, accepted an arrangement by which he furnished copy, Giroud assured production and distribution, and profits were divided equally. Having committed a breach of contract by failing to supply copy, Morénas lost his partnership. When he returned to edit the paper, it was as a salaried employee receiving an annual wage of between 600 and 800 *livres*. At this time the profits earned by the publisher from the *Courrier* were between 15,000 and 20,000 *livres* a year.[96] Panckoucke, it is true, was more generous with his editors. But then he could hardly attract the most famous men of letters of the day, such as Linguet or Mallet du Pan, without paying them well. There was no philanthropy involved. The market value of the most sought after writers was high and Panckoucke was prepared to pay high salaries to make large profits.[97] As we shall see below, on relations between publishers and writers of periodicals, as in other areas, the Revolution was to have an impact.

---

[96] Moulinas, "Les Journaux publiés à Avignon," 126-30.
[97] Levy, *Linguet*, 172; Tucoo-Chala, *Panckoucke*, 203. See also Raymond Birn, "The Profits of Ideas: *Privilèges en librairie* in Eighteenth-Century France," 154-55.

II.
The Short, Unhappy, Principled Career of
the Ami du Roi of the Abbé Royou

A. The Context: 1790

As revolutions go, 1790 was the best of times. Alphonse Aulard noted that 1790 had long been described as a time of national concord and fraternity, though it was also the time when one class gained control of the state at the expense of the others.[1] 1790 has also been called the "happy year" of the Revolution.[2] It was a period when it seemed that sweeping and long desired reforms could be carried out by consensus and France regenerated without violence or bloodshed. As a time during which the essentials of a constitution were worked out and imposed on the monarchy, 1790 has also been viewed as the revenge of the nobility for all it had lost and endured at the hands of the centralizing absolute monarchy of the seventeenth and eighteenth centuries.[3] Georges Lefebvre called 1790 "Lafayette's year."[4]

As a liberal noble who stood for a constitutional monarchy in which the prerogatives of privilege were drastically reduced and public order maintained, Lafayette represents the polit-

---

[1] Alphonse Aulard, *The French Revolution: A Political History, 1789-1804*, I, 213. What Aulard seems to have had in mind here was the poor being deprived of the franchise by the distinction between active and passive citizens and the qualification of the *marc d'argent* that precluded all but the most wealthy from standing for high elective office.

[2] F. Furet and D. Richet, *La Révolution française*, make this the title of their fourth chapter.

[3] Ibid., 114.

[4] Georges Lefebvre, *The French Revolution: From its Origins to 1793*, trans. E.M. Evanson (London and New York, 1962), title of chapter 9. Albert Mathiez entitled the sixth chapter of his classic *The French Revolution*, "Lafayette as Mayor of the Palace."

ical tone of the year well. For his parts in the American and French Revolutions Lafayette has been given the flattering title "the hero of two worlds." In 1790 he further represented a closing of the gap between liberal nobles and progressively minded members of the Third Estate. This composite elite, whose views and aspirations Lafayette at this time reflected, was further prepared to be more than usually generous—by contemporary standards— with the great mass of the people.

The year 1790 was one free of any major popular uprisings. It passed relatively quietly between the peasant risings of the summer of 1789, the taking of the Bastille and the forcible removal of the royal family from Versailles to Paris on 5 and 6 October 1789 on the one hand, and the shootings on the Champ-de-Mars on 17 July 1791, the attack on the Tuileries of 20 June 1792, the "second Revolution" of 10 August 1792, the September massacres of the same year, and all that lies beyond, on the other.[5]

The greatest event in which the masses participated in 1790 was the Fête de la Fédération in Paris, a huge public festival the leitmotifs of which were liberation, harmony and fraternity.[6] In describing the event contemporaries emphasize the immense good will generated and the wide range of social groups that cooperated to prepare and to celebrate this festival of the new France. The artists of Paris volunteered to decorate the site without charge, and the Chapter of Notre Dame offered its choir to sing the *Te Deum*.[7] When it appeared that preparations for the festival would not be finished in time there was a spontaneous rush of citizens of both genders

---

[5] J.M. Roberts has observed that "disorder ran on through 1790, though historians have long tended to overlook this fact" (*The French Revolution*, 22), and of course he is right. Lefebvre has also noted the persistence of popular unrest during 1790 (*French Revolution*, 136) and Furet and Richet have pointed out that 1790 was a year of mutinies (*La Révolution française*, 148). Unrest and disorder clearly continued through 1790. In comparison to what went before and what came after, however, this disorder seems moderate.

[6] On this festival in particular and revolutionary festivals generally see Mona Ozouf, *La Fête révolutionnaire: 1789-1799*.

[7] J. M. Thompson, *The French Revolution*, 120.

and all occupations to help. The crowd included "monks and soldiers, well-dressed gentlemen and ragged beggars, rich *bourgeoises* and women of the people, workmen of every kind and peasants from the neighbouring countryside led by their *maires* and *curés*."[8] Even Lafayette came and "put in two hours' work with the spade."[9] Despite a heavy rainfall, 14 July saw a huge crowd on the Champ-de-Mars to witness and participate in what has been called "perhaps the greatest day of the whole Revolution."[10] One historian evaluates the festival of 14 July 1790 as "An ingenuous display of a people's hopes and illusions," while a recent history of the Revolution dismisses the notion that the Fête de la Fédération was a celebration of utopia and asserts, "It was above all the reflection of a voluntary unity, confident and peaceful, which would have wished to be the dawn of a new epoch."[11] Descriptions of the festival by contemporaries, both radical and conservative, ". . . all emphasize the desire for reconciliation and happy reunion . . ."[12] If to us the illusory nature of the hopes and aspirations of the summer of 1790 seem painfully clear, to contemporaries they were not. In 1790 the French could congratulate themselves on having made the most sweeping social, political and administrative changes with remarkably little dislocation and violence. They could reasonably believe themselves to be living in the best of times.

B. The Founding of the *Ami du Roi*

On a spring day in 1790 five persons met privately in Paris to sign a contract establishing a newspaper to be entitled "The

---

[8] Gaetano Salvemini, *The French Revolution*, 178.
[9] Thompson, *French Revolution*, 120.
[10] M.J. Sydenham, *The French Revolution*, 72.
[11] Salvemini, *French Revolution*, 179; Furet and Richet, *La Révolution française*, 114.
[12] Lynn Hunt, *Politics, Culture and Class in the French Revolution*, 35.

Friend of the King, of Frenchmen, of Order and above all of Truth [L'Ami du Roy, des français, de l'ordre et surtout de la vérité]."[13] This contract, which is dated 17 May, recognized two parties. The one consisted of the printer and bookseller Jean-Baptiste Nicolas Crapart and the bookseller Pierre César Briand, who were to assure the production and distribution of the paper. The other included three figures who together undertook to write and edit the paper. These were the young priest Poujade de Ladeveze; Christophe Ventre de la Touloubre Montjoie, who subsequently earned himself a reputation as an able and restrained journalist of the right; and Anne Françoise Fréron, née Royou, the widow of the great journalist Elie-Catherine Fréron, founder of, and principal writer for, the *Année Littéraire*. There is no record of Madame Fréron ever having written for publication, though she administered the *Année Littéraire*, and would play an important part in the running of the *Ami du Roi*. She appears to have been the key figure in the partnership, for as owner of the *Année Littéraire* she had had Crapart publish and distribute it, while she was also a friend of Montjoie.[14] Ladeveze had just finished his studies, while Briand was a bookseller

---

[13] This contract was passed *sous seing privé*. It was deposited with a notary only because one of the signatories, Montjoie, anticipated controversy about his rights to the paper, and may be found in the Minutier Central (henceforth MC) LXIV[495]. For the full text of this document see Appendix 1. Maurice Tourneux pointed out that when dispute arose with respect to the ownership of the *Ami du Roi* all sides appealed to "the famous contract drawn up before Me Decaux" to support their claims, but none made it public. "Trois journaux de Paris pendant la Révolution française," *La Révolution française*, 22 (1892), 270. Montjoie, however, announced in his paper that he had deposed a copy of the act of foundation with Decaux, and that another copy was avilable for inspection by the public in his offices (Hatin, *Histoire de la Presse*, VII, 140-41). It was Montjoie's reference to Decaux that made it possible to locate the document in the Minutier Central.

[14] The *Année Littéraire* was published by Crapart from January to June 1790. Montjoie referred to himself as the "friend and collaborator" of Madame Fréron. Cited in Hatin, *Histoire de la presse*, VII, 136. Madame Fréron admitted but minimized their collaboration. She acknowledged that Montjoie had worked on the *Année Littéraire*, but said that he had only provided a few filler articles ("articles de remplissage"). "Lettre de Madame Fréron aux anciens souscripteurs de l'Ami du Roi," BN Lc² 398.

rather than publisher, and apparently a junior colleague of Crapart. Though the contract of 17 May made Madame Fréron formally responsible for editing part of the paper, she clearly participated as a businesswoman and entrepreneur. Having no part in the act of foundation was the brother of Madame Fréron and the man whose name was to be most closely associated with the paper, the abbé Royou.

The contract stipulated that half ownership of the paper went to Briand and Crapart, who were to assure production and distribution, and the other half to Montjoie, Ladeveze and Madame Fréron, who were to furnish copy. The terms accorded the editors seem reasonable enough. They were to receive 7,800 *livres* a year, which amounts to 50 *livres* a week for each of the three, payable weekly. Though another clause stipulates that the fixed salaries of the editors would not be increased for any reason, 50 *livres* remains a handsome wage.[15] Moreover, if subscriptions were good it was further stipulated that Crapart and Briand would cover all costs (presumably including the salaries of the editors), would keep the first 7,800 *livres* in profits for themselves and then divide the remaining profits, half going to themselves and half to the editors.[16] The risk would be assumed entirely by the pub-

---

[15] Fifty *livres* a week works out to a daily wage of just over 7 *livres* 2 *sous*, or nearly 143 *sous* a day. During 1789 simple laborers were effectively earning, taking Sundays and holidays into account, 15 to 18 *sous* a day, a journeyman mason 24 *sous*, a journeyman locksmith or carpenter 30 *sous*, and a sculptor or goldsmith 60 *sous*. George Rudé, "Prices, Wages and the Popular Movement in Paris during the French Revolution," 167.

[16] With 3,000 subscribers at 33 *livres* a year for an annual subscription, the *Ami du Roi* would have had a gross annual income of 99,000 *livres*. The costs of printing, paper and postage can reasonably be calculated at about 40,000 *livres* (see below, Chaps. III and IV). From the remaining 59,000 *livres* 7,800 must be subtracted for the editors' salaries, and a further 7,800 was divided equally between Crapart and Briand. Of the remaining 43,400 *livres* Briand and Crapart would get one-quarter each (10,850) while one-sixth (7,233) would go to each of the editors. If Madame Fréron and her brother had divided such an income, they would have had about 5,000 *livres* a year each, which was certainly a respectable sum. But by opening their own paper and making a success of it they could reasonably have expected to earn four or five times as much. Taking 4,800 as the average press run for 1791, J.-P. Bertaud has calculated that the gross income of the *Ami du Roi* would have been 144,000 *livres* and its profits 88,000 *livres*. *Les Amis du Roi*, 55.

lishers. This is a great improvement on the fixed salary paid
Morénas by Giroud, and it compares not badly with the contracts Panckoucke made with his more prestigious editors.[17]
But one can understand the dissatisfaction of the editors in
being deprived of a share of the first 7,800 *livres* in profits,
and then receiving only a one-sixth share thereafter, especially in that the larger the subscription list, the greater, proportionately, the profits of the publishers, while production
costs rose only marginally.[18] For a new paper the terms laid
down in the contract of 17 May seem reasonable enough,
and no doubt under the conditions of the old regime such a
contract would have been seen as more than fair. But conditions had changed.

C. The Three *Amis du Roi*

The career of the *Ami du Roi* was tumultuous and by modern standards short, its last number appearing in August
1792. Moreover, for most of the period between June 1790
and August 1792 there were two, and for a short time three,
periodicals of this name. All of them, however, were directly
associated with one or more of the signatories of the contract
of 17 May.

The first number of the *Ami du Roi* appeared on 1 June
1790 and though anonymous, was written by Montjoie and
published by Crapart and Briand. Royou collaborated with
Montjoie for just under two months,[19] then left, in circumstances that will call for further consideration, and established

---

[17] See above, Chap. I, n. 97.

[18] For the duration of Royou's *Ami du Roi*, the cost of composition remained constant
at 168 *livres* a week. The cost of printing rose from 105 *livres* for 3,000 copies to
140 *livres* for 4,000 to 199 *livres* 10 *sous* for 5,700. AN T546⁶³⁵ ¹⁴⁰ ⁶⁷.

[19] According to the testimony of both Madame Fréron and Royou himself, the abbé
wrote for the original *Ami du Roi* from 14 June to 7 August. "Lettre de Madame
Fréron aux anciens souscripteurs."

his own *Ami du Roi,* with offices at Madame Fréron's.[20] The first number of Royou's *Ami du Roi* appeared on 1 September 1790, the same day that Montjoie began publishing his own paper of the same name. As Crapart and Briand continued to publish their version of the paper, there were three papers entitled *L'Ami du Roi* appearing daily, each claiming to be the "real" one, and all claiming to be by the successors of Fréron. This led the original publishers to remark that "never had the King so many friends, nor Fréron so many successors."[21] This situation did not last long, however, for Montjoie came to an understanding with Briand and Crapart some two months after his secession. Thus from early November 1790 to May 1792, when Royou ceased publication, there were two papers called the *Ami du Roi.* Montjoie's paper was suppressed following the rising of 10 August.[22] Royou's paper thus lasted for a year and nine months, Montjoie's for a little more than two years. By the standards of the period both papers were highly successful. Jack Censer has shown that of 515 papers published in Paris between May 1789 and October 1791, 54 percent lasted less than one month, while only 9 percent lasted a year and a half or more.[23]

Royou's break with Crapart and Briand should be seen in the context of the relations between publishers and editors at the time and the way the Revolution influenced these relations. Though formal liberty of the press was achieved during the summer of 1789, this did little to redress the economic advantages of publishers over writers. What did make a difference was the unprecedented demand for news. With increased need for their skills, journalists now found that their salaries tended to rise. More than this, it now became possible for the more adventurous and better-off among them

---

[20] Royou, "Avis aux souscripteurs du journal intitulé L'Ami du Roi des françois, de l'ordre et sur-tout de la vérité." BN Lc² 398.

[21] Hatin, *Histoire de la presse,* VII, 134.

[22] Hatin, *Histoire de la presse,* VII, 132-43; Bellanger, *Histoire générale,* I, 484.

[23] J.R. Censer, *Prelude to Power,* 9-10.

to appeal directly to the public through the mechanism of the uncontrolled market. And this Royou did. He explained his decision to leave Crapart and Briand in the following terms:

Animated by the unanimous support of upright folk [honnêtes gens] and true patriots, the author [Royou] braved the clamors of the factious and scorned the outrages of a few obscure calumnators; but he has fearsome enemies in the very men responsible for the printing and distribution of his work. It is without doubt a sad state of affairs that men of letters should be dependent upon those who, by the nature of their functions, are not, and should not be, anything but their clerks . . .

. . . the author of the AMI DU ROI, overwhelmed for two months with difficulties and discouragements which often caused the pen to fall from his hands, scarcely able to get the smallest salary for his efforts, and seeing himself about to be entirely despoiled of the most precious and most sacred property in the world, that of his thoughts [pensées], has finally resolved to indicate another office to his subscribers, and to be his own publisher [libraire], and no longer to have recourse to outsiders who sell their services so dear. Since the sixth day of the month of August [1790] he has absolutely stopped working for men who were devouring the fruit of his labor.

The abbé Royou, who until now has thought it proper to remain anonymous, now declares himself to be the author of the principal and most interesting part of the journal entitled the *Ami du Roi*, and that he is going to continue it in the same style and according to the same principles that the public has appeared to relish until now, and that he will henceforth be supported in this enterprise by the same men of letters who collaborated with him in supporting the journal of the late M. Fréron, known by the name of the *Année Littéraire*. It is much less upon his own weak talents that he founds his hopes for the success of his journal than on the distinguished merit of his associates.

BUT IT IS NO LONGER at the offices of Misters *Crapart & Briand* that one subscribes for the *Ami du Roi*.

The subscription office is henceforth open at No. 37, rue Saint-André-des-Arcs, at the corner of the rue de l'Epéron on the first floor.[24]

---

[24] Royou, "Avis aux souscripteurs," 1.

If Royou's political views were conservative, his attitudes toward authors' rights and literary property were not. Moreover, his complaints here ring true. They reflect the conditions in the literary marketplace of the time too well to be dismissed as spleen. Eugène Hatin, the great nineteenth-century authority on the press, supposes that high-handed treatment of Montjoie by Crapart and Briand caused him to establish his own paper. Hatin further refers to the way Prudhomme and Camille Desmoulins had been mistreated by their publishers and observes that publishers tended to look upon themselves as the "lords and masters" of the journalists they employed.[25]

It is not possible to say whether the root of Royou's disagreement with Crapart and Briand was a refusal to treat him as one of the editors who had signed the original contract founding the paper, or whether they accorded him similar terms and he found them unsatisfactory. His comments in his "Avis aux souscripteurs" would lead one to expect the former. In any case, unlike most other writers of the time, Royou had an alternative open to him.

The abbé had had considerable experience as a journalist under the old regime. Even more importantly, his sister, Madame Fréron, for years had managed the business side of an important periodical and knew the world of publishing and bookselling thoroughly. By pooling their resources and abilities Madame Fréron and her brother were able to found a paper that became one of the leading right-wing dailies of the period of the constitutional monarchy.

D. The *Ami du Roi* of the Abbé Royou

The subject of this study is less the abbé Royou and his paper, the *Ami du Roi*, than the production, distribution and

---

[25] Hatin, *Histoire de la presse*, VII, 135-36.

readership of this paper. Nevertheless, in order to understand Royou's public, it is necessary to know something of
the paper and its editor, how they were perceived by contemporaries and what experiences they underwent.

The *Ami du Roi* of the abbé Royou was published in quarto
format, a number normally consisting of four pages of small
print arranged in two columns.[26] With a few interruptions it
appeared daily between 1 September 1790 and 3 May 1792.
It has the reputation of having been one of the more radical
monarchist papers of the early Revolution.

Of Royou's and Montjoie's papers, there is no doubt that
the former was both the more popular and the more extreme.
Both, to be sure, were royalist. But in the analogy of Leonard
Gallois, a nineteenth-century historian of the press, Montjoie
was the Brissot of royalism, Royou its Marat.[27] Jacques Godechot puts the *Ami du Roi* at the extreme right of the political
spectrum and calls Royou an ultra-royalist.[28] For Gilchrist
and Murray the paper was "one of the most extreme of the
opponents of the Revolution," and "the most celebrated of
the ultra-right-wing papers."[29] The dean of the history of
French journalism, Eugène Hatin, states that after the king's
flight to Varennes in June 1791, Royou's paper became "the
official journal of the emigration and of the clergy."[30] Two
recent studies of the right-wing press during the early Revolution, while on the whole regarding Royou's *Ami du Roi* as
less extreme than it has usually been depicted, confirm the
importance of the paper. J.-P. Bertaud calls it the leader
("chef de file") of the rightist journals, while W.J. Murray

---

[26] This was the same format as used by Montjoie's paper, the chief difference being
that each issue of Royou's paper was numbered from pages one to four, while
Montjoie's was numbered consecutively. This format was also common toward
the end of the old regime, especially for provincial papers. Feyel, "La Presse
provinciale," 356.

[27] Cited in Hatin, *Histoire de la presse*, VII, 143.

[28] Bellanger, *Histoire générale*, I, 463 and 468.

[29] Gilchrist and Murray, *The Press in the French Revolution*, 8 and 23.

[30] Hatin, *Histoire de la presse*, VII, 155.

regards the paper as the most incisive critic of the Assembly at this time and sees in its editor "the man with the best claim to be regarded as the conscience of the Right."[31] The historians just cited are unanimous in regarding Royou's *Ami du Roi* as the best known and most popular of the papers that bore that name.[32]

Though Royou's *Ami du Roi* is by all accounts the best known and most influential paper of that name, Royou himself is not well known today, nor is his paper frequently cited by students of the Revolution.[33] Yet there is reason to believe that he was fairly well known to contemporaries.[34] The success of his paper was such as to make him one of the more influential journalists of the early Revolution. Moreover, Royou's career is strangely bound up with that of one of the most famous figures of the Revolution—Jean-Paul Marat, editor of the *Ami du Peuple,* deputy to the Convention, victim of Charlotte Corday and martyr to the Revolution, in the iconography of which he came to figure prominently.[35]

Though standing at opposite ends of the political spectrum, Royou and Marat were often linked by contemporaries who seem to have been more impressed by their extremism

---

[31] Bertaud, *Les Amis du Roi,* 17; Murray, *The Right-Wing Press,* 232 and 210.

[32] Hatin, *Histoire de la presse,* VII, 143; Bellanger, *Histoire générale,* I, 484; Gilchrist and Murray, *The Press in the French Revolution,* 24; Murray, *The Right-Wing Press,* 35; Bertaud, *Les Amis du Roi,* 17.

[33] Royou figures once in Thompson, *The French Revolution,* where his name is misspelled Royon (p. 264), twice in Furet and Richet's history of the Revolution, where he is called "a clear and profound mind" (p. 109) and three times in Mathiez's basic *The French Revolution.* He also appears in Harvey Mitchell, *The Underground War Against Revolutionary France: the Missions of William Wickham, 1794-1800.* Royou is absent from the general histories of the Revolution published by Lefebvre, Salvemini, A. Goodwin, R.R. Palmer, Sydenham and Hampson, as well as from more specialized works where one might expect him to figure, such as Paul H. Beik, *The French Revolution Seen from the Right: Social Theories in Motion, 1789-1799;* J. Godechot, *The Counter-Revolution, Doctrine and Action;* and G. Michon, *Le Rôle de la presse en 1791-92: La Déclaration de Pillnitz et la Guerre* (Paris, 1941).

[34] Bertaud's assertion that "His name was as well known as those of the most illustrious orators of the Jacobins or the [National] Assembly" (*Les Amis du Roi,* 17) is perhaps exaggerated.

[35] For Marat's posthumous reputation see J.C. Bonnet, ed., *La Mort de Marat.*

than by their differing ideas. Because of his attacks on the National Assembly, Marat was accused by Brissot of being the accomplice of Royou,[36] while the deputy Girardin denounced Royou for opposing the Revolution "by a system in truth connected with, though in appearance opposite to, that of the *Ami du Peuple.*"[37] Danton pointed to the shared extremism of the two journalists, saying that Marat was "a man whose opinions are to the republican party what those of Royou were to the aristocratic party."[38] The authorities, too, seem to have looked upon Royou and Marat with equal mistrust. Following the Champ-de-Mars shooting of July 1791 the two were included in a list of suspects who were to be arrested, though both escaped.[39] In the session of 3 May 1792, the Assembly decided to issue warrants for two journalists, and only two: Royou and Marat.[40] The analogy between Royou and Marat has struck historians as well as contemporaries. Comparing the papers of Montjoie and Royou, Eugène Hatin wrote that "the *Ami du Roi* is Royou, as the *Ami du Peuple* is Marat," and Jacques Godechot has more recently made the same assertion.[41]

Thomas-Marie Royou was born in 1743 at Quimper in Brittany, the son of a magistrate in a seigneurial court who rose to the important post of *subdélégué* in the royal administration.[42] Though he entered the church and was normally addressed as *abbé*, Royou devoted most of his life to teaching and writing. For twenty years he taught a senior class at the celebrated *collège* Louis-le-Grand in Paris. He is known to have been there while Robespierre, Camille Desmoulins and

---

[36] Gilchrist and Murray, *The Press in the French Revolution*, 11.

[37] *Gazette Nationale, ou le Moniteur Universel* (henceforth *Moniteur*), 4 May 1792; reporting the session of 3 May.

[38] Mathiez, *French Revolution*, 238.

[39] *Moniteur*, 22 July 1791.

[40] *Moniteur*, 4 May 1792.

[41] Hatin, *Histoire de la presse*, VII, 132; Bellanger, *Histoire générale*, I, 484.

[42] For an account of Royou's life see M. Michaud, ed., *Biographie Universelle Ancienne et Moderne*, 36:697-99; Jean Sgard, ed., *Dictionnaire des journalistes*, 326-27; Bertaud, *Les Amis du Roi*, 18-21; and Murray, *The Right-Wing Press*, 36-39.

his nephew, Stanislas Fréron, were students in the *collège*, but there is no evidence that he personally instructed them.[43] It does not seem that Royou inspired warm regard or devotion in the students he did have.[44] While teaching at Louis-le-Grand he also wrote for the periodical press, a common practice at the time.[45] He published his own *Journal de Monsieur* from 1781 until its closure two years later. He also collaborated on the *Année Littéraire*. It is thought that this collaboration was begun while Fréron, who had taken Royou's sister as his second wife, was still alive.[46] His involvement with the *Année Littéraire* can reasonably be expected to have grown after the famous journalist died in 1776.

His first significant independent publication, *Le Monde de verre reduit en poudre*, appeared in 1779. It was a criticism of Buffon, and was well received by traditionalists.[47] On the whole his relations with men of letters under the old regime do not seem to have been congenial. Diderot and La Harpe disliked him,[48] while Rivarol included him, together with his brother, in his satirical almanac of second rate and failed writers.[49] Highly esteemed by contemporaries or not, Royou had gained considerable experience in journalism before the outbreak of the Revolution, and he had already identified himself with traditionalist values.

In light of Royou's association with traditionalism and his reputation for extremism, both with contemporaries and an older generation of historians, it is worth pointing out that

---

[43] It is unlikely that the old boy network of the school would have let this pass in silence if it were so.

[44] Murray, *The Right-Wing Press*, 36-37.

[45] From its inception in 1701 until 1762 the *Journal de Trévoux* was edited by the Jesuit professors of Louis-le-Grand. See John N. Pappas, *Berthier, the Journal de Trévoux and the Philosophes, VS* 3: chap. I.

[46] This is the opinion of William Murray in the article "Royou, T.M." in the *Dictionnaire des journalistes*, 327.

[47] Murray, *The Right-Wing Press*, 37.

[48] Ibid., 38.

[49] Rivarol, *Le Petit dictionnaire de nos grands hommes*, 163-64. The brief article devoted to the Royou brothers concerns only their literary failings.

on substantial issues he often took moderate positions. Bertaud warns against regarding the right-wing press in general, and Royou's paper in particular, as reactionary.[50] Both Bertaud and Murray note that Royou directed his arguments against principles, not persons,[51] that he was prepared to accept a considerable measure of reform[52] and that he energetically opposed violence, armed counter-revolution and war.[53] On the question of emigration he sought to remain impartial, criticizing the laws on the émigrés but never encouraging Frenchmen to leave their country.[54] Even on ecclesiastical policy, a subject probably more important to him than any other, Royou sought an accommodation going beyond what most of the Right thought acceptable.[55] Once Pius VI pronounced on the Civil Constitution of the Clergy and accompanying oath, however, the abbé accepted and firmly upheld the papal decision.

Royou's closest associates on the *Ami du Roi* were family members. His sister, Madame Fréron, whom we have seen was one of the partners in the original *Ami du Roi*, acted as his publisher, handling the organization and the business aspects of the paper. After the closure of the paper in 1792 Madame Fréron disappears from view, but is found again in her native town of Quimper, where she died in 1814.[56]

Jacques Corentin Royou was the brother of the principal editor of the *Ami du Roi* and shared his political views. By profession he was a lawyer. It was Jacques Corentin who took over much of the responsibility for the paper while his brother was in hiding. After the abbé's death, Jacques Corentin Royou

---

[50] *Les Amis du Roi*, 58.
[51] Ibid., 22; Murray, *The Right-Wing Press*, 236.
[52] Bertaud, *Les Amis du Roi*, 11, 58, 116-17 and 135.
[53] Murray, *The Right-Wing Press*, 140, 154 and 161; Bertaud, *Les Amis du Roi*, 18, 175-76 and 213-14.
[54] Murray, *The Right-Wing Press*, 145-46; Bertaud, *Les Amis du Roi*, 177-78 and 213.
[55] Murray, *The Right-Wing Press*, 145-46.
[56] J. Trevedy, *Fréron et sa famille*.

wrote for the violently anti-revolutionary *Véridique*, which appeared between October 1792 and May 1793.[57]

Also associated with Royou in writing for the *Ami du Roi* was Julien Louis Geoffroy, a minor literary figure of the period who had been a Jesuit, and like Royou, a teacher in a *collège*.[58] Geoffroy began his journalistic career under the old regime as a collaborator first in the *Journal de Monsieur* with Royou, then in the *Année Littéraire*. He left France as politics polarized, returning only in 1799. He subsequently became a particularly popular and well-paid writer with the *Journal des débats*.

Another important figure associated with the *Ami du Roi* was the abbé Maury, one of the leading spokesmen for the Right in the Constituent Assembly.[59] It does not seem that Maury actually wrote for Royou's paper, but Bertaud calls him Royou's "correspondent in the Assembly," and another journal of the time calls Royou "the echo of M. l'abbé Maury."[60] We will see below that Royou published many of Maury's speeches and pamphlets separately.

Ladeveze, a signatory of the original contract establishing the *Ami du Roi*, continued to collaborate on Royou's paper, then went on to contribute to the royalist *Courrier Universel*. Though condemned to death for his journalistic activities, Ladeveze was able to escape and reappeared during the Directory. His dramatic career notwithstanding, Ladeveze hardly figures in the records of the *Ami du Roi* and could not have played an important part in the paper. The same can be said of Pierre Etienne Regnaud, whom Bertaud describes as an "occasional collaborator" of Royou.[61]

---

[57] The principal sources used for the careers of the collaborators of Royou on the *Ami du Roi* are the *Biographie universelle*, the *Dictionnaire des journalistes* and Murray, *The Right-Wing Press*.

[58] Geoffroy lost his position in the Collège des Quatre Nations in 1792 because of his political opinions. Murray, *The Right-Wing Press*, 40.

[59] On Maury see below, Chap. IV.

[60] Bertaud, *Les Amis du Roi*, 36-37; Murray, *The Right-Wing Press*, 117, n. 57.

[61] Bertaud, *Les Amis du Roi*, 35.

E. The *Ami du Roi* and the Revolution

We have seen above that Royou's *Ami du Roi* was first published in September 1790 and ceased to appear in May 1792. Most of the great constitutional and legislative innovations of the Revolution were made or begun before Royou began publication, while the civil war, the Terror and related acts of violence by which the Revolution is most widely remembered occurred after Royou's *Ami du Roi* had been closed.

The summer of 1789 saw the enactment of a large number of the most fundamental changes in a remarkably short time. After a protracted struggle during May and June the Estates General was replaced by the National Assembly, the Third Estate, together with a minority of representatives of the other two Orders, taking that title on 17 June and the king recognizing it ten days later. Thus in a few weeks the age old principle of representation by order yielded to the principle of national sovereignty. When the National Assembly proclaimed itself Constituent on 9 July the principle of a formally drafted constitution was accepted and the crown abandoned the ideal of absolutism which it had worked so long to establish and had recently reasserted. The Declaration of the Rights of Man and the Citizen (26 August) both established equality before the law and negated the principles of social organization of the old regime.[62] The legislation abolishing noble status and titles (19 June 1790) can be seen as continuing this basic trend.[63]

Not all the achievements of the summer of 1789 were made on the legal or constitutional levels. The legislation of 4 August, which saw the voluntary renunciation of many privileges and

---

[62] On the dual nature of the Declaration of Rights, see the general histories of Aulard (I, 155), Mathiez (59), Salvemini (146-47), Lefebvre (147), who cites Aulard on this point, and Sydenham (63-64).

[63] On this question see Patrice L. R. Higonnet, *Class, Ideology and the Rights of Nobles during the French Revolution.*

certain, though not all, feudal dues, was a great economic boon to the peasantry. The popular uprisings of 14 July and 5-6 October showed that the people, who under the old regime had been feared as a source of sedition and disorder, had now emerged as a political force to be reckoned with. Traditionally, popular violence had been ill-considered, short-lived and futile. Whether by chance or by design, the uprisings of the summer of 1789, by lending essential support to the middle class professionals of the Assembly against the Court, made the people the political arbiters of the nation. On both occasions they used their strength to promote their own interests and those of their allies.

As well as many of the outstanding achievements of the Revolution, certain of the issues over which it was to come to grief had already been clearly elaborated before September 1790. During the fall and winter of 1789-90 important ecclesiastical and financial measures were taken which had grave implications for the new regime. Church property was nationalized (2 November 1789) and monastic vows were abolished while most religious orders were suppressed (February 1790). The Civil Constitution of the Clergy was passed in mid-July 1790, though the oath making acceptance of it obligatory was not imposed until November of that year, when Royou had already established himself as an important spokesman of the Right. The financial instability of the Revolution is often seen as having its source in the issuance of bonds *(assignats)* secured against nationalized Church property in December 1789 and the transformation of these bonds into legal tender four months later.[64]

The episodes and images which form the heart of the popular conception of the Revolution nearly all postdate the closure of Royou's paper. Dickens did not think it worthwhile

---

[64] In itself the idea of issuing paper money secured on Church property was sound. Problems arose when the government, faced with crushing financial burdens, failed to destroy redeemed notes and went on to print more to meet its needs. Confidence in the *assignats* failed and serious inflation followed.

to bring Darnay to Paris much before the massacres of September 1792. The action of Wajda's *Danton* is set nearly two years after Royou's death, and the image that dominates the film, that of the guillotine, which also encapsulates the Revolution for the general public, would have been unfamiliar to him.[65]

In his life Royou saw the destabilization of the ambitious settlement attempted by the men of the Constituent and Legislative Assemblies. However, he died within a day of the invasion of the Tuileries on 20 June 1792 and never heard of the rising of 10 August, the September Massacres, the execution of Louis XVI, the civil war in the Vendée, the federalist risings and their suppression, the Terror organized by the Committee of Public Safety, the White Terror that followed it, or much else. The period during which Royou published his *Ami du Roi* was not idyllic. It was a time during which much went wrong, tensions increased and the constitutional monarchy was compromised. Yet it saw relative tranquillity, and it is proper to think of it in its own terms rather than those of the period that followed it.

In mid-1790, when plans were being laid to produce the *Ami du Roi*, a block of right-wing papers was only just emerging.[66] At that time there was little concerted opposition to the Assembly, republicanism had not yet begun to be discussed seriously and virtually all Frenchmen were monarchist, even enthusiastically monarchist.[67] A few days after the appearance of the original *Ami du Roi* a hostile journalist questioned the propriety of the title of the new paper, asking "Are not

---

[65] The Assembly did not determine that decapitation should be by machine until March 1792, and the first execution by the guillotine did not take place until the following month. S. F. Scott and B. Rothaus, eds., *Historical Dictionary of the French Revolution: 1789-1799*, "Guillotine."

[66] Murray, *The Right-Wing Press*, 12.

[67] Aulard, who wrote his history of the Revolution as the history of republicanism, saw the first emergence of an embryonic republican party around Madame Robert and her salon in late 1790 (*The French Revolution*, I, 224) and asserted that "So long as Louis seemed possible as a leader of the Revolution and the guide of France, there was no Republican party" (ibid., 258).

all good citizens the friends of this virtuous prince [Louis XVI]? And does not the abbé Royou alone deserve to be excepted, since he is the apostle of aristocracy and fanaticism?"[68] Monarchism was clearly above reproach at this time, so opponents of the Revolution were designated "aristocrats" or with some other term of opprobrium.

When it was first established, then, the *Ami du Roi* was aimed at a broad section of public opinion. This partially explains why the original *Ami du Roi* in which Madame Fréron, Montjoie, Crapart and Briand were partners was an immediate commercial success. After 5 November 1790, when Crapart and Montjoie again joined to produce their *Ami du Roi* in competition with Royou's, their paper continued to do well. Madame Fréron and the abbé Royou's paper we know began by publishing 3,000 copies daily in September and nearly doubled this figure by mid-summer of the following year (Fig. 2.1). After the crises of the flight to Varennes and the shootings on the Champ-de-Mars, subscriptions began to fall (Fig. 2.2). With a peak number of 5,700 daily copies and press runs never falling below 4,000 thereafter, the *Ami du Roi* was one of the most widely circulating papers of the period.[69]

Royou's first confrontation with supporters of the Revolution was an informal one and occurred about six weeks after he had begun publishing his own paper. On 18 November 1790 a group of patriots from the Café Zoppi, formerly the Procope, near the old Comédie, decided that the right-wing press was going too far in its criticisms of the Assembly, and that it was their duty to remonstrate with the editors of the important royalist papers. They accordingly organized a deputation, which went off to find the abbé Royou, Mallet

---

[68] *Chronique*, 5 June 1790. Cited in Hatin, *Histoire de la presse*, VII, 131. It is curious that Royou should be associated with the *Ami du Roi* at this early date.
[69] See above, Chap. I, section B.

Figure 2.1: Press runs of the *Ami du Roi* from September 1790 to May 1792*

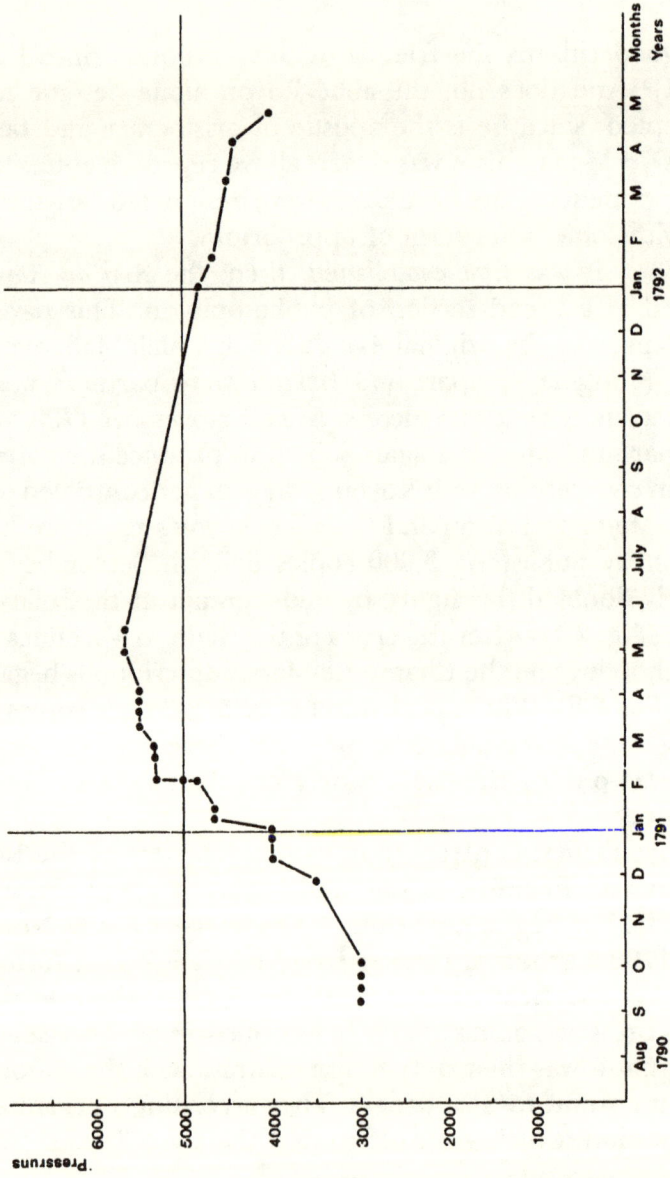

*Source: AN T546.

Figure 2.2: The Chronology of the *Ami du Roi* in the Context of the Revolution

DATE	AMI DU ROI	ASSEMBLY	COURT, CHURCH, FOREIGN RELATIONS	POPULAR MOVEMENT
1789				
5 May		convocation Estates General		
27 June		name "National Assembly" adopted		
14 July				capture of Bastille
4 Aug.		legislation on feudalism and privilege		
26 Aug.		Declaration of Rights		
5/6 Oct.			royal family moved to Paris	journée
2 Nov.		nationalization church property		
1790				
17 May	contract founding AR			
1 June	first number AR			
19 June		abolition titles of nobility		
12 July		Civil Constitution of the Clergy		
14 July			Fête de la Fédération	
31 Aug.	Montjoie deposits copy of contract with Decaux			

1 Sept.	Royou and Montjoie begin publication of their own papers: three *AR*s		
5 Nov.	Montjoie rejoins Crapart		
19 Nov.	visit of delegation of Café Zoppi		
27 Nov.		imposition of oath of acceptance of the Civil Constitution	
1791			
10 March			first papal bull on Civil Constitution
13 April			second bull condemning Civil Constitution
20 June			flight to Varennes
17 July			massacre of the Champ-de-Mars
21 July	National Guard visit offices *AR*; Royou underground; publication interrupted		
	police visit offices *AR*; Mme. Fréron arrested		
23 July	officials of section Théâtre Français visit offices *AR*; Mme. Fréron released		
1 Aug.			

5 Aug.		Assembly renounces wars of conquest		
7 Aug.	Royou's *AR* resumes publication			
27 Aug.		Declaration of Pillnitz		
14 Sept.		King accepts constitution; Legislative Assembly convenes		
1 Oct.				
5 Nov.	Mme. Fréron requests that papers be returned to her			
9 Nov.		law against émigrés		
17 Nov.	last seals removed from papers *AR*			
1792				
20 April			France declares war on Austria	
3 May	warrants issued for arrest of Royou and Marat			
4 May	last number Royou's *AR*			
20 June				crowd invades Tuileries
21 June		"patrie en danger"		
11 July				
25 July			Brunswick Manifesto	
10 Aug.	Royou dies		monarchy overthrown	journée
2-6 Sept.	Montjoie's *AR* closed			Sept. massacres
20 Sept.		Convention convenes	Valmy	
22 Sept.			republic proclaimed	

du Pan, Peltier, Rozoi and others.[70] Royou met the deputation by chance in the street but refused to allow its members to enter his home, office or printshop. There ensued a long, less than amicable argument between the abbé and the patriots in which they berated him for slanting his reporting against the Revolution and for incitement to disorder, while he argued that they had not read him correctly, that his views were sound, that he had the right to express them and that he sought to avoid civil war at all costs.[71] In his account of his confrontation with the delegation, Mallet du Pan makes two interesting points. First, the members of the delegation were "very well dressed."[72] Second, they insisted that they were good monarchists ("We love the king & we will defend his authority").[73] Mallet, for his part, assured the delegation that, "The old regime has never had and never will have a more dedicated enemy than myself, who has groaned more than anyone under its oppression."[74] When a royalist writer can openly profess and publish his abhorrence of the old regime while patriot activists assert their devotion to the king, we are far from the tensions and attitudes that characterize the Revolution in its more radical stages. But this ground was covered and the shift effected with remarkable speed.

The delegation of the Café Zoppi visited the conservative journalists in November 1790. In March and April 1791 Pius VI openly and unequivocally condemned the Civil Constitution of the Clergy, thus bringing the Roman Church into direct and uncompromising conflict with the new regime and probably costing that regime more popular support than it was to lose over any other issue. Within months Louis XVI

[70] For an account of the activities of this deputation, see Murray, *The Right-Wing Press*, 99-100.
[71] *AR*, 19 November 1790. Bertaud, *Les Amis du Roi*, 42-44, quotes extensively from Royou's account of the confrontation.
[72] *Mercure de France*, 1790 vol. 11 (27 November 1790), 291. Royou had made the same observation (*AR*, 19 November 1790).
[73] *Mercure*, 27 November 1790; 11, 289.
[74] Ibid., 288.

was brought back in disgrace from Varennes, the fortunes of the monarchy severely compromised. After 21 June, good patriots no longer felt it necessary to protest their loyalty to the crown and their readiness to defend its authority.

After the flight to Varennes the majority in the National Assembly sought to stabilize the Revolution and to retain the king. The Cordeliers Club and many of the Paris sections began to call for the removal of Louis XVI and in some cases for the establishment of a republic. The Paris Jacobins split over the question, the more moderate members, who were the majority, seceding to form a new club, the Feuillants. At the Champ-de-Mars, where a great altar to the fatherland still stood after the second Fête de la Fédération, Brissot, then a prominent Jacobin, presented a petition on 16 July calling for Louis to abdicate and to be replaced by "constitutional means." The Jacobins then reversed themselves and withdrew their support of Brissot's demands. A more radical petition calling for the abolition of the monarchy and the establishment of a republic was drawn up by the journalist Robert on 17 July and signed by five or six thousand enthusiastic supporters. Toward evening the municipality proclaimed martial law on the Champ-de-Mars and the National Guard fired on the crowd. The authorities put the number of fatalities at eleven, the sections at several hundred.[75]

The "massacre of the Champ-de-Mars," as this event is usually called, is significant as the first large-scale act of violence directed by members of the Third Estate against other members of the same Order in the Revolution. It is also the first time that republicanism appears as a major issue, and indicates a radicalization of opinion in the light of which

---

[75] Salvemini, *The French Revolution*, 229-30. George Rudé, the leading authority on crowds during this period, put the number of dead at "perhaps" 50. *The Crowd in the French Revolution*, 89.

royalism could seriously be called into question.[76] The events of 17 July 1791, then, are an important stage in the polarization of opinion.

Many royalist papers were uncertain how to respond after the flight to Varennes.[77] Royou was not. He came out unequivocally in support of the king.[78] Little wonder, then, that in the aftermath of the shootings on the Champ-de-Mars, Royou's *Ami du Roi* was one of the papers that the Assembly, seeking to quiet the situation, took action against. Warrants were issued for the arrest of Royou, as well as for his nephew, Stanislas Fréron, editor of the radical *Orateur du Peuple*, Verrières, who was believed to be editing Marat's *Ami du Peuple*, and Suleau, another prominent right-wing journalist.[79]

On 21 July 1791 the National Guard, acting on orders from a committee of the National Assembly, visited the offices of the *Ami du Roi* with the intention of arresting the abbé Royou. Failing to find him there, they seized some of his papers and put others under seals.[80] Thus began an interruption of two weeks in the publication of the *Ami du Roi*. But the visit from the National Guard was not the end of the paper's involvement with the revolutionary authorities.

Two days later, on 23 July, a number of municipal police officers, including police commissioners of two different Parisian sections, visited the offices of the *Ami du Roi* at 37 Saint-André-des-Arts. They were acting on the authority of the Comité des Rapports of the Assembly, and had come to arrest Royou.[81] The abbé still being absent, they proceeded to make

---

[76] On the importance of the shootings of the Champ-de-Mars and their significance see the general histories of Salvemini, 230; Mathiez, 131; Lefebvre, 209-210; Thompson, 221-22; Furet and Richet, 143-44; and Rudé, *The Crowd*, 80-81.

[77] Murray, *The Right-Wing Press*, 122.

[78] Bertaud, *Les Amis du Roi*, 183.

[79] *Moniteur*, 22 July 1791. In their general histories of the Revolution, Thompson (221), Mathiez (131) Lefebvre (209) and Sydenham (83-84) note the repression of the left in the second half of July 1791. Furet and Richet (144) point out that repression was directed against the extreme right also.

[80] *Moniteur*, 22 July 1791.

[81] Archives de la Préfecture de Police (henceforth APP), AA206[405].

a thorough inspection of the offices of his paper and the apartments of those associated with it, and prepared a full written report of all they saw, including the various publications found there. Having made this inspection, the police affixed seals to some documents and papers, seized others, and arrested Madame Fréron and two of the clerks employed on the paper, Candau and Serva, whom they took, together with the papers seized, to the police station.[82]

After answering questions, Candau and Serva were released, but Madame Fréron was consigned to the Prison of the Abbaye. Before being taken to prison, however, she was allowed to return home to see that an acceptable guardian of the seals to be placed on her papers was appointed. This was her employee, Serva.[83] Madame Fréron signed the police clerk's account of the day's proceedings and was then taken to prison by a National Guardsman.

Madame Fréron did not languish in prison. Two days after her arrest Perron, the police administrator who oversaw the case, wrote a note to ask that she be questioned as quickly as possible.[84] The interrogation was carried out within days and turned primarily on the running of the *Ami du Roi*, the papal briefs condemning the Civil Constitution of the Clergy, of which large numbers had been found during the police search, and Madame Fréron's relations with the émigrés.[85] On 1 August the sequestered documents (principally subscription lists) were examined in the presence of Madame Fréron and two notables and found to contain no incriminating evidence.[86] The same day Perron decided that legal proceedings should be instigated against Royou, but that Madame Fréron could be

---

[82] APP AA206[415]. The police arrived at 11:30 in the morning and left at 3:30 in the afternoon.
[83] APP AA206[415].
[84] APP AA206[409].
[85] The date of the interrogation is uncertain, but appears to have been 31 July. APP AA206[415].
[86] APP AA206[418].

freed provisionally.[87] She was taken back to her apartment at 37 Saint-André-des-Arts, more seals were affixed to papers there, and she herself was constituted their guardian.[88]

On the morning of 1 August, before Madame Fréron had returned home, two citizens of the Théâtre Français Section had seen papers being removed from her house and informed the local authorities. The Section dispatched several commissioners to look into the matter. They found copies of the *Ami du Roi,* the papal briefs mentioned earlier and "other papers" in a fourth floor apartment, placed seals on what they had found, constituted Serva guardian of the seals and withdrew.[89]

This flurry of police activity in and around the offices of the *Ami du Roi* is revealing. It shows, first, a lack of coordination among the various agencies of the newly constituted authorities. Representatives of three different bodies—the National Guard, the municipality and the sections—visited the same premises within ten days.[90] The first two visits, it is true, were carried out on the directions of a committee of the National Assembly. The third represents a local initiative by neighbors (one thinks, perhaps unjustly, of vigilant *sans-culottes*) and was intended only to prevent the removal of documents. Though the sections were soon to play a leading role in Parisian politics, here the involvement of the Section Théâtre Français was minor.

A second impression made by the National Guard, municipal police and commissioners of the sections is one of ineffectiveness. The main purpose of the visits—arresting Royou—

---

[87] APP AA206[418].
[88] APP AA206[418].
[89] AN DXXIX[b] 353[20].
[90] The composition of the police detachment that made its visit on 23 July is particularly interesting. It included Soltho, designated simply police inspector, Rameaux, police commissioner of the Section Place Vendôme, Magnus, a commissioner of the Section Théâtre Français (the Section in which Royou and Madame Fréron resided) and Marotte, a police clerk (greffier). This force thus consisted of representatives of both the municipality and the sections. APP AA206[405].

was not achieved.[91] The force of the National Guard sent to arrest him reported that "they did not find him at home,"[92] as if one gentleman had been calling on another. Royou was many steps ahead of them. Fearing the possibility of arrest, or perhaps other interference, he had gone underground several months before.[93] Moreover, though the police continued to look for the abbé, they never found him. Perhaps frustrated at missing the principal object of their descent, the police arrested Madame Fréron, a measure that exceeded their instructions.[94] This does not reflect a high level of competence.

The third point that emerges from the events of 22 July to 1 August is the respect for order and due process shown by the police. Madame Fréron was, to be sure, arrested without a warrant. But she was asked to sign the minutes of the police visit, was present when seals were affixed to documents, was allowed to choose a guardian acceptable to her and was even made guardian of the seals herself on her return home. Indeed, there seems to be an element of naivety on the part of the police in allowing an employee of a paper they were investigating, and then a partner in it, to fulfill this function. After her release Madame Fréron requested that the seals on all documents in her apartment and offices be lifted and that the sequestered registers be returned to her. In both cases she was satisfied.[95] We are far from the period

---

[91] The editors of the *Ami du Roi* claimed that they had been warned of the raids in advance. *AR*, 7 August 1791, 1.

[92] *Moniteur*, 22 July 1791.

[93] Royou announced this himself in the 4 May 1791 number of the *AR*. At the time of the police visit of 23 July, Candau asserted that he had not seen the abbé for more than three months (APP 206[412]) and Serva said that he had not seen him for more than a month (APP AA206[414]).

[94] They were explicitly authorized only to arrest Royou and sequester suspect papers. APP AA206[405].

[95] The request was formally made on 5 November 1791. On 14 November the police administrator Jolly decided to accede to her request. A note by Rameaux dated two days later indicates that the documents had been returned. APP AA206[418].

in which exceptional legal procedures had replaced regular ones.

There is, indeed, an almost obsessive concern with adherence to the law and respect for constituted procedures in the behavior of the authorities. The National Guard, the police, the commissioners of the sections, all make it their principal activity to place seals on suspect documents, and the police and the delegation of the section list these documents carefully in their reports. The use of seals was a commonplace of old-regime legal practice, and in taking over and using this device, the officials and police of the emerging order seem to have been aspiring to legitimacy and to the continuation of existing norms. The behavior of the Revolutionary Tribunals and the *armées révolutionnaires* reflects an altogether different mentality.

Though Madame Fréron was released on 1 August, it took her another week to arrange for the *Ami du Roi* to resume publication. Her brother the abbé having gone into hiding, her brother the lawyer took over editorial duties on the paper. Corentin Royou's opening notice explaining why the paper's appearance had been interrupted is a fine piece of satire directed against the revolutionary authorities. He accuses them of reverting to the worst abuses of the old regime, such as secret warrants (*lettres de cachet*), which is what he calls the warrants recently issued for the arrest of his brother and other journalists.[96] In addition to this satire in the best Enlightenment tradition, Corentin Royou also upholds a key value of this tradition: civil liberty. One expects the Royou family to be outraged that their civil liberties, recently proclaimed and enshrined in law by the National Assembly, had been violated. One is less prepared for the demand that these liberties be guaranteed to all, including, and especially, those who differ from them. Corentin says of the leftist writers

---

[96] *AR*, 7 August 1791, 1. In a similar vein the abbé Royou describes the case being brought against him as "a new blow against liberty of the press, against individual liberty and against the rights of man and the citizen." *AR*, 23 August 1791, 3.

whose arrest had been ordered and whom, in the colorful language of the time, he calls "cannibalistic journalists": "One cannot pity them; but true friends of liberty were profoundly afflicted to see violated, even toward those who encourage murder and incendiarism, toward those who preach rebellion, the protective laws of civil liberty."[97]

He observes that it may appear astonishing to see a right-wing paper pleading the case of "the murderous mob of our patriotic gazeteers," but adds forcefully, "one must defend principles without exception of persons."[98] To maintain these principles, which recall much that is best in the Enlightenment tradition, required both integrity and courage.

Despite the brave countenance shown by the staff of the *Ami du Roi* following the police raids of late July and early August 1791, the paper was adversely affected. A two-week interruption in production was a serious matter for a daily, and so too was the sequestration of subscription lists. Moreover, this sign of official displeasure might have deterred moderate readers from subscribing or extending their subscriptions. Most serious, perhaps, Royou's connection with the paper was rendered more tenuous as he does not seem to have emerged from hiding. He still managed to have articles sent to the office of the paper, and his brother and Geoffroy were certainly competent writers, but the enterprise was compromised all the same. Royou gave his landlord at 37 Saint-André-des-Arts notice that he was leaving in January 1792.[99] It is approximately from this time that from a purely formal point of view the *Ami du Roi* begins to deteriorate. The format of the paper, which had been densely packed, as if there was not enough space to say everything that needed saying, changes. Double spacing is sometimes used toward the end of a number simply to spread the copy. Items which begin to appear under headings such as "Mélanges," "Anec-

---

[97] *AR*, 7 August 1791, 1.
[98] Ibid.
[99] AN T546⁴⁰⁷.

dote," "Variétés" and "Impromptu" have the transparently clear function of filling space. The tone of the paper also becomes harsher and its attitude more confrontational. More space is devoted to foreign news, which is to say to the émigrés and to the military preparations of neighboring states, and reports of *curés* who had retracted their oaths to the Civil Constitution become a recurrent feature. Royou's paper and the Revolution did not have much left to talk about, and one could hardly expect that they could continue to accommodate one another much longer. The day the National Assembly declared war on Austria, 20 April 1792, was also the day Madame Fréron gave notice on her apartments at number 37 Saint-André-des-Arts.[100] Two weeks later the Assembly issued warrants for the arrest of Marat and Royou. Marat and the *Ami du Peuple* still had the most dramatic parts of their careers ahead of them. Royou and his paper are not heard from again.

---

[100] AN T546⁴⁰⁶.

III.
The Production and Distribution of the Ami du Roi

A. Production

Whatever its ideology and political influence, the *Ami du Roi* was a business enterprise of impressive proportions. Figure 2.1 shows that Royou's paper soon reached a press run of 3,000 copies, that this number rose quickly to nearly 6,000 and that even after losing popularity it did not fall below 4,000 copies. As the paper was produced daily, it represented a vast amount of work at a number of levels. Once the editors had furnished their copy it had to be typeset, printed, sewn or folded into envelopes, addressed, and either delivered or taken to the post office. The need to see that the paper got out daily made its production, and especially distribution, far more complicated than the production and distribution of a book of comparable bulk. So too were the finances of the paper. The public could subscribe for periods of three, six or twelve months, and they could do so either directly, through the offices of the paper, or indirectly, through booksellers or postal agents. To see that the paper appeared regularly and that it was properly managed was no small task, especially given the level of technology and the increased demand for all things connected with printing that accompanied the sudden expansion of newspaper publishing.

The *Année Littéraire* had been published with the owners of the privilege providing copy, and a series of publishers looking after production and distribution.[1] The contract of 17 May 1790 retained this division of labor for the nascent

---

[1] See above, Chap. I.

Ami du Roi. But on breaking with Crapart and Briand, Royou and Madame Fréron determined to manage all aspects of the paper themselves. The prospectus of Royou's *Ami du Roi* was printed by the veuve Herissant, as were the first five numbers of the paper. The issue for 6 September, however, was printed 'A PARIS, DE L'IMPRIMERIE DE L'AMI DU ROI.'[2] This printshop was outfitted and organized by Royou, and continued to publish his paper, with one or two interruptions, until its final closure in May 1792.

In establishing their own printshop, Royou and Madame Fréron may have had in mind their difficulties with Crapart and Briand, or they may simply have felt that given the growth in the number of newspapers and the increased demand for printing presses and workers, they would do well, the expense notwithstanding, to set up their own presses. Thus a week before the first number of his paper appeared Royou bought more than 1,000 *livres* worth of type from Firmin Didot,[3] and this must have been in use, presumably in his own press or presses, by 6 September. During January, as the number of subscribers to the *Ami du Roi* rose from 4,000 to 4,700, Royou bought another press for his printshop, and in February, when subscriptions rose above 5,000, he added yet another.[4] Royou was thus in a position to enjoy the profits as publisher, as well as chief journalist, of his paper.

Under the old regime, with its tightly organized guilds, one could not simply find the capital and go into business as a printer or bookseller. It was necessary first to win acceptance from the corporation of *libraires et imprimeurs*, and this body was closing rather than opening its ranks over the eighteenth century.[5] The Revolution abolished the guild system, allowing

---

[2] *Avis*, BN 4⁰ Lc² 398; *AR*, 6 September 1790.
[3] AN T546⁵²⁸, 23 August 1790.
[4] AN T546⁷⁶ and ⁶³². The archives also contain a bill for unspecified carpentry work carried out for Royou in October and November of 1790 (ibid., pe. 174) and an undated bill for another press (ibid., pe. 19).
[5] Birn, "Profits of Ideas," 138-39.

free access to most professions. Thus in April 1791 Royou was able, for the modest payment of 15 *livres*, to receive a license from the city of Paris allowing him "to engage in business and to exercise the Profession of Printer" for that year.[6] This proved a small investment that opened the way to large profits.

The printshop of the *Ami du Roi*, located on the rue des Cordiers near the Sorbonne, was about a ten-minute walk from the offices of the paper on the rue Saint-André-des-Arts.[7] Though Madame Fréron denied having a foreman for "reasons of economy," the weekly accounts suggest that one Perier was firmly in charge, for his signature appears consistently on the bills sent from the printshop to the offices of the *Ami du Roi*.[8] It would seem that Madame Fréron was simply attempting to protect her enterprise and her foreman from further police attention.

How the *Ami du Roi* was produced on the shop floor can be pieced together from the weekly accounts of the printshop supplemented by other bits of evidence. The basic fact governing the production of the *Ami du Roi* was that it appeared daily. This meant that the day's news, in which the proceedings of the revolutionary assemblies were prominent, had to be written up in the afternoon or early evening, typeset and printed during the night and ready for distribution in the morning. The contract founding the original *Ami du Roi*, which from the outset was conceived as a daily, stipulated that the paper was to appear punctually each morning.[9] With rare exceptions, the format of the paper was four quarto

---

[6] AN T546³⁹⁵. This document was a *patente ordinaire*, and was signed by Pétion, who was then mayor of Paris.

[7] APP AA206. This was the answer of Madame Fréron and of Serva on being asked where the printshop was (ff. 413,414). Another clerk, Candau, described its location as the Place de la Sorbonne, but this is simply another way of saying the same thing (ibid., f.405).

[8] Ibid., f.413. About twenty of these accounts are scattered throughout the extensive carton AN T546. Bertaud renders the foreman's name Perieu. *Les Amis du Roi*, 51.

[9] MC LXIV⁴⁹⁵, item 4. See Appendix I.

pages, or one folio sheet printed on both sides. Typesetting for the journal remained constant throughout its existence at 168 *livres* for seven numbers, or 24 *livres* a number. The cost of printing naturally varied with the size of the press run, but the rate remained stable at 10 *sous* for a hundred copies of the paper, which amounted to 20 *livres* a day for 4,000 copies, 25 for 5,000 and so on.[10] In addition to a set rate for piece work, the printers, though not the compositors, received an additional flat fee for nightwork. This fee is uniformly 42 *livres* a week or six *livres* a day.[11] The consistently nocturnal nature of the production of the *Ami du Roi* is reflected in the cost of candles, which varied from 8 *livres* 8 *sous* a week in winter to 5 *livres* a week in summer.

Producing a daily newspaper in press runs of 3,000 to nearly 6,000 copies was a task calculated to keep three to five simple hand presses busy for virtually the entire working week.[12] And indeed, we find that when the publishers of the *Ami du Roi* had additional printing work, they contracted it out. Such work fell into a number of categories. First, there were supplements which the paper occasionally furnished free of charge to its subscribers. We find, for example, that number 291 of the *Ami du Roi*, which was a supplement, was

---

[10] The weekly account of 13 December 1790 shows that seven daily press runs of 4,000 copies cost 140 *livres* to print. The account for 21 April 1792 shows the same size press runs at exactly the same cost for printing. AN T546[151] and [396].

[11] It is not easy to move from the expenses of the *Ami du Roi* to the salaries of its employees. At press runs of 4,000, printing cost the management of the paper 20 *livres* a day, as well as a further six for nightwork. It is unlikely that more than four presses with two pressmen each were needed for a press run of this size. But three *livres* five *sous* a day seems a rather high salary (see above, Chap. II, n. 15). There is no mention in the weekly accounts of apprentices, payment to Perier or other expenses related to personnel, so it seems reasonable to assume that these global payments were divided among a larger work force than just the compositors and pressmen.

[12] It has been estimated that in the seventeenth century a common press could produce about 150 sheets printed on both sides in an hour (Bellanger, *Histoire générale*, I, 16). Bertaud puts the daily production of a hand press during the Revolution at three thousand sheets in twenty-four hours (*Les Amis du Roi*, 51). For a description of a printshop and techniques of printing in the eighteenth century see Robert Darnton, *The Business of Enlightenment*, 238-43.

published in 5,000 copies, then reset and a further 2,500 copies printed by Caillot.[13] This shows, incidentally, that certain issues of Royou's paper were printed in press runs that far exceeded the number of subscribers at any given time, and suggests the existence of an occasional market for the paper, probably reached through street vendors and bookshops that handled pamphlets.[14] The second category of printing work the *Ami du Roi* contracted out was address forms, and the third, pamphlets. Both will be treated separately.

If work had proceeded more or less on schedule, the printshop of the *Ami du Roi* would have been prepared on most mornings in 1791 to hand over about 5,000 copies of the paper to those responsible for its distribution. This meant that the printshop furnished 5,000 folio sheets, printed on both sides, which would have had to be folded, and since most copies of the paper were intended not for sale in the streets or across the counter, but for subscribers, put into envelopes or sleeves, addressed and either distributed directly or taken to the post office. Given the level of technology of the time and the number of copies involved, these tasks demanded considerable organizational and business ability.

According to testimony given by Madame Fréron at her interrogation in late July 1791, printed copies of the *Ami du Roi* were brought from the printshop near the Sorbonne to the offices of the paper at number 37 rue Saint-André-des-Arts not directly, but by one Gentil, who had either women or an apprentice make the actual delivery.[15] Gentil is known

---

[13] AN T546[682].
[14] The supplement of the *Ami du Roi* for 6 April 1791 was printed in 6,000 copies though the paper had only 5,500 subscribers at this time. AN T546[82]. On 15 August 1792 the Municipality of Paris directed that street vendors *(colporteurs)* of a number of papers, the *Ami du Roi* among them, be arrested. (AN T604, cited in Alexandre Tuetey, *Répértoire général des sources manuscrites de l'histoire de Paris pendant la Révolution française*, vol. IV, item 3851). By this date Royou's paper had been closed for several months, Montjoie's for a few days.
[15] APP AA206.

to us from the receipts kept by Royou and Madam Fréron, and appears to have been a reliable associate in the production of the *Ami du Roi* from its inception until its closure. Written in a clear, elegant hand, Gentil's bills, of which there are about twenty, are headed 'Mémoire de reliures' or 'Mémoire de brochage' and itemize charges for a week at a time beginning on Sunday and ending on Saturday. They exactly parallel the bills from the printshop and show that the entire press run was handled by Gentil.[16] His basic fee, which remained unchanged, for handling the *Ami du Roi* was 1 *livre* 15 *sous* per thousand copies. Thus for the week of 24 to 30 October 1790 Gentil, or rather his employees, handled 3,300 copies of the *Ami du Roi* a day and a total of 24,500 for the week at a cost of 37 *livres* 10 *sous,* while six months later, when the popularity of the paper had peaked, they handled 39,900 copies a week for 65 *livres* 15 *sous.*[17] From the same source we know that Royou and Madame Fréron contracted out binding on certain pamphlets that they published. Gentil's fee for stitching the *Bref du Pape,* for example, was 2 *livres* per thousand, and for the *Lettre de l'Archevêque de Troyes,* it was 4 *livres* per thousand.[18]

In the case of the brochures there can be little doubt but that the charge is for stitching together a number of printed sheets. But such a doubt does exist for the *Ami du Roi.* A normal daily issue of this paper consisted of a single folio sheet printed on both sides. Thus a single issue might require folding, but it could hardly need stitching. Given the experience of Madame Fréron and Royou with periodicals, and assuming that their business sense was sound, it seems reasonable to conclude that Gentil and his unskilled employees

---

[16] We find, for example, that the printshop accounts for the beginning and end of May show 5,700 copies of the paper produced daily (AN T546³⁴⁵). Gentil's bills for the 1-7, 8-14, 15-21 and 22-28 May all show 5,700 copies handled (AN T546³⁴² ³⁵³ ³⁵⁶ and ³⁶⁴).

[17] AN T546²²⁶ and ³⁴².

[18] AN T546³⁶⁵ and ⁷⁶⁶.

performed an essential function in preparing the paper for distribution. Probably this was to fold, and perhaps wrap, each number of the paper in readiness for expedition.[19] Consideration of the way in which the paper was addressed may further help to clarify Gentil's role in the production and distribution of the *Ami du Roi.*

During the eighteenth century, including the period of the Revolution, newspapers were generally distributed in one of two ways. They could be sold daily by the number by street vendors or *colporteurs,* or by booksellers, or they could be sold by subscription. Economically it was preferable for a publisher to receive payment ahead of time for his paper, to know how many copies to print and who was to receive them. The system of informal distribution by street vendors and booksellers was more flexible, but less dependable. These methods were not of course mutually exclusive. But it seems likely that the economic constraints involved in sale by subscription would require that those receiving a paper by this method be fairly well off. Distribution by the number from booksellers and street vendors, on the other hand, would seem more suited to a casual and more popular clientele.

The *Ami du Roi* was distributed almost exclusively to subscribers. This meant that nearly every copy had to be individually addressed and mailed or otherwise delivered. While this appears simple enough, the distribution of a daily paper financed almost exclusively by subscription is not altogether straightforward.

Before beginning to address a publication, it is necessary

---

[19] I have no satisfactory explanation for the category "brochage" appearing regularly in a context in which, so far as I can make out, stitching was not required. However, the term "ployage," or folding, sometimes appears in Gentil's bills (AN T546[82] and [280]), and it may be that "brochage" was used generically to cover simple folding too. A Dunkirk bookseller in ordering a second subscription to the *Ami du Roi* wrote, "Ce sera deux feuilles que vous mettrez exactement tous les jours sous la même enveloppe." 5 March 1792 (AN T546[31]). Under the old regime privileged periodicals sent copies of their journals in the mail "sous bande." René Moulinas, *L'Imprimerie à Avignon,* 383. The accounts of the *Année Littéraire* for 1778 show a payment of 53 *livres* 12 *sous* for paper to be used as envelopes. AN T*546[1].

to establish lists of subscribers. These lists would have to correspond closely to the needs of the paper's organization and to mechanisms of distribution. Since mail left Paris according to the main "route" by which it would be carried, it was logical to make up lists by route, of which there were fifteen.[20] Since subscriptions were for periods of three, six or twelve months, it was convenient to subdivide the geographical lists by the period of subscription. Thus in one of the surviving subscription lists we find "cahiers" of subscriptions for three, six and twelve months, with each of these categories further subdivided into Paris and the provinces and provincial subscriptions broken down into their respective routes. An analysis of periods of subscription to the *Ami du Roi* shows that the most common form of subscription was for three months (see Table 3.1). In the provinces about 60 percent of subscriptions were for this period, 30 percent for six months, 5 percent for a year and the rest for irregular periods, most commonly eight or nine months, but occasionally also four. In Paris short term subscriptions seem to have been significantly more popular than in the provinces, but our sample here is small and should be used cautiously. It appears from Table 3.2 that in the provinces about a third of short term subscriptions, but only a sixth of longer subscriptions, were taken out through booksellers or postal agents. This is an indication of the considerable importance of booksellers in distributing the *Ami du Roi*. In Paris, where direct access to the paper was easier, fewer three-month subscriptions were taken out through intermediaries than in the provinces, while slightly more long term subscriptions were. Though the

---

[20] These include foreign routes, which are lumped as a single category, a route for the army and another for communications among provinces. Jean-Joseph d'Expilly, *Dictionnaire Géographique, Historique et Politique des Gaules et de la France*, article "Postes," vol. V, 824-37. It should be noted, however, that there are significant divergences between the official routes, as presented by Expilly, and those in fact used by the *Ami du Roi*. The former, for example, had a separate route for Lyon, which Royou's paper lacked, but had no route for Orléans, which the *Ami du Roi* did.

Table 3.1 Period of Subscriptions to the *Ami du Roi**

	3M	6M	12M	Other	Missing	Total	Total Known
PROVINCES							
LIST I**	373	233	40	35	30	781	681
	54.77%	34.21%	5.87%	5.14%	—	—	99.99%
LIST II	307	131	18	7	25	488	463
	66.32%	28.29%	3.89%	1.51%	—	—	100.00%
LIST III	51	35	1	—	8	95	87
	58.62%	40.23%	1.15%	—	—	—	100.00%
TOTALS	731	399	59	42	63	1294	1231
	59.38%	32.41%	4.79%	3.41%	—	—	99.99%
PARIS							
LIST III	94	15	8	5	3	125	122
	77.05%	12.30%	6.56%	4.07%	—	—	100.00%

*Source: AN T*546[2,3,5].
**The sample in this list is restricted to subscribers whose name begins with the letters A and B.

Table 3.2. Means of Subscription to the *Ami du Roi**

		DIRECT**		INDIRECT***		TOTAL	
PROVINCES							
3M.	L.II	191		95			
	L.III	28		7			
		219		102		321	
			68.22%		31.78%		67.30%
6M.	L.II	98		13			
	L.III	25		3			
		123		16		139	
			88.49%		11.51%		29.14%
12M.	L.II	13		3			
	L.III	1		—			
		14		3		17	
			82.35%		17.65%		3.56%
						477	100.00%
PARIS							
3M.		77		16		93	
			82.79%		17.29%		79.49%
6M.		12		3		15	
			8.00%		20.00%		12.82%
12M.		7		2		9	
			77.78%		22.22%		7.69%
						117	100.00%

*Source: AN T⁵546²·³.
*10, 18 or 33 *livres* for the provinces; 9, 16, 30 *livres* for Paris.
**9, 17 or 31 *livres* for the provinces; 8, 15, 29 and 28 *livres* for Paris.

administration of the paper normally allowed subscriptions to begin only from the first of the month, this still would require constant reworking of the registers to keep them up to date.

When they arrived, subscriptions would go to a senior clerk, Charles Norbert Serva, aged thirty-three and originally from Pont-à-Mousson, but now living at 37 Saint-André-des-Arts.[21] Having processed them, Serva passed the subscriptions along to another member of the clerical staff of the *Ami du Roi*, Candau, a young man of twenty-one from the Landes, who was described by the police as "a clerk working for the distribution section of the journal the Ami du Roi."[22] When the police arrived at the offices of the paper on the morning of 23 July 1791 they found Serva correcting a register of subscribers.[23] They subsequently confiscated fifteen such registers.[24]

Once accurate subscription lists had been established, the clerical staff of the paper faced the task of addressing the individual copies of the paper, which from January 1791 ranged between 4,000 and 5,700 daily. The simplest way of doing this was to copy the addresses from the master lists onto each wrapped copy of the day's paper. The receipts kept by Royou and Madame Fréron show that at least three clerks worked in this capacity. They were paid by the piece at a standard rate of 10 *sous* the hundred addresses, or 5 *livres* the thousand.[25] It was common for a scrivener to address about 800 copies a day, though we find both higher and lower averages. Between 15 and 18 May 1791 Longchamps addressed

---

[21] Report on the police raid on the offices of the *Ami du Roi*, 23 July 1791. APP AA206⁴¹⁴. Serva is here described as a "Commis attaché à la Reception des abonnements du Journal." He was later made guardian of the seals placed on the offices and papers of the journal. AN DIXᵇ 353²⁰.

[22] APP AA206⁴²⁴.

[23] Ibid.

[24] Ibid.

[25] The only exception is one Frampard who was paid 7 *livres* 10 *sous* the thousand. AN T546²⁶⁸.

3,069 papers, an average of 768 a day, and from the fifteenth to the twenty-first of the same month Cassin addressed 5,127, an average of 732 a day, while during December 1790 Frampard was doing more than 1,000 a day.[26]

At press runs of 5,000 copies and a cost of 5 *livres* the thousand, addressing by hand would have cost the *Ami du Roi* 25 *livres* a day or 175 *livres* a week. This was slightly more than the cost of composition. Moreover, addressing by hand was cumbersome and would have slowed distribution. It therefore makes sense that the managers of the journal very early had the addresses of subscribers printed in bulk.[27] However, as their own presses were too busy to handle the work, it was contracted out.

The records of the *Ami du Roi* show that the printer Gueffier printed 45 address forms for Royou's paper between 30 October and 24 November 1790; Caillot and Courcier printed a further 18 in March 1791; and Grand printed nine more during the same month.[28] No address "formes" have survived in the archives, but there are references to scriveners preparing address lists "for printing" and the police reported finding "a huge number of address sheets" and "a package of printed addresses" in the offices of the *Ami du Roi*.[29] A provincial bookseller asked the directors of the *Ami du Roi* not to forget to have the addresses for some new subscriptions printed up, and Royou reminded subscribers to renew their subscriptions well before the expiry date, "so that there will be no interruption in service and so that we will have enough time to have the addresses printed."[30]

---

[26] AN T546 [145] [155] [133] [164] and [169].

[27] This was not new. In an account for the *Courrier d'Avignon* for 1776 reproduced by René Moulinas we find an expenditure of 300 *livres* for "Fourniture pour papier des adresses et impression" (*L'Imprimerie Avignon*, 356). In 1778 the *Année Littéraire* paid 120 *livres* for the printing of addresses at the rate of three *livres* the "volume" or *forme*. AN T*546[1].

[28] AN T546[163] [728] [284] [285] [286] [739].

[29] APP AA206[417-18].

[30] AN T546[26]; *AR*, 28 December 1790.

Grand's bill of 26 March 1791 is more detailed than the others, and shows that a "forme" printed in one hundred copies cost five *livres* and in 180 copies seven *livres* 10 *sous*.[31] Girouiard's bill of 29 January 1792 shows that he printed eight forms of six-month subscriptions in lots of 200, and charged only 36 *livres* for them, while he printed three twelve-month forms in lots of 400, at a cost of 18 *livres*.[32] As the cost of each form remains constant, the price varying only with the number of copies printed, it seems reasonable to conclude that the "formes" were a standard size. I suggest that a "forme" consisted of a single page of about 50 addresses. A press run of 100 would suit a three-month subscription, also allowing for occasional special numbers, or supplements. Similarly, issues of 200 addresses for six months and 400 for a year would have met the needs of the journal well.[33] Assuming the estimate of 50 addresses a form to be accurate, we find that five *livres* would buy 5,000 printed addresses (one form printed in 100 copies), whereas the same sum would only have bought 1,000 handwritten addresses. In the case of longer subscriptions the efficiency increases, for seven *livres* ten *sous* bought 180 copies of a form, or 9,000 addresses. The following table shows that for short term subscriptions printed addresses cost a fifth the price of handwritten addresses, and their cost-effectiveness increases with time. For annual subscriptions the cost of printed addresses was about one-tenth of that for handwritten ones.

While representing a considerable economy to the administration of the paper, the practice of printing addresses also added a step to the process of distribution. Once printed, the addresses had to be affixed to copies of the paper. On the

---

[31] AN T546⁷³⁹.
[32] AN T546⁴⁶². Girouiard's prices are so low as to be problematic. He may possibly have undertaken the work at a reduced rate, or he may exceptionally have printed fewer addresses on each form.
[33] The press run of 180 is thus anomalous. They may have been for subscriptions that had already begun.

Table 3.3: The Cost of Handwritten and Printed Addresses

KIND ADDRESS	RATE	PER SUBSCRIPTION COST			SOURCE
		3M.	6M.	12M.	
HANDWRITTEN	10 *sous* for 100 addresses	10 *sous*	1 *livre*	2 *livres*	AN T546
PRINTED	5 *livres* per forme (50) for 100 copies	2 *sous*			pc.245
	7 *livres* 10 *sous* per forme (50) for 180 copies		3 *sous*		pc.739
	10 *livres* per forme (50) for 400 copies			4 *sous*	estimate*

*Girouiard's bill charging only 6 *livres* for 400 copies of a forme (29 Jan. 1792) seems exceptionally low, and indeed is far cheaper than Grand's charge of 7 *livres* 10 *sous* for half as many impressions (26 Mar. 1791). It is possible, given the relatively low proportion of year subscriptions, that Girouiard's formes were smaller than the standard.

basis of the evidence at hand it is uncertain whether this was done in the offices of the *Ami du Roi* after it had been delivered by Gentil's employees, or before. An item that appears in all Gentil's bills for binding is glue. This may be because in addition to folding the daily edition of the paper, his unskilled employees also cut and pasted on the address labels. In any event, once the day's edition of the *Ami du Roi* had been printed, folded and addressed, it was ready for distribution.

B. Distribution—Organization

Since the *Ami du Roi* was sold almost exclusively by subscription, it is necessary to know how subscriptions were made and how they were handled in order to understand how the paper was distributed.

The first number of Royou's and Madame Fréron's *Ami du Roi* specified three ways of subscribing to the paper: directly, to the office at number 37 rue Saint-André-des-Arts; through booksellers; and through post offices. The cost of an annual subscription in the provinces was 33 *livres*, for six months 18 *livres*, and for three months ten *livres*. The corresponding figures for Paris are 30, 16 and nine *livres*.[34] However the subscriber chose to order the paper, the cost to him remained the same. If subscriptions were made indirectly, the bookseller or postal agent kept a commission of two *livres* for an annual subscription, one *livre* for one of six or three months.[35]

Most subscribers to the *Ami du Roi* dealt directly with the offices of the paper. Despite there being no financial advantage to doing so, many nevertheless preferred to get their

---

[34] In addition to subscribing directly through the paper's office, "In the provinces one may also take out subscriptions at all booksellers and at all post offices." *AR*, 1 September 1790.

[35] Prospectus of the *Ami du Roi*, BN 4⁰ Lc² 398.

subscriptions through a bookseller or postal agent. For a provincial there was a certain advantage in having a professional handle the transaction. In this way there would be someone responsible on the spot if difficulties arose. Subscriptions taken out through a bookseller could be sent directly to the subscribers' homes, and while this was obviously convenient, some subscribers had their papers sent to their booksellers. The bookseller Vanackere of Lille received nine copies of the paper in June of 1791, and 26 in April of 1792.[36] It may have been that the paper arrived with greater punctuality and regularity if sent to booksellers, or it is possible that leisured subscribers saw in a daily trip to their *libraire* an opportunity to pick up the latest news and gossip, as well as to socialize. The booksellers clearly had a strong incentive to find subscribers to the paper, and there is reason to think that their promotion of it contributed significantly to its success. A Lyon bookseller, sending in a subscription in September 1790 concluded her letter, "I count on your punctuality [in having the paper delivered] as you can count on my zeal in getting subscribers for you."[37] From the point of view of the administration of the *Ami du Roi* the advantages of dealing with booksellers with whom they already had business contacts and the increased number of subscriptions justified the commission granted these important intermediaries.

The registration procedure followed in the offices of the *Ami du Roi* differed little whether the subscription was direct or not. When the subscriber wrote to the paper himself he was obliged to include payment, usually in the form of a postal order or *mandat*, as the policy of the paper was not to accept orders from individuals on credit.[38] By contrast, credit was extended as a matter of course to booksellers. Normally, subscription orders were sent to Madame Fréron, who saw to having the enclosed postal orders or letters of credit hon-

[36] AN T546²⁴² ⁴⁰⁸.
[37] Letter dated 8 September from the veuve Resplandy. AN T546⁴⁷⁹.
[38] *AR*, 1 September 1790.

ored. Having done this, she passed the letter along to a clerk, probably Serva, who registered the new subscriber; which is to say that he entered him or her on the list of subscribers to the paper, and began the process by which address labels would be printed for him and the paper sent out. In the case of booksellers, there was normally a period of three or four days between the time the letter was written and the time it was registered. In that these letters are almost all from the provinces, this suggests reasonable efficiency on the part of the paper. Since new subscriptions and renewals took effect from the first of the month, receipts for subscriptions naturally cluster around the end and beginning of the month.[39]

Once subscribers had been entered on the registers of the *Ami du Roi*, their address labels printed, and copies of the paper printed, folded and addressed, the paper had to be distributed. Though it is not possible to calculate the proportion of provincial to Parisian subscribers exactly, it seems that about 80 percent of the copies of Royou's paper were sent to the provinces. At its peak, about 4,500 copies of the *Ami du Roi* circulated in the provinces and about 1,000 in Paris.[40] As the methods of distribution for Paris and the provinces differed, it is necessary to treat them separately.

In Paris Royou and Madame Fréron both established their own delivery system and used the municipal postal system, known as the *petite poste*, to distribute their paper. The following table, which is based on a series of bills for postage, gives a clear picture of the use of the *petite poste* by the *Ami du Roi*.

The first point to emerge from this table is that the *Ami du Roi* must have used the Paris postal system as little as possible. It never sent more than 189 copies of the paper through the *petite poste*, even in May 1791 when its circulation was at its peak. Moreover, while press runs dropped only

---

[39] AN T*546⁵. See Figures 4.1 and 4.2 below.
[40] The complete register for provincial subscribers contains 4,630 entries (AN T*546⁵), while the peak regular press runs for the paper are 5,700.

Table 3.4:   Volume and Cost of Postage for the *Ami du Roi*
In Paris, November 1790 to December 1791*

DATES IN BILLS	NO. PAPERS MAILED	PAPERS MAILED A DAY	TOTAL COST	COST PER COPY
1-30 Nov. 1790	1721	57	431.6s**	6d.
1-31 Jan. 1791	5222	168	981.7s.3d.	4.5d.
1-15 Mar.	2390	159	441.16s.3d.	4.5d.
16-31 Mar.	2484	166	—	
1-15 Apr.	2350	157	441.1s.3d.	4.5d
16-30 Apr.	2444	163	451.16s.6d.	4.5d.
1-15 May	2837	189	531.4s.	4.5d.
16-31 Dec.	1502	100	281.3s.3d.	4.5d.

*Source: AN T546, pièces 161, 649, 709, 763, 606, 343, 361, and 419.
**Abbreviations are as follow: 1., *livre;* S., *sou;* d., *denier.*
There were 12 *deniers* to a *sou,* and 20 *sous* to a *livre.*

about 15 percent between May and December 1791, the number of papers sent through the *petite poste* fell by nearly half. The reason is no doubt one of economy. During November 1790 Royou and Madame Fréron paid a tariff of six *deniers* a copy, which amounted to about two *livres* ten *sous* for a three-month subscription.[41] By January of 1791 this tariff had dropped to four and a half *deniers* a copy and remained at this level for the rest of the year. This was a substantial reduction, but still meant postal costs of nearly two *livres* for a three-month subscription which cost nine *livres* in Paris.

From its inception the *Ami du Roi* had been distributed privately in Paris. The standard fee for a porter who delivered the paper was one *livre* a day, the payment normally

---

[41] The normal rate for letters carried by the *petite poste* was 2 *sous.* Expilly, *Dictionnaire Géographique,* "Postes," V, 837. The modern authority on the history of the French postal system is Eugène Vaillé, who has produced the *Histoire générale des postes françaises* (Paris, PUF, 6 vols., 1947-1953). M. Vaillé projected a chapter on the postal system and the press under the old regime (ibid., VI, 134, n. 6) for the eighth volume of his history, but so far as I have been able to determine, he did not publish it in that form or any other. Given the importance of the subject, this is unfortunate.

being made once a week, but on occasion fortnightly. Thus a receipt from one such porter reads: "je soussigne Reconnois avoir Recu de M L'abbe Royou la somme de sept livres pour la distribution de la feuille de la semaine dont quittance a Paris ce cinq fevrier 1791. [signed] Casomier."[42] From early September until late December 1790 the distribution of the *Ami du Roi* in Paris appears to have been subcontracted out to one Engell, who received payments of 28 *livres* (12 September), then 35 *livres* (14 November, 12 December and two undated receipts), and exceptionally 41 *livres* (for the regular numbers and one supplement) and 34 *livres* (19 December).[43] By December 1790 subscriptions to Royou's paper had risen to about 4,000, of which roughly 800 would have been in Paris. As the *petite poste* was at this time distributing only about 60 copies of the paper a day, this would have left 740 or 750 for Engell's porters. We have seen that the salary of a porter delivering Royou's paper was a *livre* a day or seven *livres* a week. From November it appears that five porters worked distributing the paper in Paris, and that each of them was responsible for about 150 copies. Assuming that our figures here are accurate, or nearly so, we find that a porter delivering 150 copies of the paper for a three-month period (which, including special numbers, would approach 100 deliveries) would cost the management about 15 *sous* a subscription. Delivering only a hundred copies, which seems low, each porter would cost one *livre* for a three-month subscription; delivering two hundred, which seems high, the cost would fall to 10 *sous*. Thus the system of distribution run by the paper itself could have cost as little as a quarter of the price of the *petite poste*, and probably would not have cost more than half.

After December 1790 there are no records of payments to Engell for the "porte" or "distribution" of the paper. Instead

---

[42] AN T546[425]. The usual formula in these receipts is "le port des feuilles."
[43] AN T546[325] [259] [173] and [146].

there are copious receipts from a dozen different carriers, some of them appearing only once, all made out for either one week or two weeks at a time, and always at the rate of one *livre* a day. Almost all these receipts are from February through May 1791, and show about seven carriers as frequently—though it is not possible to say regularly—employed during this period. It is not easy to say why the managers of the *Ami du Roi* decided to stop working with Engell. Perhaps his services did not meet their demands. Perhaps they simply wished to control distribution more closely. Whatever the reason, the employment of these carriers, some casually (Casomier, Charot, Husson, Leposme, Sologne), others more regularly (Bazard, Constantin, Delorme, Lefebvre, Primault, Salmon), raises some interesting questions.

Delivering between 100 and 200 copies of a paper consisting of one folded sheet in a concentrated section of a large city is not a day's work. Nor is one *livre* a day's pay.[44] What else did these men do? Were they street people glad of any odd jobs they could get? That they could all sign their names, as well as the responsibility involved, makes this unlikely. Were they perhaps employed in some other capacity in the offices of the *Ami du Roi*, but needed the extra work and income? And in making their rounds would they have sought to sell extra copies of the paper, or indeed of other papers, in effect working as street vendors also? That press runs were so closely determined by the number of subscribers suggests that if they had done so it would have been on a small scale, with the possible exception of special numbers and supplements. These carriers are not the least interesting members of the network that produced and distributed Royou's *Ami du Roi*. But while our sources indicate what they did with part of their time and what they were paid for this service, they provide no information on any other aspect of their activity.

---

[44] See above, Chap. II, n. 15.

Before leaving the distribution of the *Ami du Roi* in Paris, one other point requires consideration. Since it was so much cheaper to use their own carriers than the *petite poste*, why did the managers of the paper continue to use the municipal postal service at all? Firm evidence is lacking here, but it is likely that there were instances in which it was economical to do so. It would make sense if the paper's carriers handled the areas of dense subscription, while scattered subscribers and those in the suburbs received their papers through the mail. While such an arrangement is logical, we have no firm evidence to prove that it was indeed put into practice. Still, this explanation does account for the use of two systems of distribution in Paris as well as for the preference of the paper's management for their own carriers.

On the distribution of the *Ami du Roi* outside Paris we are less well informed, but the postal system clearly played the key role here. The Royal Declaration of 8 July 1759 put the cost of delivering a letter from Paris to Amiens at 6 *sous*, to Rouen at 7 *sous*, to Lyon 8 *sous*, to Quimper 9 *sous*, to Marseille 10 *sous*, and to Bordeaux 11 *sous*.[45] Assuming one hundred deliveries to Amiens over a three-month period, postage alone would have cost 30 *livres*, or three times the cost of subscription. Clearly, no newspaper could afford to pay such rates. In order to survive it would have had to have a preferential tariff. We have seen that for Paris it did indeed benefit from such a tariff. For the national postal system, or *grande poste*, we have no hard evidence for a preferential tariff, but as the paper could hardly have functioned without one, it seems safe to infer that it enjoyed such a tariff nationally, too.

René Moulinas asserts that there were reduced tariffs for French periodicals with *privilèges* during the second half of the eighteenth century which allowed these journals to be sent anywhere within the kingdom for the uniform tariff of

---

[45] Expilly, *Dictionnaire Géographique*, "Postes."

one *sou*.[46] The Assembly of the Clergy, too, benefited from a preferential postal tariff on official mail after 1755.[47] Moulinas further provides a detailed account of how the *Courrier d'Avignon* came to benefit from this tariff, first from 1740, for Provence, Dauphiné and Languedoc, and then, from 1750, with some interruptions, for the whole country.[48] Periodicals enjoying this arrangement also benefited from the cooperation of the post office in assuring subscription payments. These payments could be made locally, with the postal system assuring their being forwarded to the journal.[49] In addition to the tariff of one *sou* per copy, the *Courrier d'Avignon* also made an annual payment of about 1,200 *livres* to the post office.[50] Curtailment of this arrangement would have reduced the paper to merely local significance, perhaps even resulting in its closure, for paying regular postal rates would have made the paper prohibitively expensive, while distribution through booksellers in the south and a private delivery system had been tried and found inadequate.[51]

As the *Courrier d'Avignon* was published twice weekly, the postal rate of one *sou* a copy was manageable, but postal costs still represented by far the greatest expense of the paper.[52] In the case of the *Ami du Roi*, which was a daily, even the reduced cost of one *sou* a copy would have amounted to five *livres* for a three-month subscription. This probably would not have been financially feasible, and it seems unlikely that

---

[46] Moulinas, *L'Imprimerie à Avignon*, 383. Moulinas's article, "Du Rôle de la poste royale comme moyen de contrôle financier sur la diffusion des gazettes en France au XVIIIe siècle," is based on papers published in Avignon, and adds little to the information in his book.

[47] Vaillé, *Histoire générale des postes*, VI, 128-29.

[48] Moulinas, *L'Imprimerie à Avignon*, 382-83.

[49] Moulinas, "Les Journaux publiés à Avignon," 131.

[50] Moulinas, *L'Imprimerie à Avignon*, 383, n. 63.

[51] Ibid., 379-85.

[52] Total expenses for the *Courrier d'Avignon* for 1787 were about 30,000 *livres*, of which printing costs amounted to 5,000 *livres* and mailing 16,500 *livres*. During 1785 printing cost 6,600 *livres* and postage 17,600 *livres* out of total expenses of 42,400 *livres* (ibid., 357-58).

the paper could have paid more than 5 or 6 *deniers* a copy for postage.

The decision to grant a preferential postal tariff was not merely administrative, but also political. René Moulinas in his work on the papers published at Avignon has shown that the postal system was a highly effective means of controlling the periodical press. Granting a preferential tariff meant helping a journal to have a wide and profitable distribution, while denying it meant at best reducing it to local influence and in most cases amounted to forcing it to close. The old regime crumbled piecemeal, not all at once. Until August 1792 the king retained control of his ministers and of the postal system. The decision of the government to subsidize certain periodicals—and Albert Mathiez maintains that the *Ami du Roi* enjoyed a subsidy from the civil list[53]—no doubt enhanced a paper's profitability. But granting access to the postal system at substantially reduced rates was a concession that could decide whether a paper had a national, rather than local, influence.

C. Distribution—Efficiency

Can one expect the distribution of the *Ami du Roi* to have proceeded smoothly and efficiently? Considering the scope and complexity of the operation and the dependence of the paper on a postal system over which it had no control, it

---

[53] Mathiez, *The French Revolution*, 79. Subsidies to the press during 1793 and 1794 ranged from sums of less than 1,000 *livres* to over 100,000, and sometimes took the form of government paid mass subscriptions. Thus, for example, Fourcade's *Antifédéraliste* received 42,000 francs for 2,000 subscriptions for four months, and the *Journal Universel* was paid nearly 50,000 francs for 3,000 three-month subscriptions, which were then raised to 5,000 subscriptions for the following four months (Mathiez, "La Presse subventionnée de l'an II"). It appears from the accounts of the *Ami du Roi*, which show no mass subscriptions at all, that it did not benefit from government support of this kind. Nor do the accounts show evidence of a subsidy.

seems unrealistic to expect that the distribution of the paper, in the provinces especially, would have proceeded flawlessly. The extent of the initial task of organization must have caused many errors and omissions during the first months of the paper's existence. Royou admitted as much in a notice to his readers in November 1790. In response to the numerous subscribers who complained of the "irregularity with which this journal arrives in the provinces," Royou replied that initially there may have been errors in his registers, but that the main source of the trouble was the provincial post office, where employees who disagreed with Royou's principles were negligent in distributing his paper, while those who approved them read the paper and passed it around to their friends. He further observed that "if subscribers do not give, or have those who subscribe in their name give, the characteristic feature that clearly distinguishes the place they live, errors will be inevitable. We have already made many of this sort."[54] Royou also asked subscribers to take care to write legibly, and reminded them to give both their rank or professional standing *(qualité)* and the closest post office. Having thus excused himself for past failings and advised his subscribers what information to provide, Royou concluded: "With these precautions, and given the care that our present clerks take, I reply that henceforth there will only be those inevitable delays at the *grande poste* of Paris, which is so overburdened, that it is impossible that some errors should not occur in the intelligent activity of the clerks of this office."[55] Royou's circumspection with respect to the *grande poste* is easily understood. He was thoroughly dependent upon it. Moreover, given the sudden proliferation of newspapers and journals at this period, one can appreciate Royou's sympathy for the mammoth task which the postal service faced. A short time later the abbé informed his readers that he had discovered another

---

[54] *AR*, 21 November 1790.
[55] Loc. cit.

cause of irregular delivery. Some clerks in the Paris post office were said to have taken subscriptions intended for him to the rival office of Montjoie and Crapart.[56] While Royou saw malevolence here, it is possible and indeed likely that these incidents were occasional mistakes made by an overworked postal staff.

The interruption in publication of the *Ami du Roi* caused by the temporary closure of the paper by the police in late July and early August 1791 necessarily interfered with the distribution of the paper. Indeed, it was just after this incident that subscriptions to the paper began to drop (Fig. 2.1). It is possible that this decline in readership was as much a result of a purely technical failure to distribute the paper regularly as it was the consequence of a divergence in political views between Royou and his readers.

Bergeret, a bookseller of Bordeaux, whose correspondence with the *Ami du Roi* is the most extensive to have survived, had on at least one occasion to return money for subscriptions that were made, but never filled. In a letter of 7 December 1790 he wrote, "I have just reimbursed 4 subscriptions which I have been asking you to fill for nearly two months," and asked to be reimbursed in turn.[57] Since these orders were made so close to the opening of the paper, they may have been lost in the initial rush of organization. But we also find that an order made by Bergeret for a M. Cockerel in October 1791 was never filled, and in August of the same year a subscription which had been made in June for M. Muratel had still not been met.[58]

Irregularity in delivery is a leitmotif in the booksellers'

---

[56] Ibid., 4 December 1790. Royou also complained that Gattey, a bookseller of the Palais Royal, was taking his subscriptions to Crapart (loc. cit.). He later informed his readers that unless they indicated clearly whose *Ami du Roi* they were subscribing to, the post office would not honor their money orders. *AR*, 19 August 1791. Royou, for his part, also had at least one of Montjoie's subscribers on his registers (AN T*546²).
[57] AN T546⁵⁰¹.
[58] AN T546⁵²⁷ (1 October 1791) and ⁵²³ (6 August 1791).

correspondence with the *Ami du Roi*. There are countless reminders of individual subscribers who had not been receiving their copies of the paper for from a few days to a month, though their subscriptions were still valid. One subscriber complained that he had ordered two copies of the paper but was receiving only one, while two other subscribers who had single orders were receiving two copies each.[59] On 3 April 1791 Bergeret wrote: "The *Ami du Roi* was not delivered today, there is an irregularity in the shipments that makes people grumble, it happens very often that more recent [nouveaux] copies arrive before older ones, and very often there are some missing. Complain about this, I beg of you, at the Post Office."[60] Such complaints were repeated frequently. A week later Bergeret again noted the lack of regularity in deliveries; during the same month he reported the discontent of subscribers whose papers had failed to arrive; and not long after again observed that "much disorder still reigns in the expedition of the *Ami du Roi*."[61] Bergeret later makes a similar complaint and adds that if the offices of the *Ami du Roi* are not reorganized, he fears that he will lose subscribers, and that old subscribers will not renew their subscriptions.[62] Of the thirty or so subscribers mentioned by name in Bergeret's correspondence, there are few who did not at some time experience delays or irregularities in delivery. The great majority, however, continued, and in many cases renewed, their subscriptions.

To judge from correspondence with other provincial booksellers, Bergeret's experience was typical. Bettinger, a bookseller from Deux-Ponts, wrote Madame Fréron on 11 August 1791, the day after he had received copies of the *Ami du Roi* after a two-week hiatus. He complained that he had had no copies of the paper at all since 4 July, and had believed in

---

[59] AN T546⁵²⁹ (15 October 1791),⁵¹² (11 April 1791) and ⁵¹¹ (3 April 1791).
[60] AN T546⁵¹¹.
[61] AN T546⁵¹² (11 April 1791), ⁵¹⁴ (23 April 1791) and ⁵¹⁵ (4 May 1791).
[62] AN T546⁵¹⁷ (24 May 1791) and ⁵¹⁸ (24 May 1791).

consequence that the paper had been suppressed. Without showing any sympathy or understanding for the difficulties caused by the police raid, Bettinger threatened to ask for his money back if deliveries were not regularized, noting drily that when one has paid for a paper, one wants it delivered on time. On the other hand, he suggested that if regular delivery could be assured, he could probably get more subscriptions.[63]

Other provincial booksellers, though also complaining about irregular delivery, showed more understanding than Bettinger. Vanackere wrote with restraint from Lille on 20 June 1791: ". . . another ordinary problem[:] today instead of 8 copies of the 18th of June there was only one; so there we have 7 subscribers who will have to do without! Please send them immediately, and ask your clerk to be more careful sending the paper out."[64] Apparently a clerk had mistaken Vanackere's multiple order for an ordinary subscription, and so sent him only one copy of the paper. Not a really serious error, and one that Vanackere with good humor sought to correct as part of his day's work. Brieul of the Clermontais pointed out that one of his subscribers was missing three numbers of the paper, and asked that they be supplied.[65] In a letter of 24 June 1791, Vanackere complained that he had not had a single copy of the paper for three days, and further asked for a number of missing back copies from January to March. In a rare comment unrelated to business, Vanackere also reported on the king's flight to Varennes, which at the time of writing, he believed to have ended successfully.[66] In October of the same year, Blonet of Rennes complained that two recent subscribers had not yet begun to receive the paper,

---

63 AN T546[476] (11 August 1791).
64 AN T546[240] (20 June 1791).
65 AN T546[481] (16 May 1791).
66 "I have just received a letter from Tournay dated this morning . . . it is very certain that the king, queen and the dauphin were at Varennes yesterday, whence they have now departed to go to Brussels . . ." AN T546[242] (24 June 1791).

and that other subscribers were missing back issues.[67] A bookseller of Grenoble wrote to inform Madame Fréron that one of his subscribers had not received his paper for more than a month. The subscriber dropped in from time to time to apprise the bookseller of the fact, and the bookseller, in turn, had written the offices of the *Ami du Roi* four or five times about the same subscription, "which I assure you, is extremely annoying."[68] Chirac from Tulle wrote at the beginning of March 1792 to say that the abbé Barry, a longstanding and fully paid up subscriber, had not been receiving the paper since the first of January. According to Chirac, Barry had himself written, but received no answer. He concludes his letter with icy politeness, asking that the paper be sent regularly or payment refunded.[69] It is not possible to say whether or not the abbé Barry received his copies of the *Ami du Roi* after Chirac's letter,[70] at least until the paper closed in early May, but this case, and others cited above, suggest that administrative and business difficulties were at least partly responsible for limiting or reducing the diffusion of Royou's paper.

While the difficulties involved with the distribution of the *Ami du Roi* were serious, it is in the nature of routine business correspondence to emphasize such difficulties. In the correspondence that has survived between provincial booksellers and the office of the *Ami du Roi,* there is not a single letter from a bookseller expressing satisfaction with service received. When things went well or normally there was no occasion for comment, so that virtually all surviving letters from booksellers are either new subscriptions, renewals or complaints. Yet even from letters of this sort it is possible to learn something of the normal functioning of the paper. When Vanackere complained in a letter of 20 June 1791 that he had received only one copy of the edition of the eighteenth instead

---

[67] AN T546[472] (19 October 1791).
[68] AN T546[26] (24 February 1792).
[69] AN T546[32] (5 March 1792).
[70] The letter was registered in the offices of the *Ami du Roi* on 8 March. Ibid.

of eight, we learn that the *Ami du Roi* arrived in Lille two days after it appeared in Paris.[71] Similarly, Bettinger's letter of 10 August 1791 acknowledging copies of the seventh of the month shows that delivery to Deux-Ponts took three days.[72] In one instance a letter sent by Bergeret from Bordeaux to Paris took only two days, in another over a month. The average seems to have been around four or five days.[73] Given the level of technology and the distances involved, it would seem that the *Ami du Roi* had achieved a reasonable degree of efficiency in its system of distribution. That there would be breakdowns in this system was, in the conditions in which the paper operated, inevitable.

The pressures and constraints under which the *Ami du Roi* was produced and distributed allow us to appreciate the extent of the achievement of the paper in quickly attracting over five thousand subscribers and then remaining near that level for the duration of its existence. Though the heightened interest in politics and the quality of Royou's journalism are no doubt important factors, it is nevertheless true that other skilled journalists working in the same period failed to achieve comparable success. Part of the reason for this concerns the organization and management of the paper. It is important to recall that for fifteen years Madame Fréron had owned the privilege for, and been responsible for the management of, the *Année Littéraire*. This literary periodical lost its support and largely unnoticed ceased to appear in the middle of 1790.[74] Its place was then taken by the more topical *Ami du Roi*. Therefore, unlike so many of the journals and papers that appeared suddenly, and usually ephemerally, in 1789

---

[71] AN T546[240].

[72] AN T546[476].

[73] AN T546[550] (sent 15 October 1791, registered 17 October); pe. 511 (sent 3 April 1791, registered 11 May). More typical are a letter sent on 7 May 1791 and received on the 11th (pe. 515), and another sent on 6 August 1791 and received on the 11th (pe. 523).

[74] It changed its name to the *Année Littéraire et Politique* for the first number of 1790, but to no avail.

and 1790, the *Ami du Roi* was established by an administrator who had years of experience in all aspects of the book trade, and more specifically, in running a journal. Madame Fréron knew and dealt with the printers and booksellers of Paris, and she had long-established ties with many provincial booksellers. Thus, when the *Ami du Roi* began to appear it was quickly and professionally organized, and when it became a matter of filling subscriptions, the paper benefited from an extensive credit network already in place. In addition to the convenience to subscribers in being able to take out subscriptions locally, the journal would have gained from being able to handle numerous transactions at once and the increased flexibility that dealing with provincial booksellers gave them. Thus, for example, Madame Fréron sent a bill to a postal clerk in Arras for 328 *livres* for 32 subscriptions that he had taken out on behalf of various subscribers. Vanackere replied to a bill for 700 *livres* with a money order of just over 300 and an assurance that he would pay the rest in due course; and a bookseller in Dijon notified Madame Fréron that he was deducting the value of two subscriptions from the sum she owed him.[75] As we shall see directly, the distribution of the *Ami du Roi* was not the only reason that Madame Fréron and her brother came into contact with booksellers, both in the provinces and Paris.

---

[75] AN T546[408] and [241].

IV.
The Office of the Ami du Roi as a Center for the Dissemination of Pamphlet Literature

A. Pamphlets and Periodicals

As instruments for forging public opinion, pamphlets antedate periodicals.[1] During the great crises of the seventeenth century, such as the English Civil War and the Fronde, vast numbers of pamphlets were produced, while periodicals played only a minor role.[2] In the eighteenth century the

---

[1] For the use of pamphlets in evaluating the crises of the early seventeenth century see H. Ducchini, "Regard sur la littérature pamphlétaire en France au XVIIe siècle" and J. Michael Hayden's methodologically rigorous "The Uses of Political Pamphlets: The Example of 1614-15 in France." Also relevant is J. P. Seguin, *L'Information en France avant la périodique: 517 canards imprimés entre 1529 et 1631* and *L'Information en France de Louis XII à Henri II*; and Bellanger, *Histoire générale*, I, 27-77. Elizabeth Eisenstein points out that printing was immediately seized upon by Protestants as a means of propaganda (*The Printing Press as an Agent of Cultural Change: Communications and Cultural Transformations in Early-Modern Europe*, 304).

[2] The exception is the *Gazette de France*, founded by Renaudot at the instigation of Richelieu in 1631. Richelieu, who was sensitive to public opinion, decided to use a periodical to influence this opinion when he believed that pamphlet propaganda was inadequate to his needs (H.M. Solomon, *Public Welfare, Science and Propaganda in Seventeenth Century France: The Innovations of Théophraste Renaudot*, 108-12). Between 1648 and 1653 periodical publications were not lacking in France. Jean Sgard lists 47 such periodicals (excluding those published annually) for these years, though the distribution is far from equal. Sgard's list shows 21 periodicals appearing in 1649, 14 in 1652, but only six in 1650, four in 1651, two in 1648 and none for 1653 (*Bibliographie de la presse classique: 1600-1789*, 179-80). It is not known how many "Mazarinades" were produced during the same period, but the standard catalog, with its supplements, lists nearly 5,000 items, and it is unlikely that this is complete (C. Moreau, *Bibliographie des Mazarinades*; these volumes, which contain over 4,000 items, were supplemented by four more small volumes edited by Moreau, P. Van der Haegen, E. Socard and E. Labadie down to 1862. A catalog of the holdings of a Harvard library contains more than 100 items not listed in Moreau (J.E. Walsh, ed., *Mazarinades: A Catalogue of the Collection of Seventeenth-Century French Civil War Tracts in the Houghton Library, Harvard University*, ix). The most recent treatment of this vast and difficult literature is C. Jouhaud, *Mazarinades—La Fronde des mots*. Between 1640 and 1663

periodical press was more important in forming and directing opinion. Yet despite the obvious advantages of publications appearing at frequent and regular intervals, periodicals did not definitively replace pamphlets as a means of political persuasion.[3]

As a working definition of a pamphlet I suggest the following: a brief, self-contained publication directed at a specific issue, or fairly narrow range of issues, which is intended to influence public opinion, and is produced unofficially. On this definition pamphlets are concerned primarily with contemporary issues, usually political, and with influencing opinion. If, as they did under the old regime, governments hired pamphleteers and told them what to write, they still tended to have their works printed privately. It seems that if one appealed to the public, the rules of the game required that one pretend to be part of the public. Consequently, governments expressed their policies directly in decrees and declarations, but generally sought to influence opinion indirectly.[4] Periodicals, by contrast, appear regularly and are usually devoted to a wide range of subjects. Under the old regime most periodicals were concerned with literature and the arts and sciences, or acted as channels for local news and adver-

---

a single English bookseller collected nearly 15,000 pamphlets. See Peter Burke, *Popular Culture in Early Modern Europe*, 263.

[3] By calculating the number of pamphlets produced annually from the years preceding the Revolution to 1799, Antoine de Baecque has shown that far from being eclipsed by the periodical press after 1789, the rise in the production of pamphlets was as dramatic as that in newspapers and journals. From 1774-1786, 312 pamphlets appeared in France; during 1787 alone 217; then during 1788, 819; 1789, 3,305; 1790, 3,121; 1791, 1,923; 1792, 1,286; 1793, 663; 1794, 601; 1795, 569; 1796, 182; 1797, 245; 1798, 154; and 1799, 211. "Pamphlets: Libel and Political Mythology," in Darnton and Roche, *Revolution in Print*, 165-66.

[4] Whether in content, length or format, there is no general agreement on what constitutes a pamphlet. Hayden, for example, does not regard official government publications as pamphlets ("The Uses of Political Pamphlets," 144) while Ducchini does ("Regard sur la littérature pamphlétaire," 314). For an account of how the government sought to influence opinion by its formal publications and directives, see Michèle Fogel, "Le Système d'information ritualisée de l'absolutisme français," 142-50.

tising.[5] The government exercised close censorship of periodicals and did not tolerate independent political reporting.[6] Forced underground, or across the frontiers, much political journalism of the old regime was irregular in appearance and harsh in tone.[7]

With the Revolution, true political periodicals appear. But whether literary or political, a periodical is in some sense an institution. This follows from its permanence and continuity. Of course, in certain conditions some of these institutions last only a short time,[8] and during crises it is not unusual for pamphleteers to write series of pamphlets. The formal difference is that a journalist, whether he succeeds in doing so or not, always intends another number to follow his most recent one, while a pamphleteer generally regards the work he has just finished as his last on the subject, and awaits further developments in order to decide what, if anything, next needs writing about. Otherwise put, the journalist's genre requires him to say something at given intervals, regardless of what may, or may not, have occurred in these intervals; the pamphleteer's allows him to write or not as circumstances require. On the whole, journalism lends itself well to reporting news and supplying information, pamphleteering to forming opinion and inducing people to action.

In practice it is difficult to maintain the distinction between news and opinion, information and inducement to action. And seldom were these distinctions less clear cut than in the

---

[5] Periodicals devoted primarily to useful information of local or commercial interest developed late in France, considerably earlier in England. The French periodical press remained more learned and literary to the end of the old regime. Botein, Censer and Ritvo, "The Periodical Press," 472-73.

[6] See above, Chap. I, n. 5.

[7] Linguet is a good example of a political journalist forced abroad by the government. He published his *Annales* first in England, then Belgium, but when he risked a visit to Paris in 1780 he was arrested and detained for nearly two years in the Bastille (Levy, *The Ideas and Careers of Simon-Nicolas-Henri Linguet*, chap. 5). Robert Darnton has brought attention to the viciousness of the *libelle* in his article "The High Enlightenment and the Low-Life of Literature."

[8] Censer, *Prelude to Power*, 9-10.

years of unlimited freedom of the press in the early Revolution. In the great proliferation of pamphlet and periodical literature of the period it is often impossible, in terms of form, as well as of content, to distinguish between pamphlets and odd numbers of periodicals.[9] The advantages of periodicals—their regularity of appearance, standardized format, routine layout and rough uniformity of editorial tone and opinion—often make them foci which articulate, direct or consolidate the opinion of a selected (usually self-selected) readership.[10] But in times of protracted crisis these qualities may work against the paper. Events may move too quickly for the rhythm of publication, while routine and standardization may obscure novel or significant issues. To overcome these problems, Royou, like many other journalists, had recourse to special numbers, which were, in effect, pamphlets inserted into the flow of the regular edition. Indeed, when a number proved particularly popular Royou had it reset and reprinted.[11] In such cases the number in question became a true pamphlet, for the reprints were distributed through the channels normally used for pamphlets, namely booksellers and street vendors, the regular subscribers having already received their copies in the mail. As one might expect, the editors of the *Ami du Roi* used their paper to recommend books and pamphlets whose views they endorsed. In itself, this constitutes an important means of influencing public opinion, though admittedly a portion of the public that has shown itself willing to be influenced by its subscription to, or reading of, the journal. But Madame Fréron and Royou went well beyond this obvious and in any case well-established old-regime practice, for they also printed and distributed numerous conservative publications, most of which can be described as pamphlets. Thus this remarkable brother and sister team

---

[9] Pierre Rétat, "Forme et discours d'un journal révolutionnaire: *Les Révolutions de Paris en 1789*," 141-42.
[10] Botein, Censer and Ritvo, "The Periodical Press," 468-69.
[11] For example, the number of 1 December 1790. AN T546[158].

were able to promote ideas to which they were ideologically committed while at the same time making large profits. Naturally, they used the *Ami du Roi* to promote the pamphlets they had printed and distributed, and in this way turned their offices at 37 Saint-André-des-Arts into an important center of royalist propaganda.

When the police visited the offices of the *Ami du Roi* on 23 July 1791 they found copies of the paper, works by the abbé Maury and Cazalès, papal briefs condemning the Civil Constitution of the Clergy and, "other aristocratic and incendiary works, all in innumerable quantities."[12] In addition to the pamphlets of Maury and Cazalès and the papal briefs, the offices of the *Ami du Roi* were responsible for the production and distribution of numerous other pamphlets. These include a *Lettre à M. Lecoz, Lettre du Cardinal Zelada, Lettre de M. l'abbé Royou, Moyens de remédier à la rareté du numéraire* and an important criticism of the Assembly's religious policy, the *Principes de la foi sur le gouvernement de l'église, en opposition avec la constitution civile du clergé*.[13] This latter work, which was as much a short book as a pamphlet, sold for one *livre*, and was an immediate success. The *Ami du Roi* announced in mid-April 1791 that the *Principes* had already gone into a second edition, and that it had been pirated by two Parisian booksellers, Gattey and Arnaud. Royou warned that this edition, while supposedly augmented and corrected, was full of errors, and advised his readers to turn to the offices of the *Ami du Roi* or to a number of specified booksellers, or more generally "to the booksellers of the old guild *[librairie]*" to obtain the authorized version.[14] Royou continued to announce the availability of the *Principes* in his paper, noting at the end of May

---

[12] APP, AA 206[415].
[13] AN T546[261] [344] and [815].
[14] *AR*, 17 March 1791. Artaud and Gattey are here denounced as "real pirates and brigands." Royou and Gattey were, however, competing for the same market. In May 1790 the bookseller had come under pressure for selling aristocratic publications, and he was ultimately guillotined during the Terror. See Murray, *The Right-Wing Press*, 96 and 205.

that it had reached its fifth edition, and he was still advertising it in August.[15] While information on the relationship between the *Ami du Roi* and the *Principes* is thin, a receipt for paper shows that Royou and Madame Fréron had undertaken the publication of the pamphlet.[16]

It is clear from the many receipts from printers, paper merchants, and booksellers that Madame Fréron and her brother were responsible for the production and distribution of many pamphlets and did not content themselves with simply announcing works they approved in their paper. Since the presses of the *Ami du Roi* were busy printing the paper, the printing of pamphlets was normally contracted out. Madame Fréron or the abbé Royou then provided paper to printers,[17] took delivery of the pamphlets, subcontracted the stitching and assured distribution. Thus the brother and sister acted as entrepreneurs, having undertaken to produce and distribute numerous conservative and clerical pamphlets. As we will see below, some of these pamphlets were published in very large numbers and proved highly profitable.

B. The Main Pamphleteers Promoted by the *Ami du Roi:* Cazalès and Maury

The two pamphleteers with whom the *Ami du Roi* was most closely associated were both members of the National Assembly, and both are today regarded as among the most able defenders of royalist and traditionalist opinion. Jacques-

---

[15] *AR*, 31 May and 17 August 1791.

[16] AN T546⁵. This bill for 36 reams of paper for the printing of the *Principes* is dated 27 May 1791.

[17] Robert Darnton has shown that paper represented roughly 60 percent of the cost of production for the quarto *Encyclopédie (The Business of Enlightenment*, 186), and there is no reason to assume that the cost of paper was less important in the production of newspapers. On the manufacture, cost and regulation of paper production in the eighteenth century, see Alix Chevallier, "La Matière première: le papier," in Martin and Chartier, *Histoire de l'édition*, II, 34-41.

Antoine-Marie de Cazalès (1758-1805) was elected deputy of the nobility of Rivière-Verdun near Toulouse to the Estates General and identified with the monarchiens, first under the leadership of Mounier, then under that of his friend Stanislas Clermont-Tonnerre.[18] He was a member of the club of the Amis de la Constitution Monarchique which existed briefly from the autumn of 1790 to the spring of 1791.[19] Cazalès emigrated after the flight to Varennes, but received a cool reception from other émigrés, and returned to France, only to leave again after the rising of 10 August 1792. While a devoted monarchist and clearly traditional in outlook, Cazalès cannot fairly be described as reactionary. His integrity has caused him to be described as the "Incorruptible of the Right,"[20] and his relative moderation has been emphasized by historians who have treated his career.[21] His policy has recently been described as "social realism and political moderation aimed at halting the Revolution at a point where the aristocracy still had, or could recover, an important part in the representative system."[22]

The abbé, and ultimately cardinal, Jean-Sifrein Maury (1746-1817) was elected as a representative of the First Estate to the Estates General by the clergy of Péronne. Though elected to the Académie française in 1785, Maury came from a modest artisanal family and retained plebeian manners. He sat

---

[18] On the monarchiens see Jean Egret, *La Révolution des Notables: Mounier et les Monarchiens, 1789* (Paris, 1950). As an organized entity, the monarchiens were defeated by the end of 1789, but some of their leaders continued to play an active role in revolutionary politics after the withdrawal of Mounier.

[19] Mathiez, *The French Revolution*, 62 and 79. Mathiez identifies Cazalès with a group called the "Impartials." Furet and Richet, however, put him to the right of the monarchiens (*La Révolution française*, 106).

[20] Godechot, *The Counter-Revolution*, 22.

[21] Godechot, 24, says that Cazalès was willing to accept reforms that "perhaps" went beyond those envisaged in the Royal Program of 23 June, and Beik describes him as a politician of the Right who "remained too moderate for tastes evolving under the blows of the revolution" (*The French Revolution seen from the Right*, 26). Furet and Richet, however, associate him with the "blacks" (*La Révolution française*, 106).

[22] Beik, art. "Cazalès" in Scott and Rothaus, *Historical Dictionary of the French Revolution, 1789-99*.

with Cazalès on the committee directing the monarchiens, but then came to espouse the views of the extreme right, known as the Irreconciliables. He has been described as both one of the great extemporary speakers of the Revolution and "the ablest and most exasperating defender of reaction."[23] Yet the term "reactionary" may not be quite apposite for him either. The program he advocated was that of the Royal Declaration of 23 June.[24] Under the old regime he moved in the same circles as many *philosophes,* and continued to adhere, though with flexibility, to Enlightenment values.[25] His éloge of Fénelon was crowned by the Academy in 1771, but then condemned by the government.[26] Marmontel, of whose circle he was a valued member, called Maury "this man of so rare a talent, and of a courage equal to this rare talent."[27] Though he opposed the legislation of 4 August, Maury seems to have turned sharply against the Revolution over Church policy. Yet he was one of the last of the ecclesiastical deputies to leave the National Assembly, and having emigrated to Rome, where he was made a cardinal, he nevertheless rallied to Napoleon in 1806 and served during the Empire as archbishop of Paris. This was a compromise that a true devotee of the old regime and of absolute monarchy would not readily have made. Cazalès, though generally more moderate than Maury, refused on his return to France in 1803 to serve Napoleon.[28]

At the beginning of 1791 the *Ami du Roi* announced the availability of a pamphlet by Cazalès on the mutiny at Nancy

---

[23] Mathiez, *The French Revolution,* 62 and 79. Thompson, *The French Revolution,* 106 and 33. Georges Lefebvre agrees with Thompson on this point, and identifies him, together with Cazalès and Royou, with the "Blacks" or reactionary aristocrats (*The French Revolution, From its Origins to 1793,* 141).

[24] Godechot, *The Counter-Revolution,* 23.

[25] Beik, The *French Revolution Seen from the Right,* 23-24 and 104.

[26] Durand Echeverria, *The Maupeou Revolution: A Study in the History of Libertarianism, France: 1770-1774,* 58.

[27] *Mémoires de Marmontel,* vol. III, 311-12.

[28] Beik, *The French Revolution Seen from the Right,* 26.

and its suppression.[29] On 14 April of the same year Royou announced that another pamphlet by Cazalès on the right of inheritance was available at the office of the *Ami du Roi*. A bill dated 16 April from Caillot and Courcier shows that Royou had this pamphlet printed in 10,000 copies.[30]

The Bibliothèque Nationale in Paris has in its collection of printed works fourteen pamphlets of Cazalès that date from 1789 to 1793. These include the two pamphlets cited above and three others which were either said to be printed by, or available from, the offices of the *Ami du Roi*. The *Opinion de M. de Cazalès sur le renvoi des ministres, prononcée dans la séance de l'Assemblée nationale du 19 octobre 1790* appeared both as a pamphlet and as a special number of the *Ami du Roi*,[31] while the *Discours de M. Cazalès sur la dénonciation des ministres, par la Société logographique* (1790) appeared only as a special number. The *Opinion de M. de Cazalès sur le serment exigé des officiers de l'armée (11 juin 1791)* is simply said to be available from the offices of the *Ami du Roi*.

The other pamphleteer with whom the *Ami du Roi* appears to have had a particularly close relationship was the abbé Maury. A contemporary journal, the *Royaliste*, called Royou "the echo of M. l'abbé Maury," and a recent study describes Maury as Royou's "correspondent in the National Assembly."[32] In the first half of 1791 the *Ami du Roi* announced at least five pamphlets by Maury, most of which were available at its offices. These include a pamphlet on the Marseille affair and on the property of the clergy of Alsace, another on the question of a regency, and others on invalids, on the dowry

---

[29] *AR*, 2 Jan., 1791. On the Nancy affair see X. Maire, *Histoire de l'affaire de Nancy* (Nancy, 1861) and for a good brief summary, Mathiez, *The French Revolution*, 75-76.

[30] AN T546[283]. Composition and corrections cost 60 *livres*, printing 70 *livres* and stitching 4 *livres*.

[31] The title of the special number (supplement) changes the word "Opinion" to "Discours" but is otherwise identical. The holdings of the Bibliothèque Nationale, which themselves are not necessarily complete, again indicate the partial nature of our archival sources.

[32] Murray, *The Right-Wing Press*, 117, n. 57; Bertaud, *Les Amis du Roi*, 37-38.

of the queen of Spain, and most importantly, on the Civil
Constitution of the Clergy.[33]

In addition to the pamphlets for which we have evidence
directly from the *Ami du Roi*, the catalogue of the Bibliothèque Nationale lists another five which Royou either published or sold. Three of them, on the great Parisian court of
the Châtelet, on the organization of a supreme court and on
the sovereignty of Avignon, date from 1790. The other two,
dealing with the dowry of the queen of Spain and with the
status of Avignon, are from 1791.[34] Maury's association with
Madame Fréron and Royou, extensive though it was, did not
exhaust his activity as a pamphleteer. In addition to a number
of pamphlets that showed no place or date of publication or
publisher, from 1789 to 1792 Maury published eight pamphlets at the Imprimerie Nationale, and occasional other
pamphlets with Baudoin, Crapart, who had initially been
involved with the *Ami du Roi*, Gattey, of whom we have seen
Royou complain, a number of other Parisian publishers and
the Vatican.[35] During 1790 Maury worked most closely with
the Imprimerie Nationale and during 1791 with the *Ami du
Roi*, but he does not seem at any time to have bound himself
exclusively to one publisher.

The *Ami du Roi* also sought to promote, or to profit from,
Maury's popularity by announcing a subscription for his portrait at the substantial cost of 6 *livres*.[36] There is also a record
of a payment of 1,200 *livres* made by Madame Fréron to
Maury, but as the receipt gives no explanation of the payment

---

[33] *AR*, 12 Jan. 1791; ibid., 7 Apr. 1791; ibid., 6 June 1791; ibid., 24 Dec. 1791.
Maury's pamphlet on the Civil Constitution will be treated more fully below.

[34] The *Catalogue général des livres imprimés de la Bibliothèque Nationale* shows two distinct
pamphlets by Maury on Avignon and on the dowry of the queen of Spain, née
Louise-Elizabeth d'Orléans, the records of the *Ami du Roi* only one on each of
these subjects, despite all four appearing under the auspices of the paper.

[35] For Royou's complaints about Gattey, see above. For Maury's publications see the
Catalogue de la Bibliothèque Nationale.

[36] Maury's portrait was announced in the *Ami du Roi* of 28 Feb. 1791. The records
of the paper contain two lists of orders, one for fifteen copies (AN T546[282]), the
other for 144 (AN T546[9]).

Table 4.1:   The Publication of Maury's *Opinion sur la Constitution Civile du Clergé**

SALES	No. COPIES	DATE	NATURE OF DOCUMENT
availability announced		24 Dec. 1790	annonce
first edition sold out		12 Jan. 1791	annonce
	3,000	7 Feb.	bill for brochage
second edition sold out	7,000	16 Feb.	annonce
	3,000	20 Apr.	bill for printing (Nyon)
	28,500	23 Apr.	bill for printing (Caillot)

*SOURCES: The source for announcements is the *Ami du Roi* of the dates indicated; those for the bills are AN T546, pe. 631, 333 and 280.

it is uncertain whether, as seems likely, it represents a fee paid by a publisher to an author, or was made in some other connection.[37]

In mid-December 1790 Royou announced that Maury had found time to dictate the speech he had given on 27 November in the National Assembly concerning the oath required of the clergy.[38] A week later Royou announced that the *Opinion de M. l'abbé Maury sur la constitution du clergé* which printed up to 75 pages in-8⁰ was on sale at the offices of the *Ami du Roi*.[39] Table 4.1 summarizes what can be learned of the history of this pamphlet from the records of Madame Fréron and the abbé Royou.

This table cannot be complete, and thus gives only an imperfect impression of the popularity of Maury's pamphlet. We have no figure for the press run of the first edition, but

---

[37] AN T546[19].
[38] *AR*, 18 December 1790.
[39] *AR*, 24 December 1790.

the growing demand, which can reasonably be deduced from the February and April figures, suggests that it may not have been much bigger than the second. Further, it is implausible, given the immediate response to Maury's *Opinion*, that Royou would have waited for two months after the second edition was sold out before reprinting it. There is apparently a gap in our sources from mid-February to mid-April, so that while there is evidence for 38,500 copies[40] of Maury's pamphlet having been printed and distributed by Royou and Madame Fréron, this figure might well be doubled.

C. Pius VI as Pamphleteer: The Papal Briefs of the Spring of 1791

During July 1790 Pius VI wrote Louis XVI to warn him about legislation concerning the Church. On 24 August Louis, despite his reluctance and misgivings, gave his sanction to the Civil Constitution of the Clergy. Two months later, on 27 November, the National Assembly voted to impose on priests holding office an oath asserting acceptance of the Civil Constitution. This act has been called "the fatal moment in the history of the Revolution,"[41] and with reason, for it resulted not only in a conflict with the papacy, but also in divisions within the French clergy, and then within French society, which significantly strengthened the forces of counter-revolution, and contributed to bringing about civil war. Most historians are agreed that the members of the National Assembly sought no conflict with the Church, but were brought by the implications of the legislation of August 1789 and the nationalization of church property gradually and inexorably into such a conflict. Most are equally agreed that the conflict

---

[40] The pamphlets stitched on 7 February were almost certainly part of the second edition which was sold out by the 16th of the same month.
[41] John McManners, *The French Revolution and the Church*, 46.

was no less fateful for being unplanned, unintended and indeed unexpected.[42]

The pope's response to the Civil Constitution came slowly. Toward the end of February 1791 he made his attitude to the Civil Constitution known publicly in a brief addressed to the archbishop of Sens, Loménie de Brienne, who had taken the oath. He calls the Civil Constitution "a collection, and as it were a summary, of several heresies" and informs the juring prelate that he could commit no greater dishonor to his office than by swearing and carrying out the oath.[43] On 10 March 1791 Pius VI issued a brief in which, in relatively moderate terms, he criticized, but stopped short of formally condemning,[44] the Civil Constitution of the Clergy.[45] The implications

---

[42] Mathiez pointed out that the deputies in the Assembly acted in good faith, and believed that they could reorganize the administration of the Church without alienating the papacy. This belief was based on a careful avoidance on the part of the Assembly of infringing on dogma, on the amenability of the great majority of the clergy to the new legislation and on the recent precedent of Catherine II's reorganization of the Catholic Church in Poland and Pius VI's acquiescence therein (*The French Revolution*, 110-12). Thompson points out that Pius VI accepted initial legislation concerning the Church, the abolition of annates (4 August 1789) and the confiscation of Church property (2 November 1789) without protest (*The French Revolution*, 153). Thompson also touches on the pope's concern about unrest in Avignon, a point which McManners notes the Assembly believed it could use as a lever in its dealings with Pius (*The French Revolution and the Church*, 43). Godechot, too, believes that the breach between Rome and the Assembly came about unwanted, by force of circumstance (*Les Institutions de la France sous la Révolution et l'Empire*, 255-56). However, André Latreille in his basic study *L'Eglise catholique et la Révolution française*, vol. I, 99-102, emphasizes the importance of the differences between the papacy and the Assembly.

[43] *Traduction fidèle et littérale du Bref du Pape à Monseigneur l'Archevêque de Sens* (Paris, 1791), 4-5. BN Ld⁴ .3375. This pamphlet is 19 pages long and contains both the French translation and the original Latin. The title page states that it is available from the offices of the *Ami du Roi*.

[44] At one point the brief asks whether the goal of the Assembly is not to "overthrow and annihilate the episcopacy, as if in detestation of the Religion of which the Bishops are Ministers," and later observes that the Civil Constitution "from beginning to end offers almost nothing that is not dangerous and reprehensible" and that it contains "scarcely an article that is sanctified and completely free from error." Nevertheless, in concluding, the pope explicitly states that he had not yet condemned the legislation and asks the French bishops for their help and advice in achieving conciliation. *Bref du Pape Pie VI, à S.E.M. le Cardinal de la Rochefoucault, M. l'Archevêque d'Aix et les autres Archevêques et Evêques de l'Assemblée Nationale au Sujet de la Constitution Civile du Clergé, décrétée par l'Assemblée Nationale* (Paris, 1791),

of this brief were immediately recognized as ominous, and according to some historians, attempts were made to keep the contents secret until a compromise could be worked out.[46] The brief, however, was soon made public. The *Ami du Roi* announced on 19 March that the papal letter would appear shortly, adding disarmingly, "it is very doctrinal and very sound."[47] Four days later the paper announced that the brief was available from its offices. In a further brief, dated 13 April, Pius VI declared the Civil Constitution heretical and contrary to Catholic dogma, forbade his clergy to take the oath to it, directing them if they had done so to retract within forty days from the date the brief was issued, and declared ordinations of constitutional bishops void.[48]

Royou played a key role in bringing these briefs to the French public, for not only did he have them printed and distributed, he also, on the testimony of his sister, had a hand in their translation.[49]

The publishing history of the papal briefs condemning the

46, 74 and 93. BN 8⁰ Ld³ 547(17). This brief prints up to 94 pages in-8⁰ and was distributed by the offices of the *Ami du Roi*. The Latin version had 88 pages. I assume this to be what is later called the "first brief," the second being that signed on 13 April.

[45] Alphonse Aulard emphasized the moderation of language of the papal brief, and pointed out that technically it stopped short of formally condemning the Civil Constitution. He admitted, however, that it was generally taken as a formal condemnation (*Christianity and the French Revolution*, 70-72).

[46] Mathiez states that the French bishops kept the brief of 10 March secret for "more than a month" (*The French Revolution*, 113), and McManners asserts that the brief of 10 March was handed over to the authorities in Paris on 21 March, then kept secret until 4 May when the pope made it public (*The French Revolution and the Church*, 59). Thompson, however, maintains that on 10 March 1791, Pius VI "publicly condemned the Civil Constitution" (*The French Revolution*, 154), and he is followed on this point by Furet and Richet (*La Révolution française*, 134).

[47] *AR*, 19 March 1791.

[48] Unlike earlier briefs, which had been addressed to specific prelates or groups of prelates, this one was addressed to the entire clergy and people of France, and so was clearly intended as a definitive public statement. *Bref du Pape aux Cardinaux, Archevêques, Evêques, au Clergé et au Peuple de France* (Paris, 1791), 12 and 22-23. BN 8⁰ Ld³ 547(20). This brief was 32 pages in-8⁰ and was published by the offices of the *Ami du Roi*. See also Aulard, *Christianity and the French Revolution*, 71 and Latreille, *L'Eglise catholique*, I, 110.

[49] APP AA206⁴¹⁵.

Civil Constitution of the Clergy is both incomplete and complicated. It is incomplete because, while the office of the *Ami du Roi* clearly played an important role in publishing and distributing these briefs, it was not alone in doing so. Crapart openly printed the papal brief of 23 April addressed to the clergy and people of Avignon,[50] which Royou also handled, and we will see that the briefs of 10 March and 13 April were pirated.[51] Furthermore, though the records of the *Ami du Roi* on the publication of these briefs are substantial, they are nonetheless deficient. Even determining the numbers of briefs published is no straightforward matter. First, the same brief was published in various forms, sometimes in Latin, sometimes in French, sometimes both. Second, both the *Ami du Roi* in its announcements, and printers, binders or booksellers in their bills, frequently gave only abbreviated titles such as "brief," "bull"[52] or "Great Latin Brief," so that it is often impossible to identify it with certainty. These reservations made, it is nevertheless worthwhile to examine the role of the *Ami du Roi* in bringing the words of Pius VI to Frenchmen.

It is clear from the following table that there was an enormous demand for these briefs. There is no other way to explain single printings of 40,000 or 50,000 copies. Unfortunately we lack information on the first edition of the pope's first brief on the Civil Constitution, available from the offices of the *Ami du Roi* from 23 March, but given its obvious importance, it is not unreasonable to suggest that it was published on the same scale as the Grand Bref Latin or the Bref sur Avignon. It is not possible to say with certainty whether Gentil's bill of 27 March for stitching 12,000 copies of the brief

---

[50] L.S. Thompson, *A Bibliography of French Revolutionary Pamphlets in Microfiche*, 544.
[51] Royou foresaw the likelihood of this happening and sought to forestall it by using a special symbol on the title page of the briefs, and even by signing them. Neither method succeeded.
[52] A bull is "the most solemn and weighty form of papal letter." A brief is also a papal letter, "but it is a less formal and weighty document than a bull." D. Atwater, ed., *A Catholic Dictionary* (New York, 1941), "Brief" and "Bull." Interchanging these terms, while loose usage, is not, strictly speaking, incorrect.

Table 4.2: The Publication of Selected Papal Briefs During the Spring and Summer of 1791

DESCRIPTION OF BRIEF	INFORMATION	No. COPIES	DATE	NATURE OF DOCUMENT	SOURCE
First Brief (Quod aliquantum)	signed in Rome		10 Mar.		
"Papal Brief"	soon to be available		19 Mar.	announcement	AR
Idem, Latin and French	available offices AR; cost: 8s.		23 Mar.	announcement	AR
Brief—unspecified		12,000	27 Mar.	bill for brochage (Gentil)	pe. 766*
Brief of Cardinal de Loménie	available offices AR; cost: 6s (Paris), 8s (prov.)		1 Apr.	announcement	AR
Brief—unspecified		4,000	2 Apr.	bill for printing (Caillot)	pe. 284
Brief of Cardinal de Loménie	asserting authenticity		4 Apr.	announcement	AR
Second Brief	signed in Rome		13 Apr.		
Grand Bref Latin		40,500	14 Apr.	bill for printing	pe. 605
Brief—unspecified		4,000	20 Apr.	bill for printing (Nyon)	pe. 792

Document	Notes	Number	Date	Type	Reference
Brief on Avignon	signed in Rome		23 Apr.		
Brief—unspecified	brief being pirated		3 May	announcement	*AR*
Brief—unspecified	warning about pirating		8 May	announcement	*AR*
Second Brief	available offices *AR*; cost: 20 s., French only, 10 s.		11 May	announcement	*AR*
Brief—unspecified Latin French		6,000 15,000	21 May	bill for printing (Nyon)	pe. 317
Brief—unspecified		6,000**	22 May	receipt for paper	pe. 71; 82
Second Brief	available offices *AR*		27 May	announcement	*AR*
Brief—unspecified		35,000***	28 May	bill for brochage	pe. 365
Brief on Avignon		5,000 50,000	5 June	bill for printing (Caillot)	pe. 322
First Brief—Latin		800	idem	idem	idem
Second Brief—Latin		500	idem	idem	idem
Brief—unspecified Latin, French			20 Dec.	announcement	*AR*

*pe. indicates the number of the document in AN T546.

**This figure does not appear in the document, but follows from information provided there, namely that one ream produced 500 copies, and twelve reams were delivered.

***The cost of brochage here was two *livres* per thousand, and the total cost 70 *livres*.

was for part of the original edition, or part of a later one, but certainly Caillot's bill of 2 April for 4,000 copies was for a new edition.

The size of the printing of 14 April—40,500 copies in Latin—suggests that though the Pope's condemnation of the Civil Constitution was issued only on 13 April, Royou had nevertheless got a copy and had it printed ahead of time. His role as translator of the briefs makes this likely. Nyon's bill of only a week later for printing 4,000 more copies shows that great as was the initial printing, it did not exhaust demand. Complaints in the *Ami du Roi* of 3 and 8 May that the brief was being pirated further support this impression.

In a letter of 24 May, Bergeret, a bookseller of Bordeaux, told the offices of the *Ami du Roi* that he had only just received the 200 copies of the first brief he had ordered six weeks ago and that since two pirated editions had meanwhile appeared, he would be unable to sell most of his.[53] In a subsequent letter, in which he emphasized the importance of prompt delivery, Bergeret disclaimed responsibility for these briefs, and refused to pay for them.[54] He remained, however, a good customer for both the paper and various pamphlets.

On 21 May Nyon billed Royou for 6,000 Latin and 15,000 French briefs, and on the following day Caillot received 12 reams of paper which were sufficient to print another 6,000 briefs.[55] It therefore seems likely that Gentil's bill of 28 May for stitching 35,000 briefs would include those printed by Caillot and Nyon. If so, this would bring the number of copies for which we have records to over 75,000.

On 27 May 1791 the *Ami du Roi* announced that it would soon have a new papal brief for sale, this being a brief on Avignon, of which Caillot printed some 55,000 copies, billing

---

[53] AN T546[517]. He added that if the pamphlets he ordered were delivered promptly, Madame Fréron and her brother would find in him "un bon consomateur." Ibid.
[54] Letter of 27 August 1791. AN T546[524].
[55] AN T546[517] and [82].

Royou for them on 5 June.[56] The same bill also charges for 800 copies of the first Latin brief and 500 of the second brief. On this brief on Avignon we have no further information concerning publication by the *Ami du Roi*. But if the 35,000 briefs stitched by Gentil on 28 May were not, as suggested above, for the second brief, then they would have been for this one. In that case we would have a proven total production of 85,000 copies of this pamphlet. Taking into account the partial nature of our sources, it seems reasonable to suggest that the offices of the *Ami du Roi* were having printed and distributing 100,000, and perhaps more, copies of the pope's briefs in the spring and summer of 1791.

Who bought and read these briefs? The scattered evidence that bears on this question indicates, as one would expect, a large clerical readership. The register of accounts for the *Ami du Roi* for the spring and summer of 1791 shows that bulls were bought in bulk by a number of bishops, presumably for distribution to the *curés* of their dioceses. The bishop of Nîmes bought 103 *livres* worth of briefs on 23 May, the bishop of Uzès 808 *livres* worth on 30 May, the abbé Polonceau 1,000 *livres* worth on 15 June, and the bishop of Beauvais 100 *livres* worth on 18 August.[57] The same register shows payments to the *Ami du Roi* of 268 *livres* by the bishop of Le Mans on 21 May and of 220 *livres* by the bishop of Montpellier on 23 August without stating what the payments were made for, and shows a payment of 50 *livres* to the paper on 1 June by a curé of Abbeville for "brochures."[58] As the cost of most briefs was between eight and twelve *sous* a copy,[59] orders such as those cited above reached the hundreds, and sometimes

[56] AN T546³³³.
[57] AN T*546⁴. This register is organized chronologically.
[58] Ibid.
[59] Bishops can reasonably be assumed to have distributed briefs to the *curés* in their dioceses, and many of the parish clergy would have read them during Sunday services.

thousands of copies and help to explain how so many copies of the briefs could be sold in so short a time.

Yet it would not be correct to conclude that the public of the papal briefs was exclusively clerical. The orders of booksellers suggest that this was not so. Bertherin, a bookseller in Orléans, ordered 156 briefs in the spring of 1791, only a fifth of which were in Latin without an accompanying French text.[60] And it is common to find orders with no exclusively Latin texts at all. Barailles of Marseilles placed an order for 104 second briefs, half in Latin and French, half in French only, and for 52 unspecified briefs in both French and Latin, while Delys of Saintes ordered more than two hundred briefs, three-quarters in both French and Latin, one-quarter in French only.[61] Bergeret of Bordeaux ordered 100 copies of the first brief in Latin and French and a further 100 in French only, while Barboux of Paris took 400 first briefs, most in French without the original Latin.[62] This emphasis on the vernacular would not have been necessary for a strictly clerical readership. There are also a number of personal orders that show that laymen too bought the pope's briefs. An emeritus professor of the *collège* of Beaune ordered 25 *livres* worth of briefs, while Portier, a former principal of the *collège* of Billom and subscriber to the *Ami du Roi*, ordered two copies of a brief in French and Latin and two more of the *Principes de la foi*.[63] The countess de Broglie, a member of one of the great noble houses of France, and also a subscriber to Royou's paper, ordered three copies of a brief in Latin, three in French and two others.[64] There are also instances of an abbé and an anonymous subscriber to the *Ami du Roi* ordering two copies

---

[60] AN T546[816]. Uneven numbers are the rule in booksellers' orders because publishers usually gave their discounts in the proportion of 1:12. Thus, for example, a bookseller would pay for 48 items, but receive 52.

[61] AN T546[805 807].

[62] AN T546[511 815].

[63] AN T546[466 470].

[64] AN T546[468].

each of a brief.[65] There is no case in the admittedly small
amount of surviving correspondence with booksellers of a
customer ordering only one copy of a brief.[66]

The most interesting order for briefs comes from Brittany.
It lists six buyers, each of whom is to receive twelve copies
in French and Latin and a further six in French only. Two
of the six, Gallet, a printer, and Goujeon, an advocate and
notary, lived in Vannes. The rest lived in small centers in the
surrounding countryside. M. Guilleren, a wholesale merchant (négociant), lived in Auray; Madame de Langles, lived
in her town-house (hôtel) in Hennebout (or Hennebond); the
abbé Villeneuve was vicaire at La Roche Bernard, and M.
Lestrohau was an advocate and notary at Port Louis. Only
Madame de Langles and M. Goujeon were also subscribers
to the Ami du Roi.[67]

It is striking that none of the locations to which multiple
copies of the briefs were sent in Brittany was a mere village,
or primarily engaged in agriculture. Vannes, of course, was
a town of good size; Auray is described by Expilly as a "small
town" of about 1,000 inhabitants, a port, and the seat of a
bailliage; Hennebon is described in the same source as a wealthy
commercial town of about 3,000; La Roche Bernard, with a
population of about 2,500, had shipyards and four annual
fairs; and Port Louis, which had a garrison and whose principal industry was fishing, can reasonably be estimated to
have had a population approaching 2,000.[68] Eighteen copies
of a pamphlet delivered to centers with between 200 and 500
heads of families no doubt made the contents of the pamphlet
available to any interested resident, and likely to residents of
the immediate vicinity also.

The social composition of this small group could hardly

---

[65] AN T546[471 481].
[66] On 23 March 1791, the Ami du Roi announced that the minimal order for briefs
was three livres.
[67] AN T546[467]; T*546[5].
[68] Expilly, Dictionnaire géographique, articles on the towns in question.

be more varied: two lawyers, a cleric, a printer, a merchant and a lady of means. This is not exactly what one would have expected as the occupational profile of a group of counter-revolutionaries.[69] But then it is unlikely that they thought of themselves as such, or should be so regarded. To themselves they were probably faithful Catholics whose duty it was to learn and to inform others of the pope's position on a key issue. In the event, fidelity to the Roman Church and loyalty to the new regime being worked out in Paris proved irreconcilable. This was, no doubt, one of the great shortcomings of the Constituent Assembly, as well as one of the tragedies of those years in France. But the political implications of the papal briefs is not what primarily interests us here. Rather, it is how, by simply supplying eighteen copies of this document to six different addresses, the offices of the *Ami du Roi* contributed to, and in effect, assured, the distribution of the vastly important papal condemnation of a vital piece of legislation to the extremities of a distant province.

D. Ideology and Business

Two other aspects of the handling of pamphlet literature by the *Ami du Roi* require comment. The first is ideological, the second commercial.

I have suggested above that the *Ami du Roi* was not quite so far to the right as some historians of the press have main-

---

[69] The Counter-Revolution in the west was noteworthy for the prominence of the clergy and the broad popular support it enjoyed. Accordingly, much of the research devoted to the Counter-Revolution in the west focuses on artisans, peasants, patterns of landholding, the role of the Church in local communities and related issues. Some of the most important examinations of the west during the Revolution are surveyed by Harvey Mitchell, "The Vendée and Counterrevolution: A Review Essay." See also T.J.A. Le Goff and D.M.G. Sutherland, "The Revolution and the Rural Community in Eighteenth-Century Brittany"; Harvey Mitchell, "Resistance to the Revolution in Western France"; and Le Goff and Sutherland, "The Social Origins of Counter-Revolution in Western France."

tained, and that, having initially adopted an open-minded attitude toward the work of political renewal underway, it gradually became more hostile. I believe that the handling of pamphlets by the abbé Royou and Madame Fréron supports this view. At the time of its foundation, the *Ami du Roi* can, I believe, fairly be identified with the views of the monarchiens, who favored a constitutional monarchy and arresting the Revolution at an early stage. As we have seen, Cazalès represented this position, and Royou saw fit to print and distribute his pamphlets. Maury is the political propagandist with whom the *Ami du Roi* worked most closely, and he was to the right of Cazalès. Yet the issue on which Maury and Royou cooperated most closely was church-state relations, particularly the Civil Constitution of Clergy. With the vote of 27 November 1790 imposing an oath of loyalty to the Civil Constitution on priests, the *Ami du Roi* came into a conflict of principle with the Assembly. The briefs of the pope of 10 March and 13 April 1791 deepened and finalized these differences. Thereafter Royou merely followed the highest authority of the Church to which he belonged and to which he was devoted. Had the pope sanctioned the Civil Constitution, as many in the Assembly expected he would,[70] there is no reason to expect that Royou would have persisted in his opposition. With the pope having taken the position he did, the abbé could not well have acted differently.

To appreciate Royou's attitude and outlook one must, I think, accept that he was consistent, and that he never moved from his initial position of implicit loyalty to both the Catholic Church and the French monarchy. In September of 1790 he could reasonably expect that the great project of national reform then underway could be carried out without the state infringing on matters of doctrine and without the monarchical basis of government being called into question. With the vote imposing the oath of loyalty to the Civil Constitution

---

[70] McManners, *The French Revolution and the Church*, 46.

and then the pope's condemnation of it, Royou was forced into opposition on the question of church-state relations. With the flight to Varennes and Royou's decision to defend the king[71] he was irrevocably committed to political opposition also. No wonder his paper had so short a duration. Views that found a legitimate place in the spectrum of political opinion in the fall of 1790 no longer did do so in the summer of 1791. Yet it should be noted that Royou was forced into opposition by circumstances. His convictions remained constant while the ground around him shifted. Thus, if the *Ami du Roi* can with justice be regarded as belonging to the extreme right of the political spectrum in 1792, this should not obscure the initial moderation of its position, or the process by which the paper was driven to the right.

The French Revolution was a period of intense ideological awareness and commitment. Publishing was and is a business the object of which is profit. Madame Fréron and the abbé Royou were convinced royalists, but they were also astute managers, not only of their paper, but also of other aspects of an extensive publishing enterprise.

We have seen that Madame Fréron and her brother published pamphlets in press runs of tens of thousands. In some cases we have itemized bills for printing, and these show that publishing pamphlets was far more profitable than publishing a daily paper. The cost to the *Ami du Roi* for printing 40,500 copies of the *Grand Bref Latin* was 400 *livres* 10 *sous* while the cost for 55,000 *Bref sur Avignon* was 590 *livres*.[72] Ten thousand copies of the *Opinion de M. de Cazalès sur le droit de tester* cost 139 *livres* to set and print while 28,500 copies of one of Maury's pamphlets cost 270 *livres* 10 *sous*.[73] One *livre* thus covered the printing costs of 70 copies of Cazalès's pamphlet and of between 90 and 100 of Maury's or of the two briefs. Printing costs of course do not cover all production

---

[71] *AR*, 28-29 June 1791.
[72] AN T546^605 ^322.
[73] AN T546^283 ^280.

expenses. Most of these bills omit stitching, which normally cost about 10 *sous* a hundred items or five *livres* the thousand, and none includes the cost of paper, which was substantial. Caillot at one point informed Royou that he did not have enough paper to finish printing one of the papal briefs, that two reams had produced one thousand copies, and that he had only two more reams left.[74] The many bills for paper in the records of the *Ami du Roi* show that the price of a ream varied between eight and twelve *livres*.[75] Assuming the paper Caillot was using to have cost ten *livres* a ream, we would have to add 20 *livres* a thousand or two *livres* a hundred to the cost of the pamphlets Madame Fréron and Royou were publishing. For pamphlets such as the briefs, costs for printing, stitching and paper would have reached about three *livres* ten *sous* for between 70 and 100 copies.

That the profit involved in the publication of pamphlets was considerable can be seen both from advertisements in the *Ami du Roi* and from correspondence with booksellers. The first papal brief was advertised at two *livres* in its Latin and French version, one *livre* four *sous* in French only, and we find booksellers paying these prices for them.[76] The second brief sold for one *livre* in the provinces in both French and Latin, 10 *sous* for French only.[77] A large Parisian bookseller bought copies of this brief for 12 *sous* a copy in French and Latin, while paying one *livre* four *sous* for the first brief in Latin only, 8 *sous* for the French version, and 12 *sous* for the *Bref sur Avignon*.[78] Given that total production costs for this last pamphlet were about 3 *livres* ten *sous* for between 90 and 100 copies, and in that the charge to the retailer was 54 *livres* for the same number, the profit margin would appear to be about 1,500 percent.

[74] AN T546[82].
[75] AN T546[56 83 265 315 878].
[76] *AR*, 8 May 1791 and 20 December 1791; AN T546[469].
[77] *AR*, 11 May 1791.
[78] AN T546[815].

The only significant cost factor not so far taken into account is the purchase of the manuscript from its author. Unfortunately we have no firm evidence on this point, but it can reasonably be assumed that the payment noted above of 1,200 *livres* to Maury was of this sort.[79] There are no grounds for assuming a sudden break with the normal practice of the old regime, by which an author ceded his manuscript outright to a publisher for a cash payment.[80] On relatively small press runs the purchase cost of the manuscript could reduce the profit margin considerably, while on larger press runs the impact would be proportionately smaller. It is likely, moreover, that in publishing papal briefs the *Ami du Roi* was free from any such payment.

If the pamphlets handled by the *Ami du Roi* are at all representative, they seem to have been particularly profitable. Normally short works whose typesetting cost little, which could be done quickly, and could be printed in large numbers in response to public interest, pamphlets seem an ideal means of communicating ideas and opinions in times of crisis. Their profitability to their publishers was further enhanced by the purchasers in most cases accepting financial responsibility for distribution. Booksellers were billed for both handling and postage, and where individuals in the provinces ordered pamphlets through local booksellers, the pamphlets could be slipped in with a regular shipment. Only individuals ordering directly from the offices of the *Ami du Roi* would have caused the publishers to pay for postage. The evidence available suggests that such orders were rare. Though postal costs were in principle covered in the difference in price between Paris and the provinces, individual orders were discouraged by setting a minimum size.[81] If, then, a profit margin of 1,500

---

[79] See above, n. 37.
[80] Pottinger, *The French Book Trade*, 44. John Lough puts the average price of a literary manuscript sold to a publisher at between 1,000 and 2,000 *livres* (*An Introduction to Eighteenth-Century France*, 236-37).
[81] See above, n. 66.

percent seems high for pamphlets produced in small press runs, one cannot preclude such levels in cases, such as the papal briefs, where the author did not have to be paid or where press runs were exceptionally high. Profit margins of between 500 and 1,000 percent for most of the pamphlets handled by the *Ami du Roi* seem not unreasonable.

E. The Pamphlets and the Paper

Given the high level of activity in the offices of the *Ami du Roi* in publishing pamphlets and the profits these made, the status of Royou's paper seems diminished. This impression is confirmed by the account books of the *Ami du Roi* for May and June 1791. Figure 4.1 (p. 112) shows the daily income of Madame Fréron and the abbé Royou's publishing undertakings during the peak of their success, that is, while the *Ami du Roi* was printing 5,700 copies a day and while the various papal briefs were in high demand.

The basic fact that emerges from this graph is that during the period in question income from pamphlets exceeded income from subscriptions substantially. On 32 of the 42 days for which information is available, pamphlets brought in more money than subscriptions. What is more, they also brought in larger sums. On no day in May and June 1791 did payments for subscriptions exceed 400 *livres*, yet on four occasions payments for pamphlets amounted to between 400 and 900 *livres*, while on two others they reached a thousand. According to the bookkeeper of the *Ami du Roi*, the net income for subscriptions from 2 May to 25 June was 4,677 *livres* 12 *sous*, expenses deducted, or an average daily income of just over 111 *livres* a day for the 42 days for which we have information. The corresponding figures for brochures, which were normally listed as "briefs and other brochures" are 8,719 *livres* six *sous*, an average of between 207 and 208 *livres* a

Figure 4.1: Income of the *Ami du Roi* from Subscriptions and from Pamphlets, May and June 1791*

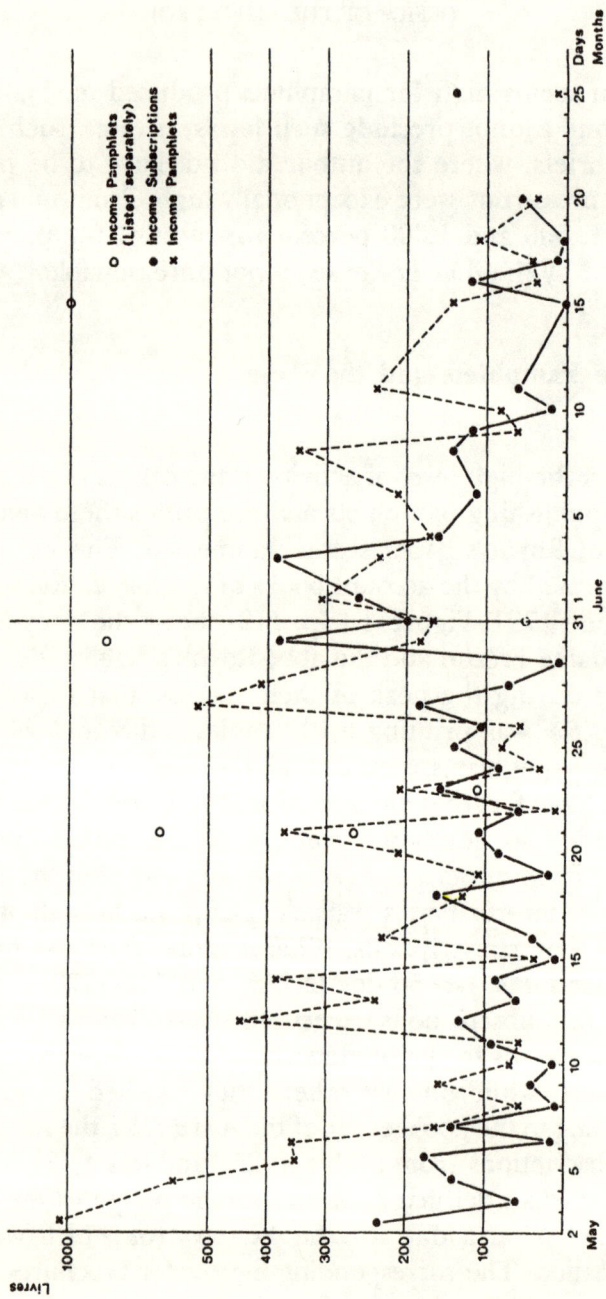

o Income Pamphlets
  (Listed separately)
• Income Subscriptions
× Income Pamphlets

*Source: AN T*546⁴.

day.[82] Total income for this period, still according to the book-keeper of the *Ami du Roi* was 25,624 *livres*, expenditures 3,968 *livres*, leaving a net profit of 21,755 *livres* for less than two months.[83]

The importance of pamphlets in the publishing activities of Madame Fréron and her brother is underscored in two bills to booksellers. From the fall of 1790 through the summer of 1791 Mame of Angers ordered over 275 *livres* worth of goods from the offices of the *Ami du Roi*. Five subscriptions accounted for 53 *livres*, the rest going for pamphlets.[84] During May and June of 1791 Barboux of Paris ordered between 800 and 900 *livres* worth of publications.[85] These include over 400 first briefs, 150 of which were in Latin, 600 second briefs, 75 briefs on Avignon and 86 *Principes de la foi*. Only a few subscriptions were included in Barboux's order.

These orders show how important pamphlets could be in the output of the offices of the *Ami du Roi*, but they should not be taken as representative. While we lack information on the production of pamphlets for most of the duration of the paper, the intensity of activity in this field during April was almost certainly atypical.[86] And many booksellers ordered subscriptions to Royou's paper and no pamphlets at all. Indeed, the financial records of the *Ami du Roi* for May and June 1791 give the impression that the paper was less important than it really was. By entering only net profits, the book-keeper obscured the extent of the cash flow of the paper. A net profit of about 2,500 *livres* a month is certainly substantial, but we learn from a different set of accounts that the gross

---

[82] AN T*546⁴.

[83] Expenses are particularly low because only net income is entered for subscriptions, which is to say that the expenses involved in producing the paper are hidden. The costs of producing the pamphlets were in any case low.

[84] AN T546⁸⁰⁵.

[85] AN T546⁸¹⁵. It is not possible to give a precise figure because no price is shown for some of the items ordered.

[86] Between 7 and 23 April the offices of the *Ami du Roi* were advertising or having published three pamphlets by Maury (*AR*, 7 and 18 April 1791; AN T546²⁸⁰) a pamphlet by Cazalès (AN T546²⁸³) and two papal briefs.

income from subscriptions to the *Ami du Roi* in one instance reached more than 13,400 *livres* for a three-week period.[87] The following figure shows the income and expenditure of the *Ami du Roi* for the three crucial months of July to September 1791.

While providing valuable information on the finances of Royou's paper, the data in this table present a number of problems. There is, first, the matter of the categories used. Payments from booksellers and payments direct from subscribers (by postal orders or *mandats*) are clear enough. Yet the first category, "subscriptions," is itemized on a daily basis and shows both the number of subscriptions received on any given day and their cash value. The basis on which the accountant of the *Ami du Roi* made this distinction is unclear, but he likely knew what he was doing.

Second, the figures for July are not compatible with those for August and September because the former included payments for pamphlets from booksellers, and we do not know which proportion of this large payment was for subscriptions and which for pamphlets. If the figure for subscriptions is high, it may well be that the figures for May and June are low, as indeed the figure for August seems to suggest.[88] This reservation made, the impression given by Figure 4.2 is that the closure of the *Ami du Roi* from 23 July to 6 August had a detrimental effect on the paper's popularity and profitability. Yet this effect was not uniform, and cannot easily be measured. Subscriptions from booksellers fell dramatically from August to September, direct subscriptions fell significantly from July to August, but then rose marginally in September, while the indeterminate but important category "subscriptions" fell by a quarter from July to August, only to recover in September. It is unfortunate that we have no fig-

---

[87] AN T546[224].
[88] The sharp drop in September was probably a reaction to the two-week closure from 23 July. The August figures would have still reflected business as usual as subscriptions were normally sent for the beginning of the month.

Figure 4.2: Subscriptions to the *Ami du Roi*, 1 July–22 September, 1971*

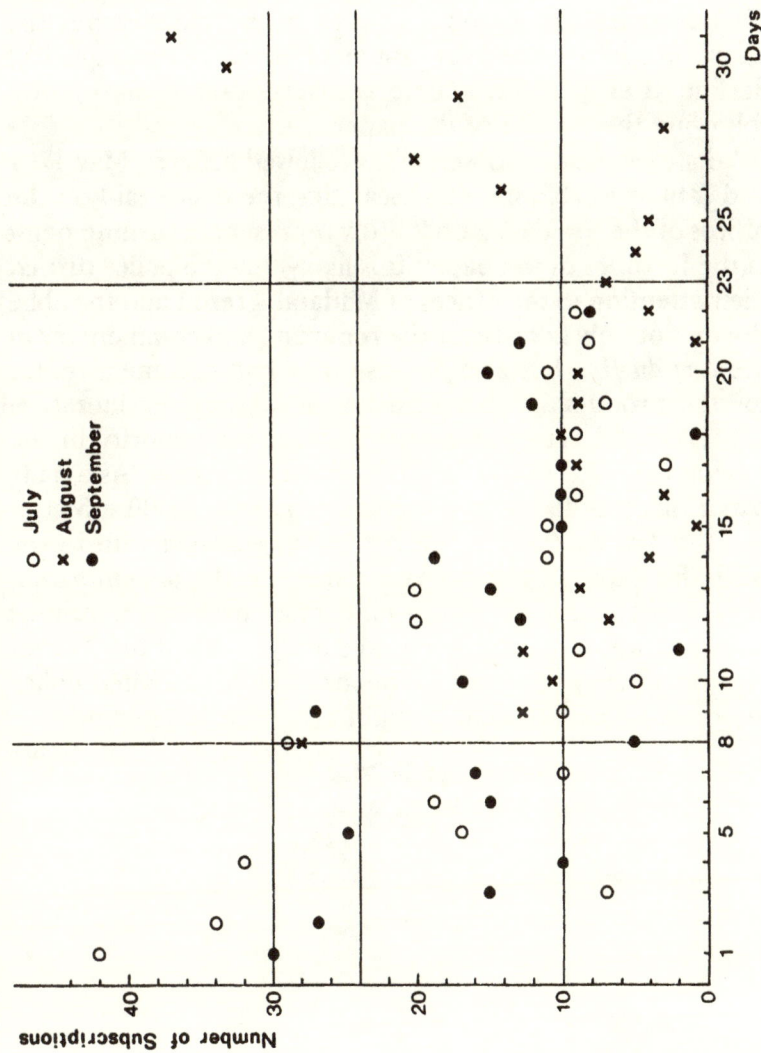

*Source: AN T546[24].

ures for press runs between mid-May 1791 and January 1792
(Fig. 2.1), for these would help to determine whether the
4,800 subscribers listed for January 1792 represent a gradual
decline after July 1791, or a recovery after a sharp drop
following the closure of the paper.

Whatever pattern subscriptions followed between May 1791
and January 1792, it seems clear that the police raid on the
offices of the *Ami du Roi* on 23 July represents a turning point
in the fortunes of the paper. It is likely that the police turned
their attention to the offices of Madame Fréron and the abbé
Royou not only because of the reporting and commentary in
the *Ami du Roi*, but also because they had become a center
for the production and diffusion of a pamphlet literature
that criticized central features of what the majority in the
Assembly hoped would be a legislative settlement. As a daily
paper that was distributed regularly to nearly 6,000 subscribers, the *Ami du Roi* was a force to be reckoned with in the
battle for public opinion. As a center for the dissemination
of tens of thousands, and in some cases probably hundreds
of thousands, of pamphlets hostile to the work of the Assembly, the offices of the *Ami du Roi* may well have invited police
intervention earlier than it might otherwise have come.

V.
The Subscribers to the Ami du Roi: Geographical Distribution, Gender and Collective Subscriptions

The extensiveness, detail and consistency of the subscription lists to the *Ami du Roi* make it possible to draw a highly detailed socio-professional profile of the readership of the paper. We have already seen that information from these lists can be used for other purposes, such as showing the duration of subscriptions. In addition, they can be made to throw light on other aspects of the collective character of the paper's subscribers. The geographical distribution of subscribers to the *Ami du Roi*, the breakdown by gender and even the problematic use of the particle "de" and its variants all add to our understanding of the people who bought and read Royou's paper.

Since the following analyses are based on three different lists of subscribers, it would be well to consider their character, and the way they have been used. The longest list, with 4,630 subscribers (List I), dates from the summer of 1791, covers only the provinces and provides fairly full information on status and occupation, but only general information on the geographical distribution of customers. A second list dates from the fall of 1790, that is, from the very beginning of the paper, and contains information on 1,211 subscribers (List II). The last list dates from early 1791 and includes 765 subscribers (List III). The two shorter lists cover Paris as well as the provinces. We have arrived at our list of Parisian subscribers by taking all subscribers from the capital in List II, comparing them to Parisian subscribers in List III, deleting the doubles, then adding the remaining Parisians from List III to those in List II. Our sample of provincial subscribers was reached in similar fashion. Provincial buyers of the paper

125

in List II were checked against List I, doubles were deleted, and the remaining subscribers added on to form the more extensive provincial list. As a high proportion of subscribers in List III already appeared in List I, it was not considered worthwhile to check provincial subscribers of List III against those in List II. This procedure would perhaps have added another 100 or so subscribers to a population of more than 5,000, and so would not have made a significant difference.

Both composite lists, then, are free from double entries. They reflect the public of the paper toward the beginning and middle of its existence. The Paris list, which is unfortunately much less full than that for the provinces, tells us who in the capital was subscribing to Royou's paper during the first six months of its existence. The provincial list covers the paper's first year, and is weighted toward the summer of 1791. These may seem fine distinctions. We shall see below that they are significant.

Where it has proven useful to compare the contents of the three lists, or to compare one list to another, no deletions have been made. This means that some subscribers will appear two, or even three times, but also that each list will reflect readership at the time it was made up. For most variables, the same information appears in all three lists and is compatible. The chief exception concerns addresses. List I gives only the postal routes of subscribers, Lists II and III both the postal routes and precise addresses. The two shorter lists contain information on the duration and cost of subscription, the longer one on duration only.

A. Geography

The distribution of the *Ami du Roi* in the provinces raises questions of general interest for the history of the Revolution. Assuming that subscription to Royou's paper is an indication of right-wing opinion, more or less along the lines of Mounier

Table 5.1: The Geographical Distribution of Provincial Subscribers
to the *Ami du Roi* by Postal Route* (n = 4630)

ROUTE	NO. SUBSCRIPTIONS	% SUBSCRIPTIONS
Amiens	361	7.80%
Bordeaux	459	9.91%
Bourbonnais	227	4.90%
Bourgogne	420	9.07%
Bretagne	420	9.07%
Châlons-Strasbourg	260	5.62%
Chartres	250	5.40%
Forbonnais-Vivarais-Dauphiné	136	2.94%
Orléans	173	3.74%
Provence-Roussillon-Languedoc	364	7.86%
Reims	146	3.15%
Rouen	520	11.23%
Saint Quentin	167	3.61%
Toulouse	272	5.88%
Troyes	119	2.57%
Foreign	156	3.37%
Variable	84	1.81%
Unknown	96	2.07%

*Source: AN T*546⁵.

and the monarchiens, what does the distribution of the paper throughout provincial France tell us about the political coloring of the different regions? Are subscribers distributed more or less evenly throughout the country, or are they concentrated in certain regions? Were readers in towns or in the countryside more prepared to pay the cost of a subscription to read Royou's analyses of events in Paris? And how do patterns of readership of the *Ami du Roi* compare to the geography of other journals of both right and left? Table 5.1 and Figure 5.1 allow us to begin answering these questions.

Two points, both fairly obvious, need to be made about the information just adduced. First, as a description of provincial subscriptions to the *Ami du Roi*, these data exclude Paris. Though explicitly noted, this omission results in a dis-

Figure 5.1:   The Distribution of the *Ami du Roi* in the Provinces*

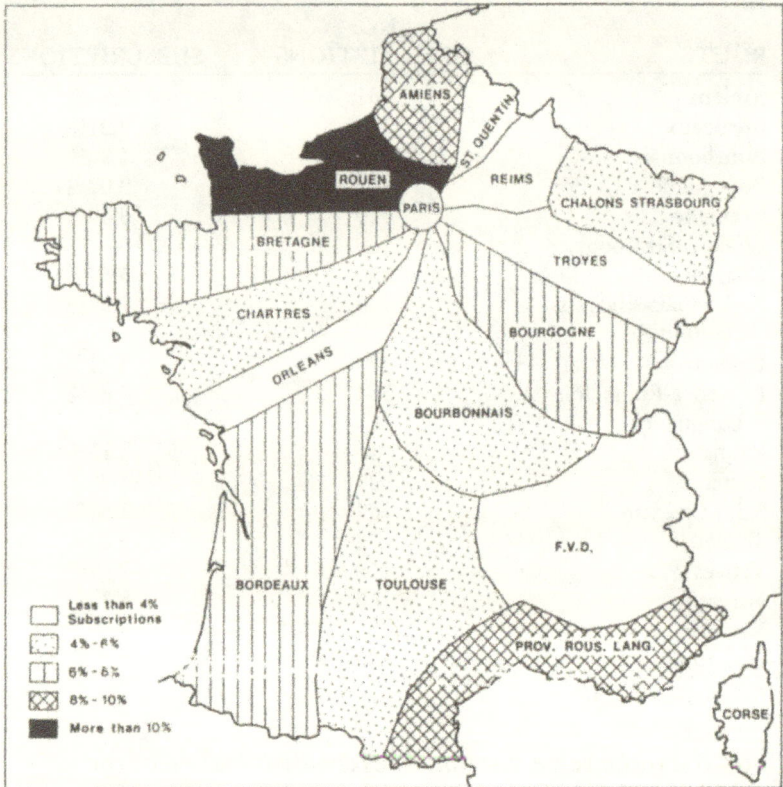

*Source: AN T*546⁵.

tortion, for Paris, with about 1,000 subscribers, was by far the largest single "regional" subscriber. Normandy, with Rouen as its center, had 520 subscribers: more than any other region, but only half the figure for Paris.[1] When discussing the regional weighting and role of urbanization among provincial subscribers, this should be borne in mind.

Second, the information on subscribers to the *Ami du Roi*

---

[1] Parisian subscriptions are approximately 20 percent of the total for Royou's paper. For the Jacobin *Journal de la Montagne,* Paris accounts for nearly 40 percent of all subscriptions. Gough, "Les Jacobins et la presse," 288-89.

in the main alphabetical list on which Table 5.1 and Figure 5.1 are based is by postal route only. After the great administrative reforms of the Constituent Assembly had been implemented, geographical divisions were normally made by département. Before those reforms, such information would be given, depending on circumstances, by *généralité, gouvernement,* province, *bailliage,* jurisdiction of *parlement* or a variety of fiscal divisions.[2] None of these corresponds exactly to any other, and none corresponds to the postal routes with which we are obliged to work. But this should not cause too much concern. The administrative geography of the old regime is not such as to permit geometric precision. But so long as we bear in mind the proposition, central to the Enlightenment, that all things cannot be known with an equal degree of certainty or precision, and so long as we are prepared to accept that our findings here will necessarily be approximate, we may proceed.

Perhaps the most basic point concerning the geographical distribution of the *Ami du Roi* as reflected in Table 5.1 and Figure 5.1 is its relative evenness. No province or postal route had less than 100 subscribers (2.57 percent), while only one had more than 500 (11.23 percent). Yet certain regions were better customers of Madame Fréron and the abbé Royou than others.

In general, the north bought more subscriptions to the *Ami du Roi* than the south, and the west than the east. Of the four regions with most subscribers, Normandy (11.23 percent) and Brittany (9.07 percent) are in the northwest, Bordeaux (9.91 percent) is in the west while only Bourgogne is toward the southeast, and its prominence here is accounted for by the inclusion within it of Lyon, the largest city in the country after Paris. The route of Amiens, which also included Beauvais, Calais and Lille, had 7.80 percent of the paper's sub-

---

[2] For an attempt to reduce these contradictory and overlapping jurisdictions to some sort of order see G. Shapiro, J. Markoff and S.R. Weitman, "Quantitative Studies of the French Revolution."

scribers, while the route of Saint-Quentin accounted for a further 3.61 percent in the north, and Chartres and Orléans, which both fanned to the west, accounted for another 5.40 percent. The northwestern routes of Châlons-Strasbourg, Reims and Troyes together account for only 11.34 percent of the subscribers to the *Ami du Roi,* while the southeastern routes of Provence-Roussillon-Languedoc and Forbonnais-Nivarais-Dauphiné add another 10.84 percent. The Toulouse route, which extended from Limoges in the north to Foix in the south,[3] provided 5.88 percent of provincial subscriptions. The center is lightly represented, but nevertheless retains a significant presence with the Bourbonnais route accounting for a further 4.90 percent of subscriptions outside Paris.

In addition to the subscriptions noted above, another 336, or 7.25 percent of the total, do not belong to any of the provincial routes. Information on the location of just over two percent of subscribers is lacking. Just under two percent had variable addresses. In most cases this meant that professional demands obliged these subscribers, frequently army officers, to move periodically. A further 156 subscriptions, or 3.37 percent of the total, were sent beyond the borders of France. These are not particularly impressive numbers, especially for a journal that has been closely identified with the emigration. Some foreign subscribers, such as Cardinal Valenti in Rome, were not French, and therefore not émigrés, though most subscribers living abroad certainly were. But while less than three and a half percent of subscribers lived outside France, three postal routes within the country, those of Reims, Troyes and Forbonnais-Nivarais-Dauphiné, had even fewer. Furthermore, while foreign subscriptions were still relatively low, they had been rising consistently. Our earliest list, that for August to October 1790, shows 1.73 percent

---

[3] Périgueux appears in both the Toulouse and the Bordeaux routes. The inconsistency of clerks in the offices of the *Ami du Roi* may also have contributed to irregularity in distribution.

foreign subscribers outside France; the list for February 1791 shows 2.27 percent; and the full provincial list with 3.37 percent, dates from the summer of 1791. On the basis of these figures one might reasonably expect the proportion of foreign subscribers to have reached 5 percent, or perhaps more, by the time the paper was closed in May 1792. Whether such a rate of foreign subscription justifies regarding the *Ami du Roi* as the official journal of the emigration and the clergy, remains a matter for individual judgment.[4]

While spread throughout all the provinces of France, the distribution of the *Ami du Roi* does show significant regional variation. The question that comes to mind is what causes this variation? Though there is no simple answer to this question, and no single answer that is valid throughout the country, it appears that density of population, degree of urbanization and political orientation all exerted an influence.

On the whole, the distribution of subscriptions to the *Ami du Roi* corresponds closely to density of population. A map based on information gathered by intendants toward the end of the old regime shows that population was thinnest in the center, south and southeast, as well as in Champagne and Lorraine. These areas had the lowest proportions of subscriptions to Royou's paper (compare Figures 5.1 and 5.2). The areas most densely populated according to the same source (1,500 inhabitants per square league) are the northwest and the Lyonnais. We have seen that the only routes with four hundred or more subscribers were Normandy, Brittany, Burgundy and Bordeaux. Density of population throughout the areas covered by the routes of Burgundy and Bordeaux were, on the whole, between 800 and 990 inhabitants per square league. Both of these routes, however, cover extensive areas, and both contain major metropolitan centers. Lyon, which received its mail through the Burgundy route,

<hr />

[4] Hatin, *Histoire de la presse*, VII, 155. It should also be borne in mind that the *Ami du Roi* carried frequent and sympathetic items on émigrés, especially toward the end of its career.

Figure 5.2:   The Distribution of the Population of France at the End of the Old Regime*

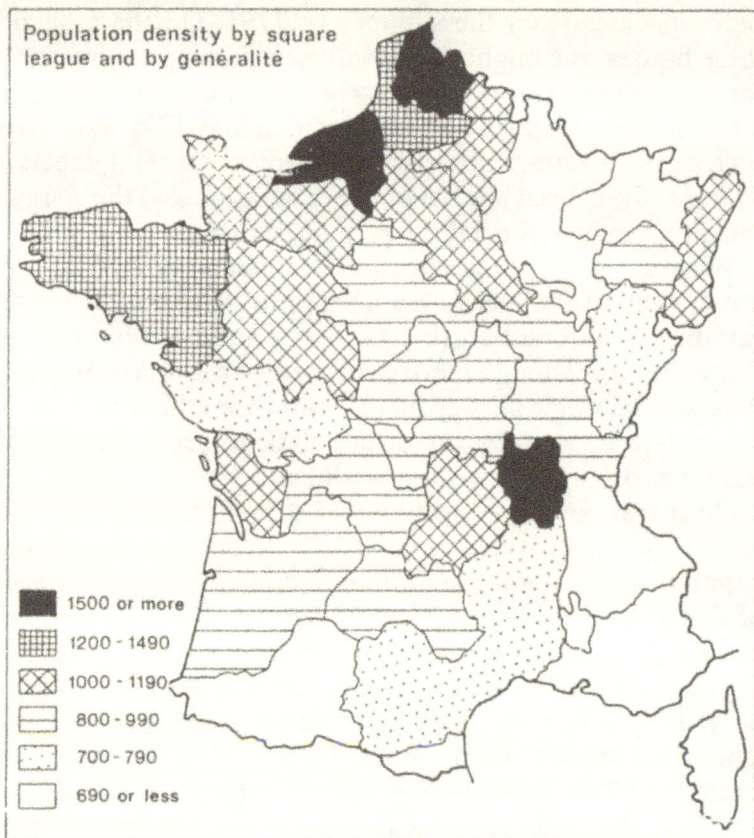

Population density by square league and by généralité

1500 or more

1200 - 1490

1000 - 1190

800 - 990

700 - 790

690 or less

*Adapted from Albert Soboul, *La Civilisation et la Révolution française*, II, 185.

was the largest city in France after Paris with just over 100,000 inhabitants, while Bordeaux, with nearly 93,000, was the third largest. Rouen, the principal urban center of Normandy, was the fourth largest town in the country, with over 86,000 inhabitants. Among the areas that bought most subscriptions to the *Ami du Roi*, only Brittany, Royou's province of origin, was without a town of the first order of importance. Rennes, the provincial capital of Brittany, had only a third the population of Bordeaux or Rouen (Table 5.2). The cases of Lyon,

Table 5.2:   The Fifty Largest Urban Centers in France in 1806*

RANK	TOWN	POPULATION
1	Lyon	102,041
2	Marseille	99,169
3	Bordeaux	92,986
4	Rouen	86,872
5	Nantes	77,226
6	Lille	61,467
7	Toulouse	51,649
8	Strasbourg	51,465
9	Orléans	42,651
10	Nîmes	41,195
11	Amiens	39,853
12	Metz	39,133
13	Caen	36,231
14	Montpellier	33,264
15	Reims	31,779
16	Clermont-Ferrand	30,982
17	Nancy	30,532
18	Rennes	29,225
19	Angers	29,187
20	Besançon	28,787
21	Toulon	28,170
22	Troyes	27,186
23	Versailles	25,974
24	Dunquerque	24,175
25	Montauban	23,973
26	Avignon	23,789
27	Brest	22,130
28	Grenoble	22,129
29	Dijon	22,026
30	Aix	21,960
31	Limoges	21,757
32	Tours	21,703
33	Poitiers	21,465
34	Lorient	20,553
35	Saint Omer	20,362
36	Arles	20,151
37	Nice	19,783
38	Arras	19,286
39	Le Mans	19,030
40	Valenciennes	19,016

Table 5.2:   The Fifty Largest Urban Centers in France in 1806*
Continued

RANK	TOWN	POPULATION
41	Douai	18,464
42	La Rochelle	18,436
43	Dieppe	18,428
44	Saint-Etienne	18,035
45	Abbeville	17,660
46	Bourges	17,552
47	Cambrai	15,608
48	Laval	15,167
49	Niort	15,066
50	Angoulême	15,011

*Source: René Le Mée, "Population agglomérée, population éparse au début du XIXe siècle," *Annales de démographie historique* (1971), 455-509.

Bordeaux and Rouen suggest that in addition to density of population, degree of urbanization played an important role in determining subscriptions to the *Ami du Roi*. The case of Brittany suggests that we should not overestimate this influence.

It comes as no surprise that the *Ami du Roi* sold best in regions that can be placed on the right of the political spectrum. A recent analysis of national elections during the Revolution has shown that the right did well in the Paris Basin, the Rhône Valley and the northwest, while the left proved strongest in the center-west and southwest.[5] With the significant exception of the Bordeaux region, the pattern of support for the right in various revolutionary assemblies corresponds quite closely to the diffusion of the *Ami du Roi*.

Other important indicators of political opinion also show that readership of the *Ami du Roi* was usually heaviest in areas where there was significant opposition to the Revolution. We have seen above that Royou was an outspoken opponent of

---

[5] Lynn Hunt, "The Political Geography of Revolutionary France," 542. This article appears in slightly modified form as chapter four of Hunt's *Politics, Culture and Class in the French Revolution.*

the Civil Constitution of the Clergy. Of the parish clergy throughout France, 54 percent accepted the Civil Constitution and were prepared to work under it, while 46 percent refused to take an oath to the new legislation, or later repudiated their oaths.[6] As usual, regional differences are huge. In large parts of Brittany, adherence to the Civil Constitution did not rise above 23 percent. In Normandy a few areas had a comparably low proportion of juring priests, though 24 percent to 40 percent were more usual figures, and the Manche and parts of Calvados and the Orne showed between 40 percent and 60 percent. These were areas in which the *Ami du Roi* enjoyed great popularity. Conversely, those areas in which the paper had fewest subscribers, particularly the center and southeast, had 86 percent or more juring clergy.[7] Yet before deducing a clearly defined inverse relationship between subscriptions to the *Ami du Roi* and adherence to the Civil Constitution of the Clergy, one should note that in large parts of the Bordeaux postal route adherence to the Civil Constitution was well above the national average, and the same is true for Burgundy.

According to Donald Greer, whose work remains the standard study of the subject, the Terror is best understood as a response to opposition to the Revolution.[8] It follows, then, that those areas whose experience during the Terror was most severe were those whose opposition to the Revolution was strongest. These include the area immediately adjacent to Paris with 2,639 death sentences; the Rhône Valley, with 1,880 death sentences in the département of the Rhône alone and a further 442 in the Vaucluse, 409 in the Bouches-du-Rhône and 309 in the neighboring Var; the north (392 death sentences in the Pas-de-Calais and 157 in the Nord); and above all in the west. The whole block of départements from

---

[6] C. Langlois and T. Tackett, "A l'Epreuve de la Révolution (1770-1830)," 248.
[7] See the map ibid., 249. This map reflects the situation for the summer of 1791.
[8] Donald Greer, *The Incidence of the Terror in the French Revolution: A Statistical Interpretation*, 70.

the Ille-et-Vilaine, Mayenne, Orne and Sarthe in the north to the Gironde in the south all had more than 100 executions, and it is in this area that the Terror took its heaviest toll: 3,548 death sentences in the Loire-Inférieure, 1,886 in the Maine-et-Loire, 1,880 in the Vendée.[9] These, of course, are the regions in which the federalist rising and civil war were concentrated. Thus, much of Normandy and Brittany and the areas around Paris, Lyon and Bordeaux had a high incidence of the Terror and subscribed well to Royou's paper. Similarly, the center of the country on the whole subscribed poorly to the *Ami du Roi*, and had a fairly mild experience during the Terror. Parts of the north and northeast, however, had worse experiences during the Terror than most of the rest of the country, yet subscribed unenthusiastically to the *Ami du Roi*. Hence the correlation between readership of Royou's paper and a high incidence of the Terror, while certainly strong, is not complete.

Given the association that is often made between the *Ami du Roi* and the emigration, one might well expect to find a strong positive correlation between subscriptions to Royou's paper and the geographical origins of émigrés. Yet no such correlation can be established, for the simple reason that proximity to the frontiers seems to have been a decisive factor in determining rates of emigration.[10] The northwest, it is true, is well represented, with eight départements having between 2,000 and 3,000 émigrés (Finistère, 2,086; Côtes-du-Nord, 2,575; Ille-et-Villane, 2,072; Manche, 2,005; Calvados, 2,080; Seine-Inférieure, 2,038; Pas-de-Calais, 2,260; and Nord, 2,635) and one, Mayenne, with 3,253.[11] Similarly, the center, which subscribed poorly to Royou's paper, shows uniformly low

---

[9] See the maps at the beginning of Greer's book (unpaginated) and Tables I and III. Ibid., 135-43 and 145-47.

[10] Donald Greer, *The Incidence of the Emigration during the French Revolution*, 38-39.

[11] It is curious that as the only département with more than 2,000 émigrés situated on neither a border nor the sea the Mayenne should have had significantly more émigrés than the adjacent maritime départements.

rates of emigration. But the northeastern and southeastern peripheries, where the *Ami du Roi* sold poorly, have the highest emigration figures in the country. The Bouches-du-Rhône and Var, which both had harsh experiences during the Terror, had more than 5,000 émigrés each, while the Alpes-Maritimes had about 3,000. It is in the northeast, however, that the incidence of emigration was highest, while subscription rates to the *Ami du Roi* were particularly low. The Haute-Rhin had 2,746 émigrés, the Moselle 3,827 and contiguous to both, the Bas-Rhin had the altogether disproportionate total of more than 20,000.[12]

A factor that one might expect to correlate negatively with the pattern of subscriptions to the *Ami du Roi* is the distribution of Jacobin clubs in the provinces. Upon examination, this proves to be the case. While subscriptions to Royou's paper were heaviest in the northwest and the Bordeaux and Burgundy routes, during the earlier stages of the Revolution Jacobin clubs were most thickly concentrated in the south and southeast. In northern France only the département of the Nord had more than 30 clubs; in the south the Gironde, Lot-et-Garonne and Bouches-du-Rhône all reached this level. Of départements with between 20 and 29 clubs, the Côte-d'Or is farthest north. Other départements reaching this level are the Rhône-et-Loire, which includes Lyon, the Dordogne, which is contiguous with the Gironde, and a heavy concentration in the south (Haute-Garonne, Tarn and Hérault) and southeast (Gard and Var). Most of the départements of the center and west had between one and nine clubs, though Morbihan, the Côtes-du-Nord, Calvados, Pas-de-Calais and Seine-et-Oise had between ten and nineteen.[13] While the inverse relationship between the clubs and the paper holds for the most part, there are also important exceptions, particularly in the Bordeaux and Lyon regions.

---

[12] Greer, *The Incidence of the Emigration*, Table I, pp. 109-11. See also the map inserted between 38-39.
[13] Kennedy, *The Jacobin Clubs*, Appendix C.

The information with which regional subscriptions to the
Ami du Roi can best be compared comes from regional subscriptions to other periodicals. For the most part this information confirms what other indicators have so far led us to
expect, namely, that Royou's paper sold best in those parts
of the country which tended to take right-wing positions on
a variety of key issues. In general, the geographical distribution of the *Ami du Roi* is similar to other right-wing papers
of the same period, has little in common with right-wing
papers of the Directory, and shows a pattern that is almost
the complete opposite of some left-wing papers.

Rozoi's *Gazette de Paris* is generally regarded as one of the
most important extreme right-wing papers of the early Revolution. In 1792 its subscribers were most heavily concentrated in Normandy (Calvados), Brittany (Loire-Inférieure),
the Gironde and the Bouches-du-Rhône.[14] The first three
areas are those in which, together with Burgundy, the *Ami
du Roi* sold best. The Bouches-du-Rhône, which contains
Marseille, the second largest provincial city in France, gives
the *Gazette de Paris* an importance in the southeast that Royou's paper lacks. A further difference between the two papers
is that Rozoi's enjoyed relatively heavy subscriptions in Alsace.
But the similarities, with the north and west showing high
rates of subscription, the center and most of the south and
east lower rates, predominate.[15]

Four right-wing papers for 1796 and 1797 show very different patterns of distribution from that of the *Ami du Roi*
in 1791. Maps constructed by Jeremy Popkin show neither
the *Gazette française* (n = 864), the *Tribune publique* (n = 180),
the *Courrier extraordinaire* (n = 1,760, but data on the south
missing) nor an unidentified paper of the right (n = 999)

---

[14] Bellanger, *Histoire générale*, I, 481. This map is based on 893 cases.
[15] Another map showing the distribution of the *Gazette de Paris* in 1790, but based
on a far smaller sample, shows high concentrations of subscriptions in the Nord,
the Pas-de-Calais and the Bouches-de-Rhône, but otherwise does not correspond
to the map for 1792. Ibid., 480.

were heavily subscribed in Normandy and Brittany. The Bordeaux region retains its prominence only in the *Gazette française*, while the area around Lyon did not have an above average rate of subscription in any of the four. In none of these papers does the center of the country seem to have played an important role, though the unidentified paper had more subscribers in the Allier than in any other département. By 1797 the predominance of the right-wing press in the northwest had been eliminated and the importance of the Bordeaux region and Burgundy much attenuated.[16]

Given the different patterns of distribution of right-wing papers in 1791-92 and 1796-97, it would be desirable to compare the pattern of readership of the *Ami du Roi* with that of left-wing papers of the same period. Unfortunately, we do not have subscription lists to left-wing papers for 1791 or 1792.[17] Those at our disposal are for later and they show very different geographical distributions from those of Royou or Rozoi's papers. The *Journal de la Montagne*, for example, sold poorly in the west, in Brittany and in Normandy during 1793-94, areas where Royou's paper did particularly well. However, the Jacobin paper enjoyed considerable popularity in the region around Lyon as well as in the north and northeast.[18] The map which results from locating the 238 provincial subscribers to Babeuf's *Tribun du Peuple* is almost a photographic negative of that with which we are familiar from the *Ami du Roi*.[19] The only areas of overlap are the Pas-de-Calais, the Nord and the Côte-d'Or. Otherwise, the west, where Royou's paper was strongest, is where Babeuf's was weakest, and

---

[16] Popkin, *Right-Wing Press*, figs. 1-4, pp. 68-71.
[17] A map showing the distribution not of subscribers, but of readers who wrote letters to the editor of Brissot's *Patriote français* between 1789 and 1791, indicates that this paper was more widely read in the south than in the north. The Rhône, the Gironde, the Isère and the Bas-Rhin are the départements most heavily represented, while the west is generally weak. There is, then, some overlap with the pattern of distribution of the *Ami du Roi*, particularly around the great urban centers of the south. Bellanger, *Histoire générale*, I, 446-47.
[18] Gough, "Les Jacobins et la presse," 289-90.
[19] Popkin, *Right-Wing Press*, fig. 6, p. 73.

the southeast where Royou was weakest is where Babeuf's paper found most subscribers. Lebois's *Ami du Peuple*, too, was weak in the northwest and strong in the southeast in 1795-96, but it also showed strength in two areas in which the *Ami du Roi* had done well, the Bordeaux region, and the area between Dijon and Lyon.[20]

Broadly speaking, the patterns of readership of the right-wing press in the early Revolution and of the left-wing press after the crisis of the Terror correspond fairly closely to regional breakdowns on various other issues, such as the Civil Constitution of the Clergy, the incidence of emigration and the incidence of the Terror. The Paris basin, the west and northwest and the Rhône valley generally tended to the right, the relatively poor and mountainous regions of the south, and especially southeast, tended to the left. Significant shifts in patterns of subscription to the right-wing press seem to have taken place by the time of the Directory, the decline in the importance of the northwest being particularly noticeable. Since the sizes of the samples on which these conclusions are based vary enormously, from over 5,000 provincial subscribers to the *Ami du Roi*, to 238 for the *Tribun du Peuple*, 180 for the *Tribune publique* and 103 for Lebois's *Ami du Peuple*, one ought not to place too much weight on these conclusions. On the other hand, the cumulative effect of these findings points to a fairly coherent pattern. Modification or revision of this pattern is a distinct possibility, but must await the discovery and analysis of more subscription lists.[21]

One way of analyzing the geographical distribution of subscribers to a paper is in terms of regions. Another is by degree

---

[20] Ibid., fig. 7, p. 74.

[21] One ought not, however, to overlook attempts to throw light on readership by other methods. Reference has been made above to the use of letters to the editor as an indication of the readership of the *Patriote français*. Melvin Edelstein used this technique in his study of the *Feuille villageoise* (*La Feuille villageoise*, 71), and Jeremy Popkin has used complaints concerning subscriptions to the *Nouvelles politiques* to get at the readership of that paper (*Right-Wing Press*, fig. 5, p. 72).

Table 5.3:   The Distribution of the *Ami du Roi* in the Provinces
             by Population Density*

SIZE OR NATURE OF SETTLEMENT	LIST II (n = 869)	LIST III (n = 617)
Château	12.54%	10.86%
Countryside and small towns	58.46%	55.75%
50 largest towns	26.22%	30.47%
Foreign	1.73%	2.27%
Unknown	1.04%	.67%
	99.99%	100.00%

*Source: AN T*546² and T*546³.

of urbanization. Our longest and most methodical list for the *Ami du Roi*, that for the summer of 1791, indicates the postal route of subscribers but does not give the full address. The two shorter and earlier lists normally give both the postal route and precise address. These lists have been analyzed according to a number of categories in an attempt to determine the degree of urbanization of subscribers. First, the fifty most populous towns, which extend from Lyon, with more than 100,000 inhabitants, to Angoulême with 15,000 were coded separately.[22] Second, subscriptions sent to a subscriber's château, or his "property" ("sa terre"), but not to his urban residence ("hôtel"), have been coded and taken to represent a rural residence. A large intermediate category includes all population centers smaller than 15,000 souls, as practical considerations precluded determining the size of every town or village that appears in our sources. The number of foreign subscribers and of cases for which information is lacking have also been noted.

Table 5.3 shows the results of this break-down for our two shorter lists. The fifty largest urban concentrations in the country together accounted for more than 26 percent of all subscriptions in the earlier list, and over 30 percent in the

[22] This list was compiled from the figures of the 1806 census as given by René Le Mée, "Population agglomérée, population éparse au début du XIXe siècle."

later one. In that these centers together contained nearly 2,150,000 residents, or 8.27 percent of the total population,[23] the larger towns appear to have had a rate of subscription three or four times greater than the national mean. This suggests that urbanization was decisive in influencing political awareness.

The category of the fifty largest towns in France is in itself far from indicating the degree of urbanization of subscribers to Royou's paper. Only those subscribers who had their papers delivered to their châteaux or to their "terres" can be said with certainty to be rural. Moreover, these rural subscribers clearly belonged to the elite. Of between 55 and 60 percent of provincial subscribers, we can only say that they lived in agglomerations of less than 15,000. The criterion of an urban center under the old regime is usually taken as a population of 2,000 or more.[24] What proportion of the 55 or 60 percent of subscribers to the *Ami du Roi* might have lived in settlements that would have qualified as urban? Bearing in mind the relative poverty and illiteracy of the countryside, the occupations of subscribers (see Chapter VI) and the residences of the Breton purchasers of papal briefs, it would seem safe to conclude at least two-thirds. If this is so, then 70 or 80 percent of the copies of Royou's paper would have gone to the 20 percent or so of the population that can be described as urban.[25] Given that the Enlightenment was so overwhelmingly urban a phenomenon and that the *Ami du Roi* was clearly in the tradition of Enlightenment journalism, this should come as no surprise.

That the *Ami du Roi* found most of its readers in towns should not be allowed to obscure the fact that it was also

---

[23] The exact figure reached by adding the 50 largest towns in France, excluding Paris, is 2,149,739. The total population of France is assumed to have stood at 26 million.

[24] Le Mée, "Population agglomérée," 456.

[25] The *Journal de la Montagne* has a proven rate of urban subscriptions of between 70 percent and 80 percent. Gough, "Les Jacobins et la presse," 290.

delivered to the smallest rural hamlets. Though the extensive alphabetical list of provincial subscribers does not contain exact addresses, it normally does give the parish of residence of curés who took the paper. Often these parishes were sparsely populated. The parish of Gouhrel in Brittany had less than ten households, Barville on the Rouen route had 40, Diarville on the Châlons-Strasbourg route had 41, Charly on the same route 45, Offlanges in Burgundy had 54, Cadolet on the Provence-Roussillon-Languedoc route 63, Boele on the Rouen route 72, Angeduc on the Bordeaux route 80, Preux on the Troyes route 86, Nouy on the Reims route the same number, Orville on the Rouen route 88, and Couville on the same route 91.[26] Few *curés* subscribing to Royou's paper lived in parishes of more than two hundred households. Moreover, one in ten provincial subscriptions in our two later lists went to châteaux in the countryside.

On the basis of the very partial information in Table 5.4 it is difficult to find any consistent pattern in the subscriptions of the larger towns in France to the *Ami du Roi*.[27] Gilles Feyel has shown that commercial and industrial readers were more receptive to provincial papers, often entitled *Affiches*, that were founded during the second half of the eighteenth century than were older legal or administrative centers.[28] Robert Darnton, on the other hand, has found that administrative and bureaucratic centers proved better customers for the *Encyclopédie* than did commercial or industrial towns.[29] Among the towns that subscribed best to the *Ami du Roi*, however, we find Bourges as well as Bordeaux, Dijon as well as Lille, Nantes as well as Rennes, Rouen as well as Toulouse. The

---

[26] The figures for the population of these villages are from Expilly, *Dictionnaire Géographique*. Variant spellings and the occurrence of numerous villages with the same name made it impossible to identify with certainty nearly half the residences of curés in List I.

[27] We saw in the preceding chapters that a single bookseller in Bordeaux, Bergeret, had more than thirty subscribers to the *Ami du Roi*.

[28] Gilles Feyel, "La Presse provinciale au XVIIIe siècle," 353-54.

[29] Darnton, *The Business of Enlightenment*, 282-86.

Table 5.4:   Towns with Eight or More Subscribers to the *Ami du Roi**

TOWN	RANK IN SIZE	NO SUBSCRIBERS List II (n = 869)	NO SUBSCRIBERS List III (n = 617)
Amiens	11	5	12
Bordeaux	3	8	7
Bourges	46	9	2
Caen	13	9	6
Dijon	29	8	6
Lille	6	11	11
Lyon	1	12	6
Marseille	2	7	9
Metz	12	12	2
Nantes	5	11	16
Reims	15	3	8
Rennes	18	6	8
Rouen	4	15	9
Toulouse	7	12	7

*Source: As in Table 5.3.

only factor that seems to exercise a consistent influence is population. All seven of the largest towns in France are represented in this list, while the rest, with only two exceptions, are among the twenty largest. The presence of Dijon (29th) and Bourges (46th) among the more avid subscribers to Royou's paper may suggest a propensity of traditional bureaucratic and administrative centers to patronize the right-wing press. But such slight evidence should not be made to bear too great a weight of interpretation.

An ambitious study of the *cahiers* described the importance of urbanization in the formation of political opinion as a "major finding" and speaks of the "downright enormous effect of urbanization" on opinion.[30] On the whole, a high degree of urbanization was found to correspond to pro-revolution-

---

[30] Shapiro, Markoff and Weitman, "Quantitative Studies," 184 and 187.

ary sentiment.[31] A more recent study of the political geography of the Revolution concurs that urbanization fosters political involvement in general, but argues that it favors the right over the left. Towns which tended to lean to the right, the author argues, were those with large, dependent floating populations that were seen as a threat.[32] These generally were commercial or industrial centers. In contrast, towns which tended to the left, were often old, well-established administrative centers, whose middle classes were relatively uniform, and dominated by the liberal professions.[33] Though some historians have questioned whether urban rates of participation in elections were regularly higher than rural ones during the Revolution,[34] our evidence suggests that towns were more politically aware and more active than were rural areas.

B. Gender

One of the most basic questions to ask about the readership of the *Ami du Roi* is whether it includes members of both sexes, and if so, in what proportions. The subscription lists show that women were a significant, not merely a marginal, part of Royou's public.

The readership of serious political and literary journals during the eighteenth century and Revolution certainly included women, but remained overwhelmingly masculine. It would not, therefore, be realistic to expect to find a majority

---

[31] Ibid., 185. The issues used as criteria of pro-revolutionary behavior or attitudes are the Civil Constitution of the Clergy, the "contribution patriotique," the Great Fear, the September Massacres, the incidence of the Terror, the incidence of emigration, and the election of Girondin deputies.

[32] Hunt, "Political Geography," 550.

[33] Ibid., 553-54. Hunt's assertion that the commercial and industrial classes of large towns should be placed toward the right of the political spectrum of course diverges from the "classical" interpretation of the Revolution.

[34] Melvin Edelstein, "Vers une sociologie électorale de la Révolution française."

Table 5.5:   The Gender of Subscribers to the *Ami du Roi* by Lists*

GENDER	LIST II (n = 1121)	LIST III (n = 765)	LIST I (n = 4630)
Male	82.00%	76.34%	82.18%
Female	17.01%	22.09%	16.61%
Collective	0.99%	1.57%	1.21%
	100.00%	100.00%	100.00%

*Source: AN T*546², T*546³ and T*546⁵.

of female readers for the *Ami du Roi,* or indeed for any other paper of the same kind during this period. Table 5.5 nevertheless shows a high proportion of female subscribers to Madame Fréron and her brother's paper, ranging between 16 and 22 percent, depending on the list.[35] Male subscriptions hover around 80 percent, while collective subscriptions, which will be treated separately, do not rise much above one and a half percent.

When the rates of subscription by gender are examined separately for Paris and the provinces, it becomes apparent that the capital had a significantly higher proportion of female subscribers than the provinces. Table 5.6 shows that nearly a quarter (23.39 percent) of Parisian subscriptions were taken out by women, while the corresponding figure for the provinces was 16.61 percent. Collective subscriptions were just

Table 5.6:   The Gender of Subscribers to the *Ami du Roi:*
            Paris and the Provinces*

GENDER	PARIS (n = 466)	PROVINCES (n = 5117)
Male	75.54%	82.26%
Female	23.39%	16.61%
Collective	1.07%	1.13%

*Source: As in Table 5.5.

---

[35] There are cases in the subscription lists, particularly in Lists II and III, in which a subscriber has his paper sent to the address of a friend or family member. When this happens the subscription is entered in the name of the subscriber, not the addressee, who is frequently female.

above one percent in both cases, while male rates varied from 75.54 percent in Paris to over 82 percent in the provinces.

It is perhaps worth noting, too, that Parisians used the particle in their names more frequently than did provincial subscribers. In Lists II and III between 42 and 43 percent of provincial subscribers included the particle in their names while nearly half (48.93 percent) of Parisians did so.

Historians have rightly been cautious in their handling of the particle, the "de," with its variants "du" and "de la," which suggests place of origin, but implies noble standing. Most nobles during the old regime did include a "de" or one of its variants in their names. And most commoners who sought to rise socially, at some stage in that often tortuously slow process began inserting the particle before their surnames when they signed documents. To do so was a claim, if not to nobility, then at least to notability. And to have the local notary or fiscal officials accept that signature was a success in the struggle for upward mobility. Yet many peasants (one thinks of Restif de la Bretonne) routinely included a particle indicating place of origin in their names, while some nobles dispensed with it entirely.[36] In names of Flemish origin the "de" was not a particle, but the definite article. Thus the particle cannot be taken as proof of noble status, though it does seem to reflect an aspiration to such status. As Pierre Goubert warns, "the particle proves nothing in itself."[37] In his analysis of the readership of the *Mercure de France* for 1763 Daniel Mornet notes that there were just under 200 subscribers with titles of nobility and then adds noncommittally "to these may be added, if one wishes, 45 names with particles."[38] A scholar with Mornet's knowledge of the old regime would not equate use of the particle with noble status. But nor did he ignore it.

Paris then, as well as having a higher proportion of sub-

---

[36] Pierre Goubert, *The Ancien Régime*, 154.
[37] Ibid.
[38] Mornet, "L'intérêt historique des journaux littéraires," 121.

scribers who used the particle in their names than did the provinces, also had significantly more female subscribers. It is unlikely that women in Paris were more conservative than women in the provinces. Rather, it appears that the higher proportion of women subscribers to Royou's paper in the capital is a function of the generally higher social standing of the Paris subscribers. The *Ami du Roi* was both a serious political publication and a direct continuation of the Enlightenment in style as well as in values. The more the social background of Enlightenment thought is studied, the more elitist the movement as a whole appears.[39] The role of women in the Enlightenment remains, it is true, minor, but it increases as one moves from lower social levels to higher ones. The importance of salons in the intellectual life of France in the eighteenth century has long been recognized, and the influence of women on the tone of Enlightenment literature as well as on advancement by patronage and elections to places in academies have received due emphasis.[40] One cannot maintain that the great mistresses of the salons of the eighteenth century from Madame de Lambert and Madame de Géoffrin to Mlle. de l'Espinasse, Madame de Doublet and Madame Necker were in any sense typical. But they do show that at the highest levels of society the sexes often achieved a cultural parity that was rarer, if not virtually nonexistent, lower down the social scale. One finds, for example, that among peasant and artisan families female rates of literacy are often half or less than half of male rates for the same

---

[39] See particularly Daniel Roche, *Le siècle des lumières en province: Académies et académiciens provinciaux, 1680-1789*; Robert Darnton, "The High Enlightenment and the Low-Life of Literature in Pre-Revolutionary France," in *The Literary Underground*; Lionel Gossman, *Medievalism and the Ideologies of the Enlightenment: The World and Work of La Curne de Sainte-Palaye*, Part I; Harry C. Payne, *The Philosophes and the People*; and Harvey Chisick, *The Limits of Reform in the Enlightenment: Attitudes toward the Education of the Lower Classes in Eighteenth-Century France.*

[40] Lewis Coser, *Men of Ideas: A Sociologist's View* (New York, 1965), chap. 2; and Lough, *Introduction to Eighteenth-Century France*, chap. 7.

socio-professional group, while among the middle and upper classes, men enjoy only a slight advantage.[41]

Literacy is only a rough indicator of cultural standing. As far as it goes, though, it is valid and underscores the way socioeconomic differences articulate differences based on gender. One can, of course, point to the exceptional intellectual activity of Madame Roland in her youth and compare this to the profound indifference of Madame de La Tour du Pin for all things literary and philosophical. Still, it remains true that women of Madame de La Tour du Pin's class had access, if they so desired, to the intellectual tools without which there was no entrance to the world of the Enlightenment, while women of Madame Roland's standing frequently did not. With its great concentration of law courts, administrative offices, educational institutions and its proximity to the Court, Paris naturally had a particularly high concentration of nobles, and of members of the liberal professions, which, at their upper levels, merged into the nobility.

There are two other sources which provide information on the proportion of male and female subscribers in Paris and the provinces. One is the list of subscribers to the *Mercure de France* for 1763 studied by Daniel Mornet. This list contains approximately 1,500 subscriptions, one half of which were sent to provincial booksellers, and the other half direct to the subscribers. Some 470 subscribers identified by name lived in Paris, 81 of them (17.23 percent) women. The names of only 286 provincial subscribers are given and of these 36 (12.59 percent) were women.[42] Female subscriptions to the essentially literary *Mercure* were thus significant, if somewhat lower than those to the political *Ami du Roi*, and the concen-

---

[41] On this point, see R. Chartier, M.M. Compère and D. Julia, *L'Education en France du XVI au XVIIIe siècle* (Paris, SEDES, 1976), chap. 3 and H. Chisick, "School Attendance, Literacy and Acculturation: *Petites écoles* and Popular Education in Eighteenth-Century France."

[42] Daniel Mornet, "L'intérêt historique des journaux littéraires," 121. Mornet adds "Le Mercure était le journal des femmes. . . ." (ibid.).

tration of female subscribers in Paris was in both cases distinctly heavier than in the provinces. The other source, Hugh Gough's analysis of the subscription lists of the *Journal de la Montagne* for 1793-94, reveals a far lower proportion of female subscribers. Globally they account for 4.4 percent of all private subscriptions to the paper. There are, however, no significant differences between Parisian and provincial subscriptions among women.[43]

The number of women subscribing to newspapers of the Directory gives added perspective on the role of female subscribers to Royou's paper. In his analysis of the readership of five papers of the Directory, Jeremy Popkin has found that two left-wing papers, the *Tribun du Peuple* and the *Ami du Peuple*, were patronized exclusively by men. The three right-wing papers, the *Gazette français*, the *Tribune publique* and one which is unidentified, had between six and nine percent female subscribers.[44] It appears, then, that women represented a significant proportion of the subscribers of the right-wing press, but not of the left-wing press in 1797. This observation should not of course be taken to imply that women played no role on the left during the Revolution.[45] It is also clear that female subscription rates to the *Ami du Roi* were far higher than comparable rates during the Directory. If our taking a high proportion of female subscribers to indicate a more elitist readership is justified, this shift could be explained by a moderation of right-wing opinion within France due to

---

[43] A calculation on the basis of all subscriptions shows 4.31 percent female subscriptions in Paris as compared to 3.75 percent in the provinces; a calculation based on private subscriptions shows only 4.38 percent in Paris, 4.66 percent in the provinces. Gough, "Les Jacobins et la presse," 289-95.

[44] Popkin, *Right-Wing Press*, Table 4, 65.

[45] On the roles of women in the Revolution see George Rudé, *The Crowd in the French Revolution*, 69, 73, and 152; R.B. Rose, *The Enragés: Socialists of the French Revolution?*, chaps. V and VI; Paule-Marie Duhet, *Les Femmes et la Révolution, 1789-94*; Harriet B. Applewhite and Darlene Gay Levy, "Women, Democracy and Revolution in Paris, 1789-1794"; by the same authors, "Women and Political Revolution in Paris"; and again by the same authors, "Ceremonial Dimensions of Citizenship: Women and Oathtaking in Revolutionary Paris."

Table 5.7:   Marital Status of Female Subscribers to the *Ami du Roi**

MARITAL STATUS	LIST II (n = 206)	LIST III (n = 169)	LIST I (n = 769)
Unspecified	—	—	0.52%
Mademoiselle	10.19%	18.34%	14.04%
Madame	85.92%	78.11%	76.85%
Veuve	3.89%	—	3.64%
Religeuse	—	3.55%	4.94%

*Source: As in Table 5.5.

the withdrawal of the émigrés and the necessity of coming to terms with a republic of some kind.

It is worthwhile to pause a moment to consider the marital status of Royou's female subscribers. During the eighteenth century virtually all social strata regarded marriage as desirable. For working-class women, establishing a household through marriage offered the best chance of economic security, other aspects of their lives aside, while for noble families, providing dowries for daughters (or establishments for sons) was a major economic burden, and the main reason why in most noble families only one or two daughters were married and the rest forced into the church or some minor domestic role.[46] Table 5.7 shows that between 80 percent and 90 percent of women subscribers to the *Ami du Roi* either were married or had been. Of the unmarried women appearing in this table between a quarter and one-seventh were nuns. Given the importance of the church in the politics of the period during which the *Ami du Roi* was active and the clearly orthodox stand of the paper, it is not surprising to find that Royou's readership extended to convents. Indeed, we will see shortly that there were a number of collective subscriptions by both convents and monasteries to Royou's paper.

---

[46] On the desirability of marriage for the lower classes, see Sarah Maza, *Servants and Masters in Eighteenth-Century France: The Uses of Loyalty*, 43, and O. Hufton, *The Poor of Eighteenth-Century France, 1750-1789*, 25-37. For the nobility see Robert Forster, *The Nobility of Toulouse in the Eighteenth Century: A Social and Economic Study*, chap. 6.

Table 5.8:   Marital Status of Female Subscribers to the *Ami du Roi:*
Paris and the Provinces*

MARITAL STATUS	PROVINCES (n = 850)	PARIS (n = 109)
Unspecified	.47%	—
Mademoiselle	14.23%	5.50%
Madame	77.18%	92.66%
Veuve	3.65%	1.83%
Religieuse	4.47%	—

*Source: As in Table 5.5.

If it is true that it was generally preferable to be married during this period than not to be, then we find again that Paris was more favored than the provinces. Table 5.8 shows that only 5.5 percent of female subscribers to the *Ami du Roi* in Paris were not, or had not been, married. In the provinces 14.23 percent of female subscribers were given the title "mademoiselle." Another 4.47 percent had entered the Church. The higher proportion of widows in the provinces suggests that remarriage may also have been more difficult, or less common, there than in Paris. In the case of Paris, however, we are speaking of only two widows, and this is too small a number from which to generalize.

C. Collective Subscriptions

While representing no more than one and a half percent of all subscriptions, collective subscribers to Royou's paper are of particular interest. Private subscriptions would, in the normal course of things, be passed around to a number of readers, though we cannot say just how many, or who they were. Collective subscriptions were always intended for a large number of readers, numbers that in the case of political clubs

Table 5.9:   Collective Subscriptions to the *Ami du Roi**

KIND OF SUBSCRIBER	NUMBER OF SUBSCRIPTIONS
General	1
Clubs—Literary and Political	44
Army—Officers	9
National Guard	3
Municipality	2
Convent—Male	7
Convent—Female	2
Seminary	1
Collège	2
	71

*Source: As in Table 5.5. This is a composite list from which doubles have been eliminated.

could reach the hundreds.[47] Where we know the status or occupation of a subscriber to a paper, we do not, as a result, necessarily know his political opinions. Membership in certain organizations, in contrast, often does provide a fair indication of political orientation.

Only a minority of collective subscriptions which appear in Figure 5.9 were held by organizations or institutions whose sympathies one would expect to belong clearly with the old regime. These are subscriptions of the army and the church. Military subscriptions, of which there are nine, were addressed to a group of officers, normally of a specific regiment, such as the Officers of the 47th Regiment of Infantry at Bayeux, the Officers of the Picardy Regiment, or the Officers of the Queen's Regiment. The Church has ten collective subscriptions: two convents which are the only female subscriptions to appear here, a seminary and seven monasteries. These last subscriptions were addressed to the priors, the religious or simply the name of the order, together with a location or name of an abbey. Thus we find subscriptions to MM. les

---

[47] See above, Chap. I, n. 35.

Bénédictins de St. Serges, MM. les Religieux de Reuil and the Priors of the abbey of Beaumont.

Nearly two-thirds of the collective subscriptions to the *Ami du Roi* were from literary or political clubs. Some of these clubs antedate the Revolution, while others were formed after 1789. The names of some clubs suggest that they were conceived as reading circles, others that they were formed for political reasons, while the names of yet others give no indication of their purpose or orientation. There is a variety of clearly literary clubs calling themselves *cabinets littéraires* (Clamecy, Lille, Poitiers) *chambres littéraires* (Langeac, Luçon, Montmorillon, Poitiers, Valogne, Caen, Troyes) or *sociétés littéraires* (Cahors, Donze, La Celle, Fouergues, Pontaudemer). The old and prestigious Société du Musée de Bordeaux, the Société de Molière of Castelnon de Montratin and the Académie anglaise of Liège can also be classed as literary clubs. Whether it is fair to see these clubs as "sociétés de pensée" which helped prepare the way for the Revolution there is too little evidence to determine. That they could serve as foci for discussion not only of literary subjects but also of current events can be taken for granted.

Some clubs had ambiguous or general names that give no firm indication of their character. These include the Associés du cercle d'Union and the Associés du cercle de Bellecoeur, both of Lyon, the Club Barbe de Moissac of Bordeaux, the Société première of Thouars, the Club des Négocians of Lille and a number of groupings designated simply as "Club" or "Société" (Noyon, Toulouse, Moulins). There is also at least one instance of a manager of a commercial *cabinet de lecture* ordering the *Ami du Roi* for his clients.[48]

There were others among the collective subscribers to Royou's paper whose names suggest a direct interest in politics, and, it seems, a sympathetic attitude toward the Revolution as it had developed down to the summer of 1791. The "clubs

---

[48] This is Landriot of Riom whose order is "pour les associés de son cabinet."

patriotiques" of Abbeville, Brioude, Chartres and Rochefort subscribed to the *Ami du Roi,* as did the Salon patriotique of Apt, the Société patriotique et académique of Vannes, the Société civique of Tiffauges in the Vendée, the Société des Amis du Bon Ordre and three branches of the Société des Amis de la Constitution in Narbonne, Cusset and Givet. There were also three subscriptions to the National Guard, two in Lille and one in Forebac.

With five collective subscriptions to Royou's paper—one for clerics, another for a reading room, a third for a merchants' club, and two more for the National Guard—Lille was far ahead of any other town in France. Four Parisian clubs, three of them in the Palais Royal, subscribed to Royou's paper, but our sources here are surely incomplete.[49] Bordeaux, Cahors, Lyon, Poitiers, Forebac and St. Pol-de-Léon all had two collective subscriptions each. While collective subscriptions tend to be concentrated in larger centers, we also find them in smaller towns such as Luçon (just under 3,000 inhabitants in 1806), Montmorillon and Givet (between 3,000 and 4,000) and Apt, Pontaudemer and Brioude (between 5,000 and 6,000).

Given the intensely anti-revolutionary reputation of the *Ami du Roi,* it seems anomalous to find groups that supported major administrative and political reform, such as the National Guard and Jacobins, subscribing to the paper. If, however, we bear in mind that this reputation is based largely on what the paper became in the course of the crisis which developed from the Civil Constitution of the Clergy and after the flight of the royal family to Varennes, this seems less surprising. I have argued above that when it was established in September 1790, Royou's paper was moderate, perhaps conservative, but certainly not opposed to all reform. One should also bear in mind that the National Guard was from its outset as much

---

[49] Two of the collective subscriptions in Paris are simply for "cabinets littéraires." The other two, both in the Palais Royal, are the Club des Valois and the Salon françois.

devoted to maintaining social order as it was to supporting moderate reform, and the Societies of the Friends of the Constitution were not yet in 1790 and 1791 what they were to become in 1793 and 1794.

In his examination of the role of the press in the Jacobin Clubs, Michael Kennedy found subscriptions to such right-wing papers as the *Mercure* and Rozoi's *Gazette de Paris* as well as the *Ami du Roi,* though none for papers as extreme as the *Actes des Apôtres.* Kennedy explains leftist clubs ordering and paying for right-wing literature by suggesting that the sub-scriptions were taken out, "before it had become apparent that these periodicals were fundamentally counterrevolutionary."[50] This seems a plausible explanation. It also lends support to the contention that initially the *Ami du Roi* was not perceived by the clubs as opposed to all significant reform. And if the Jacobins did not so view it, neither, in all probability, did the broader public. The implication for our evaluation of the subscribers to the *Ami du Roi* up to the summer of 1791 is far-reaching: our lists would reflect the make-up not of extreme right-wing opinion, but of a readership closer to the center of the political spectrum. Of course, it is possible that during the last year of the paper's existence many of Royou's readers drifted to the right with him. Indeed, this is probable. But it is not proven.

In addition to the Jacobin Clubs that appear in our lists, Kennedy notes three others. The Jacobins of Boulogne regarded Royou's paper as belonging to the right, and sub-scribed in order to learn what the other side had to say for itself.[51] They were aware of what they were doing, and acted with considerable sophistication. The Jacobins of Bourges and St. Etienne, on the other hand, apparently found that their opinions and those of the writers of the *Ami du Roi* evolved differently, so that soon there was no common ground

---

[50] Kennedy, *The Jacobin Clubs,* 58-59.
[51] Ibid., 59.

between them. In symbolic acts of outrage the Bourges club burned its copies of the paper, while the Jacobins of St. Etienne threw theirs into a cesspool, together with copies of the *Gazette de Paris*.[52] These acts took place in December of 1790 and January of 1791 and show that the *Ami du Roi* was already beginning to be seen as expounding views incompatible with those of the Societies of the Friends of the Constitution. That other Jacobins were still receiving the paper in the summer of 1791 indicates that it was not universally so regarded.

---

[52] Loc. cit.

VI.
The Subscribers to the Ami du Roi: *Status and Occupation*

A. The Readership of the *Ami du Roi:* the Views of Historians and of the Editors

Historians of the press have sometimes sought to characterize the readership of papers they have studied even though their information was less full than might have been wished. It seems logical to assume that the readership of a conservative or right-wing paper will be aristocratic and clerical, while that of a radical or democratic journal will be popular or perhaps bourgeois. We would hardly expect to find that the subscription lists of the *Ami du Roi* were predominantly sans-culotte, or that the aristocracy was particularly well represented in those of the *Ami du Peuple*. To say that a paper is right-wing or leftist implies not only that the views it expresses are characteristic of the right or the left, but also that it is likely to draw its readership from groups that constitute the social bases of this opinion. Otherwise put, a paper's ideological emphasis and its readership are interrelated and interdependent. It is not unreasonable, then, to deduce a paper's readership from its editorial policy. It would probably be correct to describe the *Ami du Roi* as either aristocratic or royalist. But the expected readership of a royalist and an aristocratic paper need not necessarily be the same.

Once one has the subscription lists of a paper, it is possible to go beyond broad generalizations about the character of the paper's readership and ask what the social and occupational composition of that readership was. This question shifts the emphasis from the self-evident interrelatedness of editorial policy and readership to the more empirical question of the make-up of a given public at a specific time. Before

158

moving on to this question, though, it is worthwhile first to consider how historians have characterized the readership of the *Ami du Roi* and how the writers of the paper perceived their public.

Hatin, who portrays the *Ami du Roi* as thoroughly reactionary, asserts that after Varennes the paper became "the official journal of the emigration and the clergy."[1] Jacques Godechot notes that the Parisian subscribers to Royou's paper lived "especially in the fine areas" of the capital, and that while there were many priests and nobles among the surviving lists of subscribers, there were also bourgeois, business people (*commerçants*), a grocer, who happened to be female, and a number of wholesale merchants.[2] Bertaud asserts that the aristocracy furnished the "greater part" of the readership of the right-wing press, but insists that the *Ami du Roi* had a bourgeois following too.[3]

Among the passages in which Royou or those associated with him refer to the readership of the *Ami du Roi*, there is one that supports the view that this readership was primarily clerical and aristocratic. It occurs in a number of the paper in which the editors congratulate themselves on being "the delight and consolation of the friends of the altar, of the throne, of the nobility and of the magistracy."[4] It might be argued, however, that Royou and his associates believed that the great majority of their compatriots, and not only a number of small elitist groups, would have supported the main institutions of the French state. This is certainly what other references to the expected readership of the *Ami du Roi* suggest.

In the "Notice to Readers" published in August 1790, which

---

[1] *Histoire de la presse*, VII, 155.
[2] *Histoire générale*, I, 485. Godechot, or his source, appears to have based these observations on fragmentary evidence in AN T546 and not to have seen the registers of subscribers of the *Ami du Roi* preserved in AN T*546.
[3] Bertaud, *Les Amis du Roi*, 58 and 213.
[4] *AR*, 6 December 1791, 4.

is in effect the prospectus of Royou's *Ami du Roi*, the abbé referred to those who subscribed to the initial *Ami du Roi* as "good Frenchmen" and to himself as having won "the unanimous approval of honest folk [*honnêtes gens*] and true patriots."[5] He goes on to state that "honest folk" groan to see the turn events are taking, and then to oppose the interests of these decent people to those of people without property. "Liberty no longer exists," Royou writes, "except for those who have nothing to lose; it is this kind of person who today forms public opinion."[6] This opposition between decent folk (*honnêtes gens*), defined as property owners, and those without property, referred to as "brigands," appears again a few months before Royou's paper was suppressed for good.[7] If Royou saw himself as upholding key values of the Catholic Church and the French monarchy, he believed that these values were cherished not only by clerics and nobles, but by the great majority of those with a stake in society through the ownership of property. The clergy and nobility no doubt played a leading role in the social order as conceived by Royou, but this position of leadership was widely, if tacitly, accepted. Thus it seems that Royou saw himself not as an agent for elitist or reactionary political interests, but as a spokesman for a broadly based and moderate conservatism. He also, it appears, believed himself to be writing for a broader public than most historians would have allowed.

At least certain of his contemporaries seem to have accepted this claim. When it became known that Royou had gone underground after the raids on the offices of the *Ami du Roi*, a provincial bookseller wrote to ask whether he was safe and

---

[5] "Avis aux souscripteurs . . ." BN 4⁰ Lc² 398. "Honnêté" has been taken as reflecting the values of commoners, specifically the bourgeoisie, and forming the basis of a nonmartial and unaristocratic set of values. On this term, see F. Brunot, *Histoire de la langue française*, vol. IX, part 2; Marcel Dorigny, "Honnêtes Gens: L'Expression dans la presse girondine, juin–septembre 1792," and François Wartelle, "Honnêtes gens: La Dénomination comme enjeu des luttes politiques (1795-1797)."
[6] Ibid.
[7] *AR*, 23 February 1792.

could be expected to continue writing and added, "all his subscribers and decent folk [*honnêtes gens*] are particularly concerned about his well being."[8]

At an annual cost of 30 *livres*, the subscription lists to the *Ami du Roi*, or of any other periodical of comparable price, cannot be expected to yield a cross section of French society. Thirty *livres* represented two or three weeks' income for most working families. Only after costs of food, clothes, housing, as well as other necessary and socially obligatory expenses had been met, could one think of the luxury of a subscription to a journal. It follows that probably only the top 30 percent or so of French society could have subscribed to a journal if they so wished. We have seen above that the readership of a paper was normally much wider than its subscription lists.[9] Even so, Royou was certainly correct, perhaps in a more literal sense than he intended, in saying that his public was one of property owners. And even if 60 or 70 percent of the population can be expected to be absent from the subscription lists of the *Ami du Roi*, the analysis of the top third or so of French society at the end of the old regime and during the first few years of the Revolution is no simple matter.

B. Problems of Classification

The surviving subscription lists to the *Ami du Roi* were seized by the authorities at the end of July 1791 and so reflect the readership of the journal before the polarization of opinion that occurred in the wake of the king's flight to Varennes and the massacre of the Champ-de-Mars. During the fall of 1790 and the summer of 1791 many of the institutions of the old regime had not yet been dismantled, though some of the new legal and administrative agencies that had just

---

[8] AN T546⁵²⁵. Letter from Bergeret of Bordeaux, 6 August 1791.
[9] See Chapter I.

been legislated were beginning to function. As a result, subscribers to Royou's paper in positions of authority identified
themselves as belonging to either the new or, more often, to
the institutions of the old regime. This is a rare situation,
and one that could have occurred only after 1790 and before
1793. The old regime flavor of the lists is further strengthened by the presence of a high proportion of nobles and
clerics. Having to take into account the institutions and special status groups of the old regime will greatly complicate
our analysis, but it will also enrich it. This blending of the
old and new in which the old still predominates also serves
to underscore the transitional nature of the period and the
sources we are dealing with. Yet if the presence of old-regime
categories complicates but ultimately enhances our study of
the subscribers of the *Ami du Roi*, the fact that our analysis
must necessarily be carried out on the largely formal criteria
of status and occupation tends to undue simplification.

The subscription lists of the *Ami du Roi* normally include
the status of subscribers when this information is relevant,
indicating that the subscriber in question is a cleric, a noble
(marquis, count, chevalier and so on), a member of an order
of chivalry or a commoner with a distinct standing (bourgeois,
elector, notable; see Appendix 2). The lists likewise usually
indicate the profession or occupation of the subscriber, identifying him or her as a bishop, curé, monk or nun, army
officer, merchant, artisan, lawyer, administrator and so forth.
Royou had specifically asked his subscribers to identify themselves by their status or profession (*qualité*), as this would
facilitate delivery.[10] Status and occupation are not, of course,
mutually exclusive categories. Almost all clergymen could be
classed according to both status, as belonging to the church,
and by occupation, taken as the function performed within

---

[10] *AR*, 21 November 1790.

Table 6.1:   Information on the Status and Occupations of Subscribers
to the *Ami Du Roi**

	List II (n = 1,211)	List III (n = 765)	List I (n = 4,630)
Status and Occupation	35.34%	25.10%	28.40%
Status only	14.45%	11.76%	12.16%
Occupation only	19.57%	16.34%	17.88%
Neither status nor occupation	30.63%	46.79%	41.56%

*Source: AN T*546[2,3,5].

the church.[11] Nobles could also be classed according to status
and profession when both were given. D'Agrin, for example,
has both the title of baron and the commission of captain of
cuirassiers, and so will appear with both status and occupation.[12] Almost all women have entries for status only. Under
the old regime it was exceptional for women, whatever their
social standing, to give an occupation in legal or fiscal documents.[13] Commoners rarely used a title indicating status,
and either gave their occupations or no personal information
at all.

Table 6.1 shows what proportions of subscribers provided
information on their status and occupations in the three subscription lists at our disposal. Between a quarter and a third
of subscribers in all three lists provide information on both
status and occupation, between 11 and 15 percent indicate
status only and between 16 and 20 percent indicate occu-

---

[11] Occasionally a subscriber has clerical status, but a nonclerical function, as in the
case of the abbé Bonnevie, who was a professor of rhetoric, or of churchmen
who sat as deputies in the National Assembly. There is therefore a small discrepancy between the number of subscribers with clerical status and those with clerical
functions. See below, Section C.

[12] Unless otherwise indicated, examples are taken from the register AN T*546[5],
which is alphabetical.

[13] It was, however, more common for lower class women to do so. Adeline Daumard
and François Furet, *Structures et relations sociales à Paris au milieu du XVIIIe siècle*,
65. See also Roland Mousnier, *La Stratification sociale à Paris aux XVIIe et XVIII e
siècles: L'Echantillon de 1634, 1635, 1636*, 22.

Table 6.2:   Availability of Information on Status and Occupations of
             Subscribers to the *Ami du Roi* in Paris and the Provinces*

PROVINCES	MALE (n = 4209)	FEMALE (n = 850)
availability info. status	44.83%	27.06%
availability info. occupation	55.57%	9.18%

PARIS	MALE (n = 352)	FEMALE (n = 109)
availability info. status	43.47%	41.28%
availability info. occupation	52.84%	8.26%

*Source: As in Table 6.1.

pation only. Only in our shortest list does the proportion of
subscribers about whom we have no personal information
reach nearly half. In the other two they are just over 30 and
40 percent respectively.[14]

It seems that the assiduousness of the scribe is the prime
factor in determining how complete personal information on
subscribers is. The fullest list is fullest in all categories and
that with least information is weakest in all. This suggests
that there was no conscious effort to favor one category at
the expense of another. Nor is there deterioration over time,
for though the earliest list has most information, the middle
list, and not the last, has least.

There is, however, another factor that influences the frequency with which information on status and occupation is
provided. This is gender. Table 6.2 shows that men indicate
their occupations five or six times more frequently than women
do, and this holds for Paris as well as the provinces.

With regard to status, the difference is less great. In the
provinces 44.83 percent of men give some indication of their
status while 27.06 percent of women do so. In Paris, however,
men and women are more or less on an equal footing in this
respect. In the capital 43.47 percent of Royou's male sub-

---

[14] Collective subscriptions are coded as having no status or occupation even though
   these categories are not applicable. Accordingly, the proportion of subscribers
   for whom we have no information should be lowered slightly.

scribers can be identified by the criterion of status while 41.28 percent of female subscribers can be so identified. Thus in the provinces the number of women in the subscription lists to the *Ami du Roi* significantly reduces the proportion of subscribers for whom there is information on status and occupation, while in Paris women indicated their status as frequently as men but gave occupations even less often than in the provinces.

A number of questions arise about the use of the information on the status and occupations of subscribers, among them the problem of the treatment of multiple statuses and occupations, the question of the significance of the relatively large proportion of subscribers for whom no personal information is given, and most fundamentally, the value of conclusions drawn from the formal criteria of status and profession, whether alone or combined.

One difficulty in analyzing information on status and occupation is entirely of my own making and follows from my decision to code only one status and one occupation for each subscriber. Yet some subscribers had more than one title or several occupations. Thus, for example, de Beaumont appears both as a count and a chevalier of the Order of St. Louis, Brissaud as both archiprêtre and curé, Delalande as both advocate *(avocat)* and notary, Desportes as both a president (of a court) and a treasurer of France, Gonidec as both chief cantor *(grand chantre)* and vicar general, Madillac is qualified both as marquis and chevalier, Farsac is both vicar general and canon, and Sylvain was both curé and mayor of his village. In most cases there is little difference between the two statuses held or occupations exercised. For purposes of coding, the higher, more permanent or more prestigious status or occupation was used. Thus Beaumont's status is given as count, Brissaud's occupation as archiprêtre, Delalande's as advocate, Sylvain's as curé. Something of the fullness of the social reality is lost here. The inability to note that Sylvain simultaneously carried out functions in the church and the municipal administration gives the impression of false simplicity. The same is true for a number of subscribers to the *Ami du Roi* who were both curés and deputies to the National Assembly, or a nobleman who gave as his double status the elegant combination of count and citizen, a combination which, unique though it is, speaks volumes about the climate of opinion at the time. Though our coding procedure does oblige us to do violence to the complexity of social and professional reality, it does so infrequently, instances of double status or occupation occurring in fewer than one case in a hundred. A more serious problem is the lack of information.

Three out of ten subscribers in List II, four out of ten in List I and 47 percent in List III give no indication of either status or profession. These are large proportions, and it is important to form some idea of who these men and women were.

To begin with, we should distinguish between status and occupation. The overwhelming majority of those for whom we have information on status are members of the clergy and nobility. This should cause little surprise since commoners' titles, such as "bourgeois," "elector" or "notable," were rarely used. That we have the status of 40 percent of the subscribers in List I and nearly 50 percent in List II reflects the high proportion of the privileged among Royou's readers. The figures on status we have to work with, then, require no apology. On examination, the same will be found to be true of the figures on occupation.

With the exception of those who have retired, we tend today to think of nearly all adults as having an occupation or profession. The same was not true in the eighteenth century. Titles of nobility, if they implied wealth, also implied a lifestyle of unlimited leisure (or idleness). Male nobles might indeed serve the king, primarily in the army or the law courts, but it was not acceptable for women to have professions of their own. At most they were designated by their husbands' professional titles as, for example, Madame la Présidente or

Madame la Maréchale. As noted above, women indicated their occupations far less frequently than men. The nearly 20 percent of female subscribers to the *Ami du Roi* tends to depress the number for whom occupations are given.

Adding the few *rentiers* and bourgeois to the nobles and women, we still have not explained the absence of occupational designations for perhaps 15 percent of all subscribers to the *Ami du Roi*. Three hypotheses may account for the remaining omissions.

First, it may have been that a significant number of subscribers to Royou's paper were fashionably indolent, perhaps retired, or from comfortable families, and lived from incomes from land, state bonds or some other source. In these cases the lack of occupational designation would reflect the lack of an occupation. It is likely that a significant portion of Royou's subscribers belonged to this category, but it is not possible to say how many.

A second hypothesis is that certain subscribers sought to conceal their occupations for the reasons the Marquis de Ferrières dropped his title of nobility.[15] Further, those performing functions or holding offices in institutions that had been abolished by recent legislation may have hesitated to identify themselves with such institutions. But this does not seem very likely. If so inclined, a seigneur could give his occupation as property owner or agriculturalist, and an advocate in a parlement could identify himself simply as an advocate or lawyer *(homme de loi)*. Moreover, the fact that so many subscribers continued to identify themselves by their noble titles or offices in old-regime institutions suggests that at the time these lists were compiled feelings had not yet turned strongly against these things.

A third way of explaining the absence of occupations for a significant number of subscribers is clerical bias. This is not to have recourse to chance, but rather to attempt to evaluate

---

[15] Alfred Cobban, *The Social Interpretation of the French Revolution*, 81.

the social weight or prestige attaching to various occupations and to treat critically the documents we are working with, which are, after all, mailing lists. Other serial documents of the old regime, such as tax rolls, normally give either the status or occupation of everyone appearing in them. There are other documents, such as parish registers, which identify those appearing in them as seldom as one time in ten and as often as eight times in ten.[16] Whether occupations are given frequently or infrequently in parish registers, and indeed in most old-regime documents, such as notarial records, they are not given randomly. There were people in the community that any curé or his scribe would not dare list with their names alone, as this would constitute an affront to their dignity. These were persons of power and prestige whose status or functions brought them recognition and honor. Such, for example, were the seigneur of a parish, a municipal officer, a local commander or army officer, a high functionary in the legal or administrative system, a financier or a wholesale merchant *(négociant)*. As one descends the social scale to the level of merchants, master artisans and shopkeepers, the scribe might or might not feel that it was necessary or desirable to include the occupation of the person in question, and that person, if he wanted his occupation to appear, might, or might not, depending on temperament, family ties, wealth and an array of other factors, have the social weight to have his occupation included in the document against the clerk's will and the complex set of social judgments it represented. It is, I suspect, from the intermediary levels of merchants, independent artisans, shopkeepers and the more humble members of the liberal professions, and not from nobles grown shy of their titles, or from the working population, that could not in any case have afforded the paper, that most subscribers without designations for status or occupation come.

---

[16] I am drawing here on my experience with the parish registers of Amiens and the surrounding countryside in the second half of the eighteenth century.

The most fundamental question to be asked of the subscription lists of the *Ami du Roi* concerns not those subscribers for whom personal information is missing, but the nature and value of the conclusions that can be drawn from the largely formal criteria of status and occupation.

Most social historians are agreed that no very satisfactory analysis of social structure can be carried out on the basis of any single criterion. Daumard and Furet regard information not only on profession, status *(qualité)* and fortune, but also on the form of wealth possessed, lifestyle and marriage patterns as necessary for a complete analysis of any social group.[17] In discussing methodological problems involved in the analysis of old-regime society, Jacques Dupaquier has similarly maintained that the necessary elements for such an analysis include information on socio-professional standing, status, *qualité*, income and collective psychology.[18] Roland Mousnier, who emphasizes the importance of *qualité* in determining a person's place in the society of orders he believed the old regime to have been, does not himself overlook levels of fortune or life style in his study of Parisian society in the mid-seventeenth century.[19] More recently, in an important study of the structure and values of old-regime society, François Bluche and Jean-François Solnon have suggested dignity, power, wealth and consideration as the criteria for comprehensive social analysis.[20]

The information available in the subscription lists of the *Ami du Roi* falls far short of what we would like to have. The status of subscribers tells us something of their *qualité*, but this category is normally applicable only to corporate or privileged groups. Occupation, especially for males, is more gen-

---

[17] Daumard and Furet, *Structures et relations sociales*, 16-17.

[18] J. Dupaquier, "Problèmes de la codification socio-professionnelle," 162-64. See also A. Daumard, "Une référence pour l'étude des sociétés urbaines en France au XVIIIe et XIXe siècles: Projet de code socio-professionel."

[19] Mousnier, *La Stratification sociale*, 8, 21 and 22.

[20] F. Bluche and J.-F. Solnon, *La Véritable hiérarchie de l'ancienne France: Le Tarif de la première capitation:1695*, 67 and 86.

erally available, but in itself tells us nothing about the wealth, prestige or prosperity of the subscribers. This is the most serious shortcoming of the formal categories at our disposal. There is a vast difference between a curé of a small rural parish receiving the statutory minimum of 750 *livres* a year and the curé of a wealthy urban parish with an annual income of 20,000 *livres*. Similarly, the title marquis might be borne by the well-established owner of a number of large estates with a supplementary income from state bonds or other sources, or by an impecunious country squire, the ebb of whose fortunes has brought him to the brink of derogation. An advocate might equally well be a modest city dweller who had taken a degree in law without ever having practiced professionally, or a wealthy and influential member of the legal profession. Or again, the term merchant could be applied to a prosperous employer of dozens of workers and clerks, or to a small retailer, or even to an artisan who had failed to achieve the status of master.[21] Without further information on wealth, income and lifestyle, then, socio-professional categories can tell us little about any given case. Taken collectively, however, such categories do provide a fair profile of the social composition of a group, provided that it is large enough.

Status and occupation do not exist in isolation, but are closely interrelated with wealth, lifestyle and prestige. A particular day laborer might have acquired a respectable fortune. But we know from numerous detailed studies that on the whole journeymen were better off than unskilled laborers, that master artisans were better off than journeymen, that merchants were better off than artisans and that members of the liberal professions, especially law, were on a level with comfortable merchants, but often in a position to rise above them. Office holders formed a large, varied social group which at its upper limits reached into the highest levels of

---

[21] Mousnier, *La Stratification sociale*, 35 and 53.

the law and administration, and whose members were noble. These holders of important offices themselves blended with titled nobles, who, with their great wealth in land, annuities, offices and pensions, formed the apex of the society of the old regime.[22] Thus, if on the basis of the subscription lists of the *Ami du Roi*, we are unable to say how things went economically with any given subscriber, we can still characterize the readership of the paper by the main corporate, professional and occupational groups in these lists. If such an analysis will not reveal the subtleties of social structure, which often emerge only after a comparison of formal to economic criteria,[23] it should provide a reliable profile of the readership of an important journal during a vital formative phase of the Revolution.

C. The Status of the Subscribers

Whether defined as dignity, *qualité* or social rank, status is an important reflection of social standing. But by itself it is a very imperfect reflection of that reality.

Status does say a good deal about the titled nobility, the qualifications made above about the utility of purely formal categories of social classification notwithstanding. For the clergy, status is of value largely for indicating those whose training or qualifications associate them with the church, but who performed no recognized clerical function. To gain a more adequate understanding of the subscribers to the *Ami du Roi* it is necessary to examine their occupations also. Very few members of the third estate appended a title indicating status to their names, but as I have suggested above, the great

---

[22] The literature on the social structure of the old regime is vast. For a sampling of it see the bibliography in E. Labrousse, P. Léon et al., *Histoire économique et social de la France*, vol. II, 754-58 and Albert Soboul, *La Civilisation et la Révolution Française: La Fin de l'Ancien Régime*, section III of the bibliography, 591-606.
[23] See P.H. Thore, "Essai de classification des catégories sociales l'intérieur du tiers état de Toulouse."

majority of those for whom no indication of status is given are commoners.

The following table shows that both in the provinces and in Paris nearly 60 percent of all subscribers gave no indication of status,[24] and were thus most likely commoners. In Paris no commoners used titles indicating status, while in the provinces less than 1 percent of all subscribers (34) did so. These include 20 "bourgeois," four "citizens," one "active citizen," a few electors, notables, *rentiers* and the holder of an unspecified *doctorat*.

Together the clergy and nobility completely dominate the category of status. In the provinces 56.25 percent of subscribers whose status is known belonged to the clergy, just over 42 percent to the nobility. Interestingly, these proportions are reversed in the capital. Despite the smallness of the contingent of Parisian subscribers, this would confirm what has been said about Paris as a center of power and prestige.

In absolute numbers, the *Ami du Roi* was better subscribed by the clergy than by the aristocracy. This remains true even if we include the archbishops and bishops, who were certainly noble,[25] together with the *grands vicaires* and archdeacons who were almost certainly so and a proportion of canons and abbots of convents who came from aristocratic families.[26] Assuming about 150 clerics to have been noble, we still have a hundred more clerics than nobles (1,234 to 1,124).

In terms of status, then, most subscribers to the *Ami du Roi*

---

[24] Technically, somewhat more failed to give an indication of status. In coding information on subscribers I have taken certain occupations to imply noble standing, and so have assumed nobility under a distinct code for these occupations (status 322). The occupations for which nobility has been assumed are the army at level of sub-lieutenant and above (the cut-off point for the Ségur Law), the parlements at the level of avocat général and above, and all positions in the king's household (maison du roi). Certain positions in the church also implied nobility, specifically the positions of archbishop and bishop. One can also reasonably assume nobility for a proportion of the other superior and intermediate secular clergy and for the abbots and abbesses of most convents. See R. Mousnier, *The Institutions of France under the Absolute Monarchy, 1598-1789*, I, 324-27.

[25] Marion, *Dictionnaire*, "Clergé," 95; Mousnier, *The Institutions*, I, 324-25.

[26] Ibid., 326-27.

Table 6.3: Status of Subscribers to the *Ami Du Roi**

	PROVINCES			PARIS		
		T = 5117	Known = 2048		T = 466	Known = 194
Clergy	1152	22.51%	56.25%	82	17.60%	42.27%
Nobility:						
Titled	653			97		
Presumed	208			15		
	861	16.85%	42.09%	112	24.03%	57.73%
Third						
Determined	35					
Presumed	3069					
	3104	60.64%	1.66%		58.37%	—
		100.00%	100.00%		100.00%	100.00%

*Source: As in Table 6.1.

Table 6.4.:   Status of the Clergy Subscribing to the *Ami Du Roi**

	PROVINCES (n = 1152)			PARIS (n = 82)	
General	539		46.79%	12	14.63%
Abbé-Title	166		14.41%	24	29.27%
Abbé**	226	19.62%		34	41.46%
Prêtre**	79	6.86%		—	
Degree holders in theology**	3	0.26%	27.43%	—	
Beneficiers**	8	0.69%			
Reguliers***	131		11.37%	12	14.63%
			100.00%		99.99%

*Source: As in Table 6.1.
**Without further qualification.
***Includes abbots of monasteries.

(about 60 percent) were commoners, just over 20 percent were clerics and just under 20 percent were nobles, allowance made for cases of double status for aristocratic churchmen. These figures hardly justify characterizing Royou's paper as primarily aristocratic, but they do bring out the strength of the paper's clerical and aristocratic following. In that members of the third estate made up more than 95 percent of the country's population, one would not wish to overemphasize their majority of 60 percent in the subscription lists. The privileges of the first two orders extended to the field of culture also.

An examination of the status of the clergy is useful primarily for distinguishing those members of the first order who performed some specific function within the Church from those who did not. Some of the categories used in Table 6.4 require explanation. Unlike laymen, clerics almost always are classed as having both an occupation and a status. A bishop, curé or vicar about whom we have no further information has automatically been coded as having "general" clerical status so as to avoid confusion with subscribers who have no special status. Their specific function is shown under occupation. I have also coded separately subscribers who, in addition to a specific occupation within the Church, are given the honorific title of abbé before their names. Thus, for example, M. l'abbé Bancarel, curé, is classed as a curé with respect to occupation but as an abbé (title) with respect to status. Similarly, the abbé Bonnel, chanoine, is classed as an abbé (title) for status, and as a canon for function.[27] For practical purposes, the categories "general" and "abbé (title)" can be taken together. Monks and nuns are classed by occupation under their order, but for status as members of the regular clergy.

The more interesting categories in Table 6.4 are those which are purely honorific or which indicate a qualification without an occupation. This is clearly the case for the one bachelor of theology and two doctors of theology that appear without any further qualification. It was true in the eighteenth century, as it is today, that to have earned a degree is not necessarily to have employment. To have been ordained a priest is likewise to have qualified to administer the sacraments; it is not to be given the care of souls, or, as the English straightforwardly put it, a "living." When the subscriber appears without further qualification, which is to say when he is not shown as the abbé of any specific institution and does not exercise any other clerical function, the title indicates a person who is somehow affiliated with the Church, but who has no position in the Church and derives no income from it. It should come as no surprise that there were in the eighteenth century many who had studied theology without succeeding in finding a position in the Church. The Church was the leading employer of the functionally literate at the time, and created its own supply of candidates for the jobs it offered. In the eighteenth century this supply exceeded demand. It is no coincidence that we find clerics in general and unemployed clerics in particular playing a central role

---

[27] The abbé Bonnevie, professor of rhetoric, is classed as an abbé (title) with respect to status, but as an educator with respect to function. This is a case in which clerical status does not correspond to a clerical function.

in the intellectual life of the time. Many educators, from professors at prestigious *collèges*, such as Royou and Geoffroy, to simple tutors, bore the title abbé. So too did some of the key figures of the Enlightenment, such as the abbés Condillac, Morellet, Mably and Raynal. The ubiquitous abbés of the period include such men as the encyclopedists de Prades and Yvon, and a clerical counterpart of Rameau's nephew, La Senne.[28] Also classed with those who had clerical status without having clerical occupations were the few lucky holders of benefices, who had an income from the Church without having to fulfill any clerical function. Together, the abbés without incomes, priests without parishes, holders of theological degrees and holders of benefices and prebends account for more than a quarter of Royou's clerical subscribers in the provinces. In Paris the abbés without function alone accounted for more than 40 percent.

With 11.37 percent in the provinces and 14.63 percent in Paris, the regular clergy represented a small but by no means negligible proportion of churchmen subscribing to the *Ami du Roi*. In the provinces more than 60 percent of clerical subscribers were classed as having general status. In the capital this was the case for only 35 percent. The difference seems to lie in the high proportion of clerics on the fringes of the Church in Paris.

Since it does not make much sense to consider clerical status apart from clerical function, we will examine what positions the clergymen who subscribed to the *Ami du Roi* held before considering the status of the other subscribers to the paper.

The most fundamental formal distinction in the Catholic clergy is that between the secular and regular hierarchies.[29] The secular clergy were those who lived in the world (their time, or *siècle*) and whose function it was, whether directly or indirectly, to minister to the faithful. The geographical

---

[28] La Senne's career has been brought to light by Robert Darnton in his article "A Pamphleteer on the Run" in *The Literary Underground*.
[29] See Marion, *Dictionnaire*, "Clergé" and Mousnier, *The Institutions*, I, chap. 7.

framework for the secular hierarchy was the diocese, which was administered by an archbishop or bishop, aided by a grand vicaire or an archdeacon and by the canons who comprised the chapter of his cathedral. At the local level the unit of ministration for the secular clergy was the parish, the basic administrative as well as ecclesiastical unit of the old regime. Charged with the care of souls in the parish, and often much else, were the *curés*, also called *recteurs* in the west of France, and vicars. At the end of the old regime there were in France 19 archbishoprics, between 120 and 130 bishoprics[30] and about 40,000 parishes.

The regular clergy were not normally ordained, but lived according to a rule *(règle)* and, at least originally, had withdrawn from the world to seek their salvation in prayer, meditation and spiritual exercises. The monastic ideal still existed in this form in the eighteenth century, but by this time also included orders whose members saw their vocations in the world. These orders include mendicants, such as the Franciscans and Dominicans, which were founded in the thirteenth century, and the Jesuits and others that date from the Counter-Reformation. Some women's orders, such as the Filles de la Charité, also performed useful social functions, for example, as nurses in hospitals and poorhouses. But cloistered female orders often acted as dumping grounds for young women from better off families unable or unwilling to provide dowries for them. Members of the regular clergy normally lived in monasteries or convents and were governed by abbots or abbesses, priors or prioresses. There were probably between 40,000 and 80,000 nuns at the end of the eighteenth century, and half as many monks.[31]

---

[30] Marion gives 121 bishoprics *(Dictionnaire,* 95), Latreille *(L'Eglise catholique,* 20) and Mousnier *(The Institutions,* I, 322) 130.

[31] There is no agreement on the numbers of regular clergy at the end of the old regime. Marion cites Expilly to the effect that the secular and regular clergy together totaled 406,000 souls of whom 80,000 were nuns, and another eighteenth-century demographer, Moheau, who gave 130,000 as a total maximum. He himself refused to make an estimate on the grounds that the necessary infor-

In addition to the horizontal division into regular and secular clergy, there was a no less important series of vertical cleavages within the Church. The prestige and power of a prelate cannot be compared to those of a country curé, and the position and connections of an abbot of a rich monastery were not the same as those of a novice or simple monk. Hence the divisions within each branch of the clergy are as significant as those between the two branches.

Table 6.5 (p. 171) breaks down the clerical subscribers to the *Ami du Roi* into four broad categories. A "general" function has been ascribed to clerics who were addressed as abbé, but about whom we know nothing else, and to others such as holders of benefices or prebends. In the provinces this amorphous category accounts for just over one-quarter of Royou's clerical subscribers, in Paris for nearly half. The category "other" is composed almost entirely of heads of seminaries, and accounts for between two and three percent of clerical subscribers.

Members of the regular clergy form 12.83 percent of Royou's clerical provincial subscribers and 17.39 percent of those in the capital, but again, the Parisian numbers are very small. Among the best represented orders in the provinces are the Order of Malta, a religious order of chivalry for membership in which nobility was required, with ten subscribers, the Benedictines with eight, the Oratorians with seven and the Capuchins with five. Women account for only sixteen (including four from charitable institutions) of the 146 provincial regulars in our lists. What is perhaps most striking here is the

---

mation was lacking (*Dictionnaire*, 101). Latreille, apparently following Moheau, states that there were 20-25,000 monks and 40,000 nuns in France at the end of the eighteenth century (*L'Eglise catholique*, I, 20). Mousnier, going beyond Expilly asserts, "The male members of the clerical order constituted 1 per cent of the total population. . . ." and that "the number of nuns was probably higher" (*The Institutions*, I, 320). As most estimates put the population of France at this time at about 26,000,000, Mousnier's estimate would yield more than a quarter of a million nuns. Michel Vovelle seems to have confused Expilly's and Moheau's estimates, asserting that the first order had a total of "130,000 personnes, 2% peut-être des français" (*La Chute de la monarchie: 1787-1792*, 27).

Table 6.5:   Occupations of the Clergy Subscribing to the *Ami Du Roi**

	PROVINCES (n = 1138)		PARIS (n = 69)	
General	301	26.45%	32	46.38%
Secular				
Upper				
Cardinal				
Archbishop				
Bishop	63	5.54%	10	14.49%
Grand vicaire				
Archiprêtre				
Archidiacre				
Chapters				
Canon	156	13.71%	4	5.80%
Officer				
Lower				
Curé				
Recteur				
Prieur-curé	448	39.37%	9	13.04%
Vicaire				
Diacre				
Chapelain				
Regular				
misc.				
various orders				
abbé				
prior				
celerier	146	12.83%	12	17.39%
female order				
sup.-female				
sup.-male				
missions				
charitable inst.				
Other				
sup. seminary	24	2.10%	2	2.90%
nonce apol.				
		100.00%		100.00%

*Source: As in Table 6.1.

vertical cleavage. Nearly half (68 of 146) the regulars who subscribed to Royou's paper were either abbots, superiors, or priors of their houses. In Paris this was true of five in twelve.

The secular clergy forms nearly 60 percent of Royou's clerical readership in the provinces, but only a third in Paris. The provincial secular subscribers include two cardinals, two archbishops and fourteen bishops. Together with the other important functionaries at the diocesan level, the upper secular clergy accounts for 9.44 percent of the 667 provincial secular clerics. The intermediary level, which consists of the officers and canons of the cathedral chapters, accounts for a further 23.39 percent. This leaves the lower clergy, predominantly the parish curés and vicars, as a clear majority of the provincial secular clergy with 67.17 percent. Of the 23 members of the secular clergy in Paris, four times as many belong to the upper clergy (43.48 percent), only 17.39 percent to the intermediary levels and 39.13 percent to the lower clergy, though one might expect Parisian curés, of which there were five, to be much better off than their rural counterparts. These figures again reinforce the aristocratic character of the Parisian readership of the *Ami du Roi*.

There is an element of ambiguity in the makeup of Royou's clerical readership. In the provinces we find that more than one bishop in ten and about one curé in a hundred took the *Ami du Roi*. Does this mean that the paper was more to the taste of prelates than of more humble clerics? Or does it reflect a greater likelihood that prelates, and the social milieu from which they came, were more likely to read anything at all than the curés and vicars and the social strata to which they belonged? Whatever the explanation, it is true both that a very high proportion of prelates subscribed to Royou's paper and that the great majority of the clerical readers of the *Ami du Roi* were relatively humble foot soldiers of the Church. But the makeup of subscribers belonging to the regular clergy was less democratic than that of the secular.

Under the old regime nobility was a true status or *état* which "raised those who possessed it above the other subjects of the King."[32] Nobility, it has been fairly said, was "the ideal of all Frenchmen . . . the model to which nearly everyone tried to conform."[33] But while comprising a true status with attendant legally sanctioned privileges, it is a status exhibiting considerable internal differentiation.[34]

The culture of the old regime distinguished sharply between families whose nobility dated from time immemorial and those whose ennoblement was recent. It also differentiated nobility won by service in the army from that achieved by service in the courts or bureaucracy or by the purchase of office. Similarly, of two noblemen who bore the same title, one could be immensely wealthy, the other nearly destitute. Above all, nobility could be won and it could be lost.

Nobility was primarily a question of heredity only for the authors of dictionaries and theoretical treatises. In practice it was closely related to wealth and lifestyle. By achieving sufficient wealth and living in the prescribed way, commoners could attain noble status. The most usual ways of doing this were buying a seigneurie and living nobly (without directly engaging in mechanical or commercial activities), by serving the crown at a sufficiently high level, whether in the army, courts or administration, or by buying an ennobling office. In most cases nobility was acquired gradually over a number

---

[32] Marion, *Dictionnaire*, "Noblesse," 392.

[33] Mousnier, *The Institutions*, I, 121.

[34] There is no agreement on the size of the nobility at the end of the old regime. Estimates range from roughly 100,000 to 400,000. See Marion, *Dictionnaire*, 392 and Mousnier, *The Institutions*, I, 147. Goubert inclines to accept the frequently used figure of 300,000 (*L'Ancien Régime*, I, 167), while after a careful discussion of the sources, Franklin Ford suggests that France had about 190,000 nobles in 1700, or about one percent of the total population (*Robe and Sword: The Regrouping of the French Aristocracy after Louis XIV*, 29-31). More recently Guy Chaussinand-Nogaret has examined data on the convocation of the nobles to the Estates General and on the *capitation* and concluded, "We must give up the high figure of 400,000 individuals and settle for 110 or 120,000, or about 25,000 noble families in 1789" (*The French Nobility in the Eighteenth Century: from Feudalism to Enlightenment*, 28-30).

of generations,[35] but full nobility could be acquired immediately in some cases, as in the purchase of the office of *secrétaire du roi*, while there also existed a form of personal nobility that could not be transmitted to the next generation. A noble might suffer derogation, that is, lose his noble status, if he engaged directly in an artisanal craft or retail business, activities he would undertake only in extreme financial distress. Thus it is misleading to think of nobility as a static state of being or as a status that could be enjoyed independently of other social determinants. Rather, it was a highly variegated status enjoyed by those who had risen to a certain level in the unending struggle for wealth, power and prestige. Its significance consisted in the formal recognition of success in this struggle and in conferring prestige, together with certain material advantages, upon those who already enjoyed wealth and power. The threat of derogation was a constant reminder that prestige could not sustain itself.

One might paraphrase the observation of detractors of socialism that under this system all are equal, but some are more equal than others, and say that under the old regime all members of the second order were noble, but some were more noble than others. There was, after all, a formal hierarchy of noble status descending from princes to dukes to marquis to counts, viscounts, barons, chevaliers (knights) and finally écuyers (esquires).[36] Moreover, while the titles of duke, marquis and count unequivocally designate noble status, the titles of chevalier and écuyer only imply it.[37] Indeed, it often happened that commoners aspiring to noble status usurped these titles.[38]

The status conferred or implied by an award of the Order of Saint Louis brings out the ambiguities surrounding noble

---

[35] Goubert, *The Ancien Régime*, 179-86; Mousnier, *The Institutions*, I, 129.
[36] Marion, *Dictionnaire*, "Noblesse."
[37] Goubert, however, regards these terms as fairly reliable indications of noble status. *The Ancien Régime*, 154.
[38] Marion, *Dictionnaire*, "Ecuyer," 197.

and near-noble status. This order was established in 1693 as a military decoration. It could be won either by outstanding feats of arms or for extended service in the army at officer level. It was not necessary to be noble to qualify for the Order of Saint Louis, nor was a commoner ennobled by receiving it. Knights of this order, some of whom were noble in their own right,[39] and so overlapped the nobility, formed a milieu "intermediary between true nobles and people 'living nobly'. . . ."[40] In some cases membership in the order freed commoners from payment of the *taille*, perhaps the main criterion of common status. In others it assured nobility for the second generation, and it exempted sons of common officers who were also knights of the Order from the provisions of the Ségur Law of 1781, which required four quarters of nobility for officers above the rank of sub-lieutenant.[41] Thus the Order of Saint Louis was one way near-nobles could cross the threshold from the formally common to the formally noble world. The distance was not great.

Similarly, a dowager or someone receiving a royal pension need not necessarily be noble. They have nevertheless been classed with the nobles on the assumption that a woman living from property set aside from her late husband's estate, or a man close enough to the centers of power to be awarded a royal pension,[42] were sufficiently well off to be included in the elite of wealth and power of which noble status was the formal recognition.[43]

There are other subscribers to Royou's paper who have

---

[39] The combination "count" and "chevalier de Saint Louis" is fairly common in the subscription lists. In such cases status is coded for the higher value, which is count.
[40] Bluche and Solnon, *La Véritable hiérarchie*, 60-61.
[41] Mousnier, *The Institutions*, I, 131 and 196. Mousnier gives the cut-off point of the Ségur Law as second lieutenant, Marion as sub-lieutenant (*Dictionnaire*, "Grades, Militaires").
[42] I assume that not everyone receiving a royal pension, but only those for whom the pension was a primary source of income and who exercised no common profession, would have so described themselves.
[43] On the diverse social and institutional origins of this elite see Goubert, *L'Ancien Régime*, II, 210.

been assumed noble on the basis of their functions. These include officers of the royal household, army officers from the level of sub-lieutenant and officers of the sovereign courts from the level of advocate general. It may be that some of Royou's subscribers who were really noble have escaped us, and that others who had achieved only personal nobility, or were still seeking ennoblement, or were merely wealthy or professionally well established, have been assumed to be noble. But in terms of the social reality of the time it seems more reasonable to class such people with the nobility than not to do so.

A glance at the subscription lists of the *Ami du Roi* would seem to support those who described the paper's readership as essentially aristocratic. The names of many of France's great aristocratic families appear among Royou's subscribers. In the provinces we find d'Armestadt (duchess), Béthune (count), Beauvray (duchess), Beuvron (duchess), Broglie (countess), Castres, also rendered Castries (duke), Caylus (marquise), Clermont-Tonnerre (count), Colbert, Condé, Crouy (duke), d'Epinay (marquis), Grammont (count), Mailly (duke), Maupou (marquise), Modène (duke), Montmirail (countess), Montmorency (two princes, one princess and one duchess), Narbonne (duke), Rochechouart, a Madame de Besse, née Rochechouart, Rochefoucault, Rohan (a cavalry captain), Rohan-Chabot (duchess), le Tellier, d'Uzès (duchess) and Villeroy (duchess). Among the Parisian subscribers we find more of the great names of the aristocracy, some of them names we have just seen, whether different members of the same family or the same subscriber who has shifted his or her residence. The Paris subscribers include two members of the royal family, Madame Adelaide and Madame Victoire, the dukes of Brancas, Brissac and Chabot, the duchesses of Gesvres, Grammont, Mailly, Montbazon and d'Uzès, the marquises of Choiseul and Louvois and the count of Clermont-Tonnerre.

There were also numerous nobles from less illustrious families closely attached to the Court, ranging from Barthouille, the commander of the Louvre, and Champlost, governor of the Louvre, both resident in the palace, to Belleroi, an usher (*huissier*) of the king's bedchamber, Bernis, a gentleman of the bedchamber of Monsieur, Camssan, secretary of the queen's cabinet, Saint Pardoux, a gentleman attached to the household of Madame Elisabeth, and Saint Robert, a sub-governor of the duke d'Enghien, to Madame de Mericourt, a lady in waiting to Madame Adelaide, Madame de Makau, a sub-governess of the royal family, and the countess de Montléard, a lady in waiting to Madame at the Luxembourg Palace. We also find among the Paris subscribers to the *Ami du Roi* a number of ministers of state, such as d'Invau,[44] de la Luzerne (marine) and Saint Priest (king's household), the Austrian ambassador and confidant of Marie-Antoinette, Mercy-Argentau, a number of councillors of state, Bertin, de la Morlière and Royer, and three farmers general, Desmarets, Puissen and Saint Amand.

Subscribers classed as noble account for just over 16 percent of provincial subscribers, but for nearly a quarter of Parisian ones (see Table 6.3). The following table shows that not only do the provinces and Paris differ in the proportion of nobles they have, they also differ in the makeup of their respective nobilities.

In Paris nearly 84 percent of nobles are titled, in the provinces just over 60 percent. In both cases the somewhat questionable categories of chevalier and écuyer play only a small role with less than one titled noble in five, the solid titles of duke, count and baron predominating. The proportion of dukes among titled nobles is three times as high in Paris as in the provinces, but in the case of princes the provinces for once have the better of the capital.

Few Paris subscribers made their membership in an order

---

[44] D'Invau is shown as a "ministre d'état" in AN T*546[2]. He does not, however, appear in either the basic general histories of the Revolution or the list of ministers in Colin Jones, *The Longman Companion to the French Revolution*.

Table 6.6:   The Status of Noble Subscribers to the *Ami Du Roi**

	PROVINCES (n = 861)		PARIS (n = 112)	
Titled				
Prince	10		1	
Duke	18		9	
Marquis	150		24	
Count	184		36	
Viscount	32		4	
Baron	54		3	
Chevalier	67		14	
Ecuyer	3		3	
	518	60.16%	94	83.93%
Orders				
Saint Louis	109		3	
Saint Michel				
Saint Esprit				
Du Roi	2			
	111	12.89%	3	2.68%
Presumed Noble	209	24.27%	15	13.39%
Other				
General	3			
Seigneur	3			
English	3			
Russian	1			
Dowager	10			
Pension Holder	2			
Châtelain	1			
	23	2.67%		
		99.99%		100.00%

*Source: As in Table 6.1.

of chivalry their chief identifying characteristic, while in the provinces 111 (12.89 percent) did so. We have seen above that a knighthood in the Order of Saint Louis did not necessarily imply nobility, though it certainly suggested close proximity to that coveted status.[45] Since titled nobles who were also knights of the Order of Saint Louis were classed on the criterion of status by their titles, the high proportion of these knights in the provinces confirms the superior standing of the Paris subscribers.

Another category which leads to the same conclusion is that of subscribers whose positions imply that they are noble, principally army officers and members of the sovereign courts. Nearly a quarter of provincial subscribers, but only 13.39 percent in Paris, were deemed noble by virtue of their functions or offices. Though their noble status was above question, high legal officers seldom used formal titles of nobility in the subscription lists. In the army and navy the assumption of nobility for officers above the level of sub-lieutenant is less certain, but in the light of the Ségur Law and their similarity in lifestyle, still worth making.

There are, finally, a number of nobles, or presumed nobles, who fit into none of the categories discussed above. These include ten dowagers, a few foreign gentlemen, two holders of royal pensions, three hardy souls who, more than a year after the peasant risings of the summer of 1789 and the legislation following the night of 4 August, still publicly identified themselves as seigneurs, and one more circumspect châtelain. One wonders what the proportion of seigneurs would have been had these lists been compiled two or three years earlier. In this particular the Revolution seems to have had an immediate and dramatic effect.

---

[45] The humor in Sterne's portrayal of a chevalier of the Order of Saint Louis selling pastries in the street while wearing his decoration derives both from the contrast between the implied and actual status of the decorated pastry salesman and the literalness and liberty with which he accepts his common status. See *The Sentimental Journey*, section entitled "Le Patissier de Versailles." Similarly, Diderot remarked that "there are holders of the Cross of Saint-Louis who don't have bread to eat. . . ." *Le Neveu de Rameau, Oeuvres Romanesques,* ed. Henri Benac (Paris, classiques Garnier, 1962), 440.

Table 6.7:   Occupations of Subscribers to the *Ami Du Roi**

| | PROVINCES | | PARIS | |
	Total (5117)	Known (2417)	Total (466)	Known (195)
Clergy	1138	22.24%	47.08%	69	14.81%	35.38%
Military	333	6.51%	13.78%	13	2.79	6.67%
Agriculture	10	.20%	.41%	—	—	—
Arts & Com.	296	5.78%	12.25%	9	1.93%	4.62%
Lib. Prof.	640	12.51%	26.48%	104	22.32%	53.33%
Undesignated	2700	52.76%	—	271	58.15%	—

*Source: As in Table 6.1.

D. The Occupations of Subscribers

I have divided the occupations of subscribers to the *Ami du Roi* into five broad categories. The first of these, the clergy, accounts for just over 22 percent of all provincial subscribers to Royou's paper, and 47 percent of subscribers whose occupations are known. While forming a slightly lower proportion of provincial subscribers whose occupations are known than of subscribers with an identifiable status, the clergy remains by far the largest occupational group in the provinces. In Paris, however, their numerical importance is much reduced, and the clergy takes second place to the lawyers, administrators and others who make up the category of liberal professions.

Whether in Paris or the provinces, the common professions of agriculture and trades and commerce account for a small proportion of Royou's subscribers. Together these categories make up 12.66 percent of provincial subscribers whose occupations are known, and only 4.62 percent of Parisian ones. The army accounts for 13.78 percent of subscribers who indicate their occupations in the provinces, but only half that figure in the capital. The greatest occupational difference in the readership of the *Ami du Roi* in Paris and in the provinces concerns the liberal professions. Whereas a quarter of provincial subscribers who indicate their occupations come from this group, more than half the Parisian ones belong to it. Thus the provincial list is the more balanced, having nearly half its subscribers from the clergy, just over a quarter from the liberal professions, and roughly an eighth each from the army and trades and commerce, as well as token representation from agriculture. In Paris the liberal professions dominate with well over half the subscribers whose occupations are known. The clergy is the only other large group in the capital, the army being reduced to 6.67 percent and trades and commerce to 4.62 percent of subscribers whose occupations are known.

Of the more than 2,600 subscribers to Royou's paper who indicate their occupations, only ten were actively engaged in agriculture. This amounts to less than one-half of one percent in a country in which about 80 percent of the population made its living directly from farming. Moreover, these subscribers are in no way representative of the peasant community. Four were *fermiers*, that is, large scale leaseholders and agricultural entrepreneurs, and six were *laboureurs*, or independent proprietors, who together with the *fermiers*, formed the elite of rural communities. This near exclusion of the peasantry from the subscription lists of an important conservative daily is perhaps more complete than one might have expected, but not surprising. The masses of dependent peasants had neither the cultural tools nor the material means necessary to acquire and read a sophisticated daily paper. They formed a cultural community apart from the advanced circles of the capital, whether progressive or conservative.

One way the peasantry does reflect the rest of the readership of Royou's paper is in its elitist makeup. Whatever sector of the economy subscribers to the *Ami du Roi* come from, they represent the elites of those sectors. As we will see when we have examined trades and commerce, the army and the liberal professions in more detail, the makeup of the clerical readership of the paper was the most nearly democratic.

Table 6.8:   Occupations of Subscribers in Trades and Commerce
to the *Ami Du Roi**

	PROVINCES (n = 296)		PARIS (n = 9)
Businessman	6	2.03%	—
Banker	1	.34%	—
Négociant	129	43.58%	—
Merchant (unspecified)	20	6.76%	—
Merchant (specified)	21	7.09%	—
Master artisan	5	1.69%	1
Artisan independent	12	4.05%	1
Book trade	80	27.03%	6
Hospitality	12	4.05%	1
Transport	10	3.38%	—
	296	100.00%	9

*Source: As in Table 6.1.

The 296 subscribers to the *Ami du Roi* who were engaged in the trades or commerce represent 12.25 percent of subscribers whose occupations are given in the provinces, and the nine in Paris, 4.62 percent. Table 6.8 shows that these artisans and businessmen are no cross section of the commercial community. Broadly speaking, merchants are engaged in exchange, workers and artisans in production. In preindustrial societies the former are generally less numerous, but wealthier, than the latter. There are no dependent artisans *(ouvriers, compagnons)* whatever in these lists; independent artisans account for 4.05 percent of provincial subscribers in the trades and commerce, and master artisans 1.69 percent. Thus those primarily engaged in production account for slightly more than one subscriber in twenty in the category of trades and commerce.

Merchants whose businesses are specified account for 7.09 percent of this category, subscribers identifying themselves as merchants without further qualification for 6.76 percent.[46] The group that completely dominates this category is that of *négociants,* or wholesale merchants, who were by far the wealthiest stratum of the commercial community, financiers aside, though in the eighteenth century finance and large-scale commercial activity were often carried on by the same people. By themselves, the *négociants* account for 43.58 percent of those occupied in the trades and commerce in the provincial lists.

The only group that approaches the *négociants* in numerical importance is the book trade. Printers and booksellers make up 27.03 percent of Royou's subscribers in trades and commerce in the provinces and six of nine in Paris. But these can hardly have been customers in the ordinary sense. Rather, they would have been taking the *Ami du Roi* as part of their business dealings and selling the paper without necessarily reading it.[47] Another group who probably took Royou's paper for professional reasons rather than for their own personal use are the 4 percent engaged in providing accommodation or food and drink. It was common practice at the time for innkeepers and café owners to provide a variety of papers for their clients. It is probably fair to say that nearly a third of Royou's subscribers engaged in trade and commerce took his paper not from personal interest, but as part of their business. If so, this further diminishes the already small role of those engaged in the trades and commerce in the readership of the *Ami du Roi.*

---

[46] If we ask what trades these merchants and artisans engaged in, we find that the food trades and textiles were most prominent. Of the merchants, ten dealt in food, four in textiles; of the master artisans three in food and two in textiles; and of the independent artisans, three in food, three in luxury goods, two in textiles and two in manufacturing. But the vertical, not the horizontal, differences are the more striking.

[47] This would certainly have been the case for the 52 booksellers *(libraires)* and for the 12 printer-booksellers *(imprimeurs-libraires)* in the lists. It is also likely that the 15 printers *(imprimeurs)* who took the *Ami du Roi* were distributors as well as producers of the printed word. One would not expect Madame Fréron and Royou to send their paper to potential pirates.

Table 6.9:   Ranks of Military Personnel Subscribing to the *Ami Du Roi**

		PROVINCES (n = 333)		Paris (n = 13)
Maison/Roi Mil.	18	5.41%		1
Army				
Noncommissioned officer	7	2.10%		
Off. Particulier	113	33.93%		1
Off. Supérieur	57	17.12%		1
Off. Général	28	8.41%		5
Off. Unit	51	15.32%		1
Military Surgeon	4	1.20%		
Navy (all officers)	22	6.61%		1
Paramilitary				
Maréchaussée	11	3.30%		
Nat'l. Guard	10	3.00%		
Administration	12	3.60%		3
	333	100.005		13

*Source: As in Table 6.1.

The artisans, merchants and businessmen just discussed were all, by definition, commoners. Subscribers of the *Ami du Roi* who served in the army were nearly all nobles. Only seven of the 333 military personnel in Table 6.8 held ranks that imply common status. These are five soldiers of various sorts, one sergeant and one *maréchal des logis,* or cavalry sergeant. It was difficult for commoners to gain promotion above the rank of *maréchal des logis* in the eighteenth century, this rank acting as a significant social barrier.[48] There were three broad classes of commissioned officers during our period.[49] The first and most numerous was that of *officiers particuliers* within which lies the cut-off point for the Ségur Law, the rank of sub-lieutenant. None of the officers within this grouping is below this rank (see Appendix 2), and only two are

---

[48] Guy Cabourdin and Georges Viard, *Lexique historique de la France d'Ancien régime*, "Armée."
[49] This classification is borrowed from Marion, *Dictionnaire*, "Grades (Militaires)."

sub-lieutenants. There are eight lieutenants, but it is the rank of captain that completely dominates with 103 of the 113 officers in this category.

There are 57 field officers *(officiers supérieurs)*, amounting to 17.12 percent of all military personnel among Royou's provincial subscribers. These include 14 majors, 19 lieutenant-colonels, two *mestres de camp*, which were roughly equivalent, and 20 colonels. These are ranks that imply high social standing.

At the top of the chain of command come the general officers. Numerically predominant among the 28 general officers in the provincial lists are 20 *maréchaux de camp* and five lieutenant generals. It appears, then, that Royou's military readers included four times as many officers of the highest rank than noncommissioned officers or simple soldiers. There is, perhaps, no stronger indication of the interest of the aristocracy in Royou's paper than this. As usual, the Paris lists heighten this impression. Leaving aside three administrators dealing with army affairs, five of the ten military subscribers shown for the capital are general officers.

In addition to the officers whose ranks place them precisely in the military hierarchy, there are a number of others whom it is less easy to place. These include 18 members of the military establishment of the royal household and 51 officers who specify their units, but not their rank. The navy is represented by 22 officers, all presumably, but not certainly, noble.

Officers of two paramilitary forces, the *maréchaussée* and the National Guard, also appear among the provincial subscribers to the *Ami du Roi*, though neither in large numbers. The *maréchaussée*, which acted as a rural police force under the old regime, has 11 subscribers, six of whom held the relatively high rank of lieutenant. It may seem odd to find ten officers of the National Guard among the readers of the *Ami du Roi*, for that force, which superseded most of the police agencies of the old regime, has rightly been described as a bulwark of the Revolution.[50] Though the exclusion of the working poor (as passive citizens) gave the National Guard a distinctly middle-class character,[51] it should be borne in mind that this force was formed in the uncertain days of the summer of 1789 with the primary purpose of assuring the security of persons and property. Marat even denounced the National Guard as the "hired assassins of the King,"[52] and it was this force, not the army, that fired on the crowd in the Champ-de-Mars. Given the common interest in the defense of property and Lafayette's conception of the National Guard as a pillar of an essentially "conservative revolution,"[53] it should not be surprising that at this relatively early date eight commanders and two officers of the force took Royou's paper. We have seen above that there were also three collective subscriptions to the *Ami du Roi* from companies of the National Guard, as well as a number from the Jacobins.

There are two more groups included among military subscribers that might arguably have been classed elsewhere. These are the four military surgeons and the 12 provincial and three Parisian administrators who handled the supplies and monies of the armed forces. If one prefers to emphasize professional skills rather than the institutional framework, he would put the surgeons with other practitioners of medicine and the administrators with the appropriate subdivision of the category liberal professions, which we are about to consider.

The category "liberal professions" is defined broadly here. It includes not only law, medicine and other learned professions, but also the worlds of administration and bureaucracy, from key decision-makers to humble, or relatively humble,

---

[50] Thompson, *The French Revolution*, 66.
[51] Aulard, *The French Revolution*, I, 217; Lefebvre, *The French Revolution*, I, 131; Thompson, *The French Revolution*, 66; Sydenham, *The French Revolution*, 50, n. 2; and Furet and Richet, *La Révolution française*, 119.
[52] Salvemini, *The French Revolution*, 202.
[53] Furet and Richet, *La Révolution française*, 111.

Table 6.10: Members of the Liberal Professions Subscribing to the
            *Ami Du Roi**

	PROVINCES (n = 640)		PARIS (n = 104)	
Medicine	39	6.09%	2	1.12%
Applied Sciences	5	.78%	—	
Education	40	6.25%	5	4.81%
Clerical	15	2.34%	2	1.92%
Law				
General	138	21.88%	8	7.69%
Old Regime	98	15.00%	32	30.77%
Revolution	27	4.22%	—	
Gov't. & Admin.				
General	40	6.25%	1	.96%
Old Regime	37	5.78%	19	18.27%
Revolution	21	3.28%	21	20.19%
Finance	84	13.13%	11	10.58%
Services	58	9.06%	2	1.92%
Other	38	5.94%	1	.96%
	640	100.00%	104	99.99%

*Source: As in Table 6.1.

clerks. The common denominator of these occupations is that they all presuppose functional literacy.

Together the categories of law and government and administration, to which it would be fair to annex finance and services, make up the overwhelming majority of members of the liberal professions subscribing to Royou's paper. But this is not to say that the role of other groups is insignificant.

Table 6.10 shows that medicine accounts for just over 6 percent of subscribers classed as belonging to the liberal professions in the provinces and just over 2 percent in Paris. The practitioners of the medical profession outside Paris include 21 doctors, 11 surgeons, whose status was much lower than that of doctors or of their contemporary counterparts, and five apothecaries; those within, a doctor and a midwife. The only other subscribers who practiced a profession based on the exact sciences were three engineers and two architects, all from the provinces.

The educators who appear in Table 6.10 are for the most part attached to universities and secondary schools (*collèges*), but also include a number of tutors, masters of boarding schools, and the like. In the provinces ten subscribers are attached to universities, one as a principal, one as an administrator and eight as professors, while nineteen are attached to *collèges*, twelve as principals and six as professors. All five educators in the Parisian lists are associated with *collèges*.

There is also among Royou's subscribers one seminary professor from the provinces, who brings to mind the 25 directors or superiors of seminaries that appeared in our analysis of the occupational breakdown of the clergy. Had they been classified as educators, they would have increased this category by more than half, and their functions would have justified our doing so. It is not possible, however, to put the same subscriber into two different occupational groups. On the whole I have made the institutional framework in which a person worked rather than the function performed determine where that person was classified. Thus I have put a brother responsible for the economic affairs of his monastery with the Church, and not with finance, and have classed military doctors with the army rather than the medical profession. The opposite procedure is, of course, both reasonable and legitimate.

The category "clerical" is comprised primarily of secretaries. In Paris these are secretaries to an official and to a private individual. In the provinces we find one secretary who does not indicate whom he serves, two secretaries of institutions, five of clubs and three of bishops.[54] The other subscribers classed as clerical are an archivist, two librarians and a journalist. None of these positions suggests wealth or power, and

---

[54] Secretaries to institutions, officials or private individuals would derive their incomes from these functions; secretaries to clubs probably would not.

together they account for just over two percent of subscribers who lived by their pens in the provinces and just under this figure in the capital.

Members of the legal profession account for roughly 40 percent of subscribers to Royou's paper who belonged to the liberal professions (see Table 6.10). These judges and lawyers have been classed in three broad categories. The first, labeled "general," includes those subscribers who indicate their function, such as advocate *(avocat)* or notary, but not the court or jurisdiction to which they are attached, if indeed they are attached to any. The second category takes in members of the profession who hold an office or perform a function in one of the many courts of the complex legal system of the old regime. The third category is reserved for members of the legal profession who have accepted positions in the new system of courts put in place by the Constituent Assembly.

Table 6.11 shows that in the provinces more than half the members of the legal profession subscribing to Royou's paper gave no institutional affiliation. Of these, 62 called themselves simply advocates, 33 notaries and 22 attorneys *(procureurs)*, while a further 16 referred to themselves as legal practitioners *(hommes de loi)*. Of the 92 who identified themselves with the courts of the old regime, 58 owned offices in, or worked with, *parlements* or sovereign courts, which were the highest ordinary legal authorities in the land. Thus more than half the judges and lawyers who held offices in the legal system of the old regime came from institutions at the apex of that system. Moreover, 28 of the 58 parlementaires in question held the elevated title of *président* within their courts and 17 had the title councillor.[55] Though advocates and attorneys

---

[55] There were fifteen sovereign courts in France in 1789, including *conseils supérieurs* (Ford, *Robe and Sword,* 38). The Parlement of Paris consisted of eight different chambers, or jurisdictions, which together had 24 presidents. Provincial parlements usually consisted of five or six chambers, each normally having more than one president. Councillors came after presidents, but before advocates and attorneys in order of precedence. Marion, *Dictionnaire,* "Parlements."

Table 6.11:   Members of the Legal Profession Subscribing to the
*Ami Du Roi**

	PROVINCES (n = 263)		PARIS (n = 40)	
General				
avocat	62		5	
notaire	33		2	
homme/loi	16		1	
procureur	22		—	
other	5		—	
	138	52.47%	8	20.00%
Old Regime				
parlement	58		24	
bailliage	28		1	
prévôté	4		—	
directoire	2		—	
special juris.	4		7	
feudiste	2		—	
	98	37.26%	32	80.00%
Revolution				
national	1		—	
département	—		—	
district	8		—	
commune	12		—	
other	6		—	
	27	10.27%		
		100.00%		100.00%

*Source: As in Table 6.1.

were far more numerous in the sovereign courts than either
presidents or councillors, we find only two advocates and five
attorneys practicing in parlements in our provincial lists.[56]
This discrepancy can be explained in two ways. First, it may
be that the higher and more prestigious an office, the more
the holder of that office tends to identify himself publicly

---

[56] The term "avocat" was broadly and variously used. An "avocat" without further
qualification was someone who had taken a legal degree at a university. An "avocat
au parlement" and an "avocat en parlement" both owned their offices within the
sovereign court. Marion, *Dictionnaire*, "Avocat."

with the institution in which he holds that office. Second, it may be that some of the advocates and attorneys in the "general" category had in fact practiced law in the parlements, but given the reforms that were under way did not want to identify with them.[57]

There are no representatives of the courts immediately beneath the parlements, the *présidiaux*, among Royou's subscribers, but there are 28 officers of *bailliages* or *sénéchaussées*, the courts below the *présidiaux*. These include five *baillis*, 11 *lieutenants du roi* and six *procureurs du roi* and a number of other office holders. In general the superior officers of the sovereign courts were noble, those of the *bailliages* were notables, but not normally noble.[58] There were also four judges from the more humble *prévôtés*, the courts immediately below the *bailliages*.

The other members of the legal profession in the provinces who worked within the framework of the old regime are two judges of the Eaux et Forêts, and two more from the Cour des Aides, a court with jurisdiction over taxes. They are both special jurisdictions, the latter with the standing of a sovereign court. There were also two members of the *directoire*, a court in Alsace reserved for nobles. Finally, we also find here two *feudistes*, or specialists in feudal law, who were normally employed by seigneurs seeking grounds to reimpose lapsed seigneurial dues or to increase the yields of existing ones. That this professional designation should have lingered for more than a year after the legislation of August 1789 should come as no surprise. Feudalism was not finally abolished in France until July 1793, and Robert Forster has shown that peasants in Normandy were still paying seigneurial dues until early 1791.[59]

---

[57] The parlements stopped functioning after the summer of 1789 and were formally replaced in the Constitution of 1791. Holders of offices in these courts were, however, compensated.

[58] Goubert, *L'Ancien Régime*, II, 97.

[59] R. Forster, *The House of Saulx-Tavannes: Versailles and Burgundy, 1700-1830*, 137-38.

That a significant proportion of subscribers to a conservative daily had a very real stake in the old regime by ownership of office in institutions of that regime, or made their livings by interpreting or arguing the law of that regime, is to be expected. That a proportion of these subscribers should have accepted positions in the new legal structures put in place by the reforming Assembly is less so. Yet 27, or just over 10 percent of the provincial subscribers to the *Ami du Roi* who practiced law, worked within the new legal system. But unlike their counterparts in the courts of the old regime, Royou's subscribers who held positions in the new legal system do not seem to have belonged to the elite of the legal profession. Only one subscriber, an *avoué au tribunal*, held a position on the national level. There were no provincial subscribers with legal posts in their departmental administrations. Eight had positions in district courts, mostly as lawyers, and twelve had positions within their communes, six as justices of the peace and six as municipal prosecutors (*procureurs de la commune*). The rest for the most part exercised clerical functions in the new courts.

What are we to make of the presence of these members of the legal profession who both subscribed to a conservative paper and played an active role in the institutions that replaced those of the old regime? Their position would be consistent only if they favored the reform and rationalization of state institutions while at the same time wishing to see the fundamental values of both old-regime society and the monarchy retained. As I have suggested above, a demand for significant reform was not incompatible with a broad conservatism in the earlier phases of the Revolution.

As usual, the Paris subscribers are drawn more heavily from the elites than were provincial subscribers. There are, first, no members of the legal profession in the capital who belonged to any of the new tribunals, at any level. Of the 40 men of law in the Paris lists, only eight fall under the category "general." The rest identify themselves with the legal institutions of the old regime. Some 24 owned offices in the greatest law court of the realm, the Parlement of Paris.[60] To these parlementaires should be added the seven members of the courts of special jurisdiction of Paris which were on a level with the sovereign courts: the Châtelet (three), the Grand Conseil (three), and the Cour des Aides (one). Only one Paris subscriber can be classed as belonging to a *bailliage*, and none is below this level.

Those directly involved in government and administration account for 15.31 percent of Royou's subscribers belonging to the liberal professions. If we broaden our definition of administration and include in it most of those engaged in finance and various services, then this figure rises to 37.50 percent.[61] Broadly conceived, then, government and administration are a near second to the closely related legal profession in the subscription lists to the *Ami du Roi*.

Within the narrowly defined category "government and administration" we can again distinguish those who identified themselves with institutions of the old regime from those who worked within the newly established structures. In the provinces 37 subscribers still worked within old-regime agencies. These include 14 members of the king's domestic household, the majority of whom were connected with the stables and the hunt, three ministers of state, two state councillors *(conseillers d'état)*, two members of the foreign ministry and the lieutenant general of police. Reflecting the fading and by now superseded provincial administration are one provincial governor, one subdelegate, one secretary to an intendant and three agents of *élections*.

Twenty-one provincial subscribers held positions in the newly created political and administrative bodies. These include

---

[60] These include six presidents (a quarter of the total number), four councillors and 11 *procureurs*.
[61] All but a few of those engaged in finance and services worked for the national administration. The exceptions are a few concierges, a porter and a fiscal agent *(receveur)* of a seigneurie.

two deputies to the National Assembly, together with one back-up deputy *(suppléant)*, four departmental administrators, six district officials and eight municipal clerks and officers. Those who held positions in the new system, unlike those who identified with the old, tended to be concentrated in the lower levels of that system.

There are also among the provincial subscribers 40 who could not be placed within the administrative framework of either system. These include 14 *conseillers du roi*,[62] ten *commis du roi*, whose titles at least derive from the old regime, and ten mayors. It is impossible to tell from their titles alone whether the mayors derived their authority from before or after the convocation of the Estates General, but in that the "municipal revolution" took place in the summer of 1789 it is likely that the mayors serving after the middle of 1790 had been newly elected.

In Paris only one of the 41 subscribers to Royou's paper classed with government and administration had an indeterminate function. This was a *commis du roi*. All 21 subscribers associated with the new regime were deputies in the National Assembly.[63] Their membership in that body need not, naturally, be taken as support for or acceptance of the new regime. Among the 19 Paris subscribers who had places within old-regime institutions are seven members of the domestic household of the royal family, three ministers, two *conseillers d'état*, one member of the foreign ministry, two *maîtres des requêtes*,[64] two intendants and two agents of *élections*.

---

[62] This title had originally designated those who in fact sat in one of the king's councils, but by the eighteenth century it came to be conferred on a wide range of officials in both the administrative and legal systems. See Marion, *Dictionnaire*, "Conseiller du Roi."

[63] These were Achard de Bonvouloir, Bengy de Puyvallée, Belboeuf, the abbé de la Boissière, d'Eymar of Guadeloupe, Le Fort, the abbé and curé Fournes l'Angenois, de Guilhemery, the curé Guyon of Castelnaudary, d'Hodicq, Labrousse Beauregard, the abbé Landreau, Laporte, Laslier, Le May, the curé Letellier, the abbé Rivière, curé of Vic, Sentez, Thomas, curé of Mormans, the abbé Vaneau and the abbé Yvernault.

[64] *Maîtres des requêtes* were important officials attached to both the Court and the Parlement of Paris. Marion, *Dictionnaire*, "Maîtres des requêtes," and Mousnier, *The Institutions*, II, 140-43.

Between 10 and 15 percent of the members of the liberal professions who subscribed to the *Ami du Roi* were engaged in finance (see Table 6.10). As the assemblies which governed France after 1789 were slower in reforming the tax system than in making sweeping administrative changes, almost all those involved in finance in these lists worked within the fiscal framework of the old regime.

Of the 84 provincial subscribers in this category, 32 had the title *receveur*, their jurisdictions being specified in 24 cases. Twelve were *trésoriers*, six of whom indicated the jurisdictions in which they worked, and 17 were directors of various agencies or jurisdictions. The rest were clerks, administrators, inspectors, *controlleurs* and agents of various financial administrations.

The titles of *trésorier, receveur* and *payeur* normally implied the ownership of venal offices that might cost hundreds of thousands of *livres*.[65] The wealthiest and most powerful of these officials, the *trésoriers généraux*, the *receveurs généraux* and the *fermiers généraux*, were all nobles as well as very rich.[66] Among the provincial subscribers to the *Ami du Roi* were five *receveurs généraux* and six *trésoriers de France*, while the Paris lists show one *receveur général* and three *fermiers généraux*.

Under the old regime "finance" was normally understood to mean state finance. This is reflected in the jurisdictions served by the financial officials among Royou's subscribers. In the provinces 22 officials were involved with indirect taxes, eight in the *aides*, six in the tax farms, six in the *régie*[67] and two in the salt tax. Only two of the provincial subscribers worked with direct taxes, one with the *taille*, the other with the *vingtième*. Of the 25 subscribers managing or working in

---

[65] John F. Bosher, *French Finances, 1770-1795: From Business to Bureaucracy*, 68.
[66] Goubert, *L'Ancien Régime*, II, 151.
[67] The tax farms were contracted out for a set sum, in principle payable in advance by the tax farmer, whose profit consisted in the difference between what he paid for his lease and other expenses and what he was able to collect. In the *régie*, by contrast, the *régisseur* received a set sum from the government for collecting the tax. See Marion, *Dictionnaire*, "Régie."

special jurisdictions, 12 were occupied in the affairs of the royal estates or domaine. Two others held offices at the mint *(monnaie)*, three in the army, two in the Eaux et Forêts, three in the lottery and three in the *enregistrement*. The only fiscal officials who appear to have been connected with the new regime are a customs officer and a district financial official. There is also a single *receveur* of a seigneurie in these lists.

Royou's subscribers engaged in finance appear to have been part of the state fiscal bureaucracy especially concerned with the administration of indirect taxes and special jurisdictions. Like many members of the legal professions, many of those engaged in finance owned their positions or *offices*. They thus had a vested interest in the old regime. Yet at the same time this milieu of high *officiers* was one of the areas in which Enlightenment culture took root and flourished.

The category "services" accounts for just over 9 percent of provincial subscribers to the *Ami du Roi* who were classed as belonging with the liberal professions, and just under 2 percent in Paris (see Table 6.10). This category is completely dominated by officials of the post office who make up 46 of the 58 provincial subscribers in services and both the Parisian ones.[68] The post office was, of course, another government agency. Given the complete dependence of the *Ami du Roi* on the post office for distribution outside Paris, it is virtually certain that these subscriptions represent not interested readers, but necessary business contacts. This would, then, somewhat decrease the importance of the liberal professions in Royou's public.

Only ten subscribers classified with services are unconnected with the post office. Six of them were also part of government bureaucracies, being concerned with the inspection or regulation of trade and commerce, navigation, or

---

[68] These officials were 26 *directeurs des postes*, five *maîtres des postes* and a variety of clerks, controllers, secretaries and *receveurs*. There were, furthermore, two officials of the *messagerie* in this category.

roads. The other four include three *concierges* and a petty official of the Hôtel Dieu of Paris.

There is, finally, the catch-all category "other" in Table 6.10. In fact it includes only two designations, *secrétaire du roi*, of which there are three, and *officier* without further qualification, of which there are 35. The office of *secrétaire du roi* was by the eighteenth century "a title without functions,"[69] and above all a speedy means for very wealthy commoners to acquire noble status. The *officiers* for whom it is impossible to give any function or jurisdiction have been put with the liberal professions and not the army on the assumption that there were more, and more vaguely defined, civil offices than military ones in these years.

In evaluating the character of the readership of the *Ami du Roi* on the basis of its subscription lists, we find a broad measure of agreement between the criteria of status and occupation, with the Paris subscribers generally holding more prestigious positions and showing higher social standing than their provincial counterparts.

The nobility, whether titled or their noble status deduced from function or office, account for 16.85 percent of Royou's provincial subscribers, 24.03 percent of those in the capital. Including clergymen whose standing in the ecclesiastical hierarchy implies noble origins, we have well over 1,000 noble subscribers to the *Ami du Roi*. If we accept the recent estimate of a maximum of 25,000 noble families in France in 1789,[70] then it would seem that one noble family in 25 took Royou's paper. This figure certainly justifies the claim that the *Ami du Roi* appealed to the nobility—provided that this is not taken to mean exclusively to the nobility.

In absolute numbers more clerics than nobles subscribed to Royou's and Madame Fréron's paper. In the provinces the clergy accounted for 22.51 percent of all subscribers, in Paris

---

[69] Marion, *Dictionnaire,* "Secrétaire du roi."
[70] Chaussinand-Nogaret, *The French Nobility,* 30.

17.60 percent. While it is true that the upper levels of the ecclesiastical hierarchy are proportionately better represented than the lower ones, a feature that is also common to all secular institutions or frameworks examined, the clerics of common origins who performed the more humble tasks in the Church still predominate. Certainly the *Ami du Roi* was the paper of the clergy, the more so when one bears in mind the central place of the debate over the Civil Constitution in its editorial policy. But it was not the paper of the clergy alone.

The presence of roughly 60 percent of all subscribers who cannot be identified with either of the privileged orders reminds us that it was possible to be both a commoner and broadly conservative in one's politics. It is true that whatever the institution or enterprise examined we found that the upper levels of that institution were best represented. Military subscribers were almost exclusively commissioned officers, the largest single group in the category of arts and commerce consisted of *négociants,* and in the liberal professions, whether law or administration, more powerful and prestigious institutions were better represented than less important but more numerous ones, and holders of high office are found with disproportionate frequency.

Why should this have been so? An obvious answer is that the better integrated one was into the structures of the old regime, the more one potentially had to lose by the reform or abolition of those structures, and so the more likely one was to be conservative. The nearly universal readiness for significant reform in the early years of the Revolution might require qualification of this explanation, but a more basic objection could be raised on grounds of culture rather than politics. What cultural or economic levels, or combination of these, would have to be achieved before it made sense for a person or a family to subscribe to a paper such as the *Ami du Roi?* Did the image the potential subscriber had of himself in relation to his community play a role here? The great majority of those who indicated an occupation were in some sense community leaders or public figures—ministers of the Church, commanders in the army, magistrates in the legal system, government administrators—and so would naturally have thought it their right to participate in, and be informed about, politics. Though we have seen what kinds of people subscribed to Royou's paper, we have not yet explained why they did so. This question is a complex one, and is perhaps best approached indirectly. We may begin by comparing the public of the *Ami du Roi* with the publics of other papers of the Revolution and other related enterprises.

VII.
Enlightenment and Counter-Revolution

The readership of the *Ami du Roi* as described above was composed almost entirely of the elites of old-regime society. Both the nobility and the clergy are present in disproportionately large numbers in the lists of subscribers to Royou's and Madame Fréron's paper, and this disproportion increases as we move from the provinces to Paris. Members of the third estate who took the *Ami du Roi* held positions or exercised occupations that placed them among the intellectual and economic elites. And we have found that one in five of Royou's subscribers was female. These results, it should be remembered, reflect the readership of the *Ami du Roi* during the first nine months or so of its existence, and before the polarization of opinion that followed the flight to Varennes and the shootings in the Champ-de-Mars.[1] Having gone to the trouble of analyzing the data on the subscribers to the *Ami du Roi*, I am not inclined to belittle the results. But nor do I think that we should be content with the quantitative findings in themselves. One wants to know what they mean and what they imply. To answer these questions it is probably best to begin by comparing the readership of the *Ami du Roi* to the readerships of other journals of the period, and to the audiences of other comparable cultural undertakings.

A. Subscribers to the *Ami du Roi* and Subscribers to Other Journals of the Revolutionary Period

At present there are no figures available for subscriptions to newspapers of either right or left for the period 1789-

---

[1] Despite the importance of these events, it is difficult to imagine the collective character of the subscribers to the *Ami du Roi* changing significantly. The fact remains, however, that we have little or no hard evidence of the readership of the paper from the fall of 1791 on.

1792, so we are unable to compare the immediate readership of Royou's paper to that of other papers of the same period. Given that social and political conditions after 1792 changed in ways that are directly relevant to our study,[2] this is unfortunate. The subscription lists for three right-wing papers dating from 1797 are our closest point of reference, but while only five or six years later than the lists for the *Ami du Roi*, they were produced in significantly different circumstances. A summary of the findings for these papers, as well as for two left-wing ones of the same period, is presented in Table 7.1.[3]

A glance at the following table shows that there was little continuity in the immediate publics of the right-wing press from 1791 to 1797.[4] There are no indications of separate status for subscribers to Popkin's three papers for the simple reason that by 1797 all members of society were deemed to have the same status: that of citizen. An entire dimension of our analysis of the subscribers to the *Ami du Roi* is inapplicable here. In occupational terms, however, where our categories are compatible, there is only one area of obvious continuity, that of the liberal professions. Just over 22 percent of the subscribers to the *Ami du Roi* whose occupations are known were engaged in the liberal professions, while 21 percent of subscribers to the *Tribune publique*, 22 percent of subscribers to "Paper X"[5] and 28 percent of subscribers to the *Gazette française* were similarly employed. This should cause little

---

[2] I refer here not to the establishment of a republic, but to the new legislation and hardening of attitudes that precluded the use of noble titles and sensibly diminished the number of clergymen who were prepared to identify themselves as such.

[3] Popkin, *The Right-Wing Press*, 65. The figures for the *Tribun du peuple* are taken by Popkin from Soboul's article "Personnel sectionnaire et personnel babouviste" and for Lebois's *Ami du peuple* from Max Fajn's article "The Circulation of the French Press."

[4] So as to be compatible with Popkin's figures, those for the *Ami du Roi* are for provincial subscribers only, and given as proportions of subscribers whose occupations are known, not of the total number of subscribers.

[5] Popkin found one subscription list without the name of the paper it belonged to. Hence the designation "Paper X." See *The Right-Wing Press*, 65-66.

Table 7.1: Occupations of Provincial Subscribers to the *Ami Du Roi* Compared to Occupations of Subscribers to Papers of the Directory*

	AR (n = 2417)	RIGHT WING			LEFT WING	
		Paper X (n = 563)	Gaz Fr. (n = 218)	Trib. Pub. (n = 108)	Trib. Peup. (n = 238)	Ami Peup. (n = 103)
Agriculture	0.41%	12%	22%	13%	6%	2%
Commerce	11.05%	24%	19%	14%	28%	34%
Artisans	0.70%	8%	6%	—	9%	15%
Hospitality	0.50%	8%	2%	10%	10%	6%
Government	4.06%	22%	21%	34%	22%	33%
Lib. Profs.	22.42%	22%	28%	21%	16%	8%
Army	13.78%	3%	1%	—	9%	2%
Church	47.08%	—	—	—	—	—
Other	—	1%	1%	8%	—	—
	100.00%	100.00%	100.00%	100.00%	100.00%	100.00%

*An T*546² and ⁵ and Popkin, *The Right-Wing Press*, p. 65.

surprise, as the central role of *officiers* and lawyers in the political life of France has long been recognized.

In all other areas there is no significant correspondence between subscribers to the *Ami du Roi* and the three right-wing papers of the Directory on which we have information. Less than one-half of one percent of Royou's subscribers identified themselves as being engaged in agriculture. The corresponding figures for Popkin's papers are 12, 13 and 22 percent. But there is probably more continuity than meets the eye. It would be natural for wealthy proprietors who identified themselves by their noble status or rank in the army in 1789 to refer to themselves discreetly as "property owners" or "agriculturists" in 1797. Royou's farmers *(laboureurs, fermiers)* were indeed actively engaged in working the land. What proportion of subscribers to the 1797 papers were likewise working farmers and what proportion gentlemen or large proprietors, it is impossible to say.

Taking the categories of "commerce," "artisans" and "hospitality" together, we find that only 12.25 percent of Royou's subscribers belong in this broader category which we earlier referred to as "arts and commerce." Twenty-four percent of subscribers to the *Tribune publique*, 27 percent of those to the *Gazette française* and 40 percent of those to Paper X fit into these categories. The 1797 papers had proportionately more merchants among their immediate readers than did the *Ami du Roi*, but especially noteworthy are the increased numbers of artisans and owners of cafés. The significant increase in the number of artisans taking right-wing newspapers in two of three cases in 1797 seems to suggest increased awareness and politicization, a reasonable hypothesis given the intensity of political life in the intervening years. The even higher proportion of artisans who subscribed to left-wing papers seems to support this notion. No less significant is the higher proportion of papers of both right and left in 1797 taken by coffee houses and similar institutions. Even taking into account collective subscriptions to the *Ami du Roi*, we find the habit of making newspapers available to wider, often casual, audiences had become more widespread in 1797 than it had been six years earlier.

Only 4 percent of Royou's subscribers whose occupations are known held government positions. Of the three rightwing papers whose subscription lists were seized by the police in 1797, none had less than 20 percent of their subscribers so engaged, and one had 34 percent. Moreover, the figures for the two left-wing journals are comparable (see Table 7.1). One would like to have the breakdown of the positions of the 1797 subscribers to these various papers, and to know at what levels and in what capacities they were employed. But even without such precise information, one can reasonably assume that two complementary factors account for the dramatic rise in the category "government" among newspaper subscribers. First, the administrative reforms of the Constituent and Legislative Assemblies, by creating councils and supporting offices at the departmental, district and municipal (or communal) levels, greatly increased the number of government and administrative positions in the country. Second, the habit of reading newspapers seems to have spread further down the social scale in the years between 1791 and 1797, for one suspects that many of the 1797 subscribers were relatively humble local notables serving on municipal councils.[6]

There are only two areas in which the *Ami du Roi* had significantly higher proportions of subscribers than the rightwing papers closed in 1797. The first is the army. While the *Tribune publique* had no military subscribers, the *Gazette française* had 1 percent and Paper X 3 percent, the *Ami du Roi*

---

[6] If this were so it would raise a further question about the usual occupations of these men. A public position enhances prestige, and so is likely to be used as an identifying label. But a city councillor who attended council meetings one evening a month might well be a landowner, merchant, lawyer, doctor, businessman or cleric in his normal daily activities. It would be desirable to know what proportion of those engaged in government had full time positions and what proportion simply served on boards and councils.

had nearly 14 percent. This no doubt reflects the aristocratic nature of the army up to 1791—it will be recalled that nearly all Royou's military subscribers were officers whose ranks implied nobility—and its having undergone a process of republicanization thereafter. This would also explain the relatively high proportion of military subscribers to the left-wing *Tribun du peuple* (9 percent).

The second category in which the *Ami du Roi* had far more subscribers than the papers of 1797 is the clergy. Here the difference is dramatic. Nearly half of Royou's subscribers whose occupations are known were clerics (47 percent), while no known subscribers to the *Gazette française*, the *Tribune publique* or Paper X so identified themselves. That a fall in clerical readership might be expected is arguable, but so complete an eclipse is puzzling. The French clergy played a central role in the Enlightenment, and we have seen that they were active in the early stages of the Revolution. Though many churchmen may have had a difficult time during 1793 and 1794, by the time of the Directory their position was regularized, at least with respect to the state, and there were no formal constraints on their appearing and functioning publicly. Moreover, one would not expect deeply ingrained habits, such as following and commenting on public affairs, to be abandoned in a short period, the more so as newspaper reading was a means of following current events in which clerics, in their capacity as public figures, were more or less directly interested. In short, the fall of the clergy from a dominant position among the subscribers of an important right-wing journal in 1791 to their total elimination from the subscription lists of three right-wing papers six years later is a problem to which I have no solution. By 1807 clerics can again be shown to be subscribing to newspapers, but still not in the numbers we find in the lists of the *Ami du Roi*.[7]

---

[7] The *Feuille nantaise* had only two clerics among its 418 subscribers, and the *Publicateur*, also of Nantes, a more substantial 24 of 213 (11.27 percent) of subscribers whose occupations are known. Jeremy Popkin, "Les Abonnés des journaux nantais en 1807," 386.

The immediate readership of two left-wing journals of the Directory has been analyzed by Albert Soboul and Max Fajn, and conveniently summarized by Jeremy Popkin. The breakdown of the subscribers to Babeuf's *Tribun du peuple* and Lebois's *Ami du peuple* appear in the two columns at the far right of Table 7.1. Popkin rightly comments on the similarity between the readerships of the left- and right-wing papers of the Directory.[8] Though it is possible to discern a higher proportion of subscribers in the broad category "arts and commerce" among the left-wing papers (47 and 55 percent as opposed to between 24 and 40 percent) and though the left-wing papers have a lower proportion of subscribers in the liberal professions (8 and 16 percent as opposed to between 21 and 28 percent) and in agriculture (2 and 6 as opposed to between 12 and 22 percent), the similarities are greater than the differences. Indeed, subscribers of left- and right-wing journals of the Directory have more in common with each other than the right-wing journals have with the *Ami du Roi*. The only obvious exceptions are the category "liberal professions," in which all right-wing papers are remarkably similar, and the separate category of gender. Whereas the *Ami du Roi* had nearly 20 percent female subscribers and the right-wing papers of the Directory between 6 and 9 percent, the *Tribun du peuple* and *Ami du peuple* had none.[9] In any case, it seems clear that in terms of social and occupational composition, there was considerable discontinuity in the immediate readership of the right-wing press between 1790-92 and 1796-97.

---

[8] Popkin, *The Right-Wing Press*, 75.
[9] The complete absence of female subscribers from the lists of left-wing papers is problematic. If we assume the readers of the left-wing press to be of lower social standing than their counterparts on the right, then the suggestion made above of the cultural enfranchisement of men occurring lower down the social scale than that of women would provide a partial explanation.

B. Subscribers to the *Ami du Roi* and to Two Literary Periodicals of the Old Regime

I noted in the opening chapter of this study that subscription lists to old-regime journals are particularly hard to come by. The industry of Daniel Mornet has uncovered one such list, already cited above, that for the *Mercure de France* for 1763, and the revolutionary police, in seizing Madame Fréron's and her brother's papers, inadvertently confiscated an unevenly kept account book for the *Année Littéraire* which contains, among other things, a list of about two hundred recipients of Fréron's journal for 1774-76.[10] The records of the *Mercure* include a total of about 1,500 copies, but refer to only 756 subscribers by name, the rest going to booksellers and vendors. The fragmentary records of the *Année Littéraire* give the names of 169 subscribers at a time the press runs of the paper can reasonably be estimated at 1,500 copies.[11]

Despite certain inconsistencies in the data on subscribers and the way they were compiled and analyzed, it is clear that the readership of the *Ami du Roi* has far more in common with the literary periodicals of the old regime than it did with the political papers of the Directory. The importance of nobles and clerics as well as the larger proportions of female subscribers in the subscription lists of the old-regime journals recalls the pattern of subscription to the *Ami du Roi*. But before being able properly to compare the subscribers to Royou's paper to those of the *Année Littéraire* and *Mercure* it is necessary briefly to discuss the data on which our information is based.

Table 7.2 summarizes what is known of the status and

---

[10] Mornet, "L'Intérêt historique"; AN T*546¹.

[11] We have seen above that the *Année Littéraire* was printing 2,000 copies or more during the 1760s. In 1778 its press run was 1,250 copies, and in the following two years its subscriptions fell below 1,000 (AN T*546¹). The estimate of 1,500 is simply the mean between the two.

Table 7.2:   The Status, Occupations and Gender of All Subscribers
to the *Ami Du Roi* and Two Old-Regime Periodicals*

	AR (1790/91) (n = 5883)	Année Lit. (1774/76) (n = 169)	Mercure (1763) (n = 756)
Agriculture	0.18%	—	—
Commerce Artisans	5.46%	8.28%	5.82%
Hospitality Gov't. Admin.	2.49%	—	—
"Fonctionnaires"	—	—	25.00%
Lib. Profs.	10.48%	16.59%	12.04%
Army	6.20%	2.37%	—
Church	22.10%	17.16%	6.48%
Nobility	13.43%	?0.12%	26.46%(?)
Women	18.50%	18.93%	15.48%
Other	—	2.96%	—

*AN T*546[1,2,3,5] and Mornet, "L'Intérêt historique."

occupations of subscribers to the *Ami du Roi,* the *Mercure* and the *Année Littéraire.* It should be noted, first, that the figures in Table 7.2 are not discrete, but allow for multiple entries for the same individual under categories of gender, status and occupation. In this Table 7.2 differs from Table 7.1, which gives percentages in terms of subscribers whose occupations are known, and whose figures are discrete, the category of gender excepted. More important than this formal difference is the geographical weighting of the readerships of the papers in question. All subscribers to the papers studied by Popkin were provincials. More than 90 percent of the total number of known subscribers to Royou's paper were also provincials. By contrast, 62.17 percent of the *Mercure's* subscription lists and 74.56 percent of the *Année Littéraire's* were drawn from the capital. In light of the differences in status and gender in the Parisian and provincial subscribers to the *Ami du Roi* noted above, the significance of the geographical origins of subscribers is clear. The figures for noble and female subscribers to the *Ami du Roi* would have been higher had more than 9 percent of the total been from the capital, the figure for clerics lower.

Even without taking the geographical origin of subscribers into account, it is obvious that the readership of the *Ami du Roi* belongs to the model of readership of the literary periodicals of the old regime. But there is one major divergence in the patterns of readership of the three journals in question. The *Année Littéraire* shows no subscribers in the category government and administration; the *Ami du Roi* has 2.49 percent; but the *Mercure*, under the analogous category "fonctionnaires" has a full 25 percent.

Most historians of the old regime prefer to distinguish *officiers*, who owned their positions, from *commissaires*, who served at the king's pleasure. The term "fonctionnaire" is not much used to describe government officials before Napoleon. To complicate matters further, Mornet used the term loosely to include "functionaries of the State, or functionaries in the service of provinces, princes, etc."[12] This "etc." can reasonably be taken to include towns as well as provinces and important noble households as well as princely establishments. In that case the "functionaries" in question would include stewards, secretaries, librarians, readers and historiographers, and possibly chaplains. While there are no grounds for assuming that members of the royal administration are lacking among the 1763 subscribers to the *Mercure*, it is likely that had the categories of classification used for the *Ami du Roi* and *Année Littéraire* been applied to the *Mercure*, the category "government and administration" would have been significantly smaller, and other categories, especially "liberal professions" but also perhaps "army" and "church," somewhat larger. In other categories the similarities are clear enough.

Agriculture, which accounts for one-fifth of one percent of subscribers to the *Ami du Roi*, is not represented among

---

[12] Mornet, "L'Intérêt historique," 121.

subscribers to either the *Mercure* or *Année Littéraire*. The category "arts and commerce" accounts for between 5 and 8 percent of subscribers to the three journals, and in the cases of the *Ami du Roi* and *Année Littéraire*, this category is composed almost exclusively of those commercially interested in the papers and the elites of the commercial community.[13]

Members of the liberal professions account for between 10 and 17 percent of subscribers of all three papers, the *Année Littéraire* being particularly well represented in this category.[14] The larger role of the army in the *Ami du Roi* as compared to the old-regime journals is likely the result of the conditions obtaining in 1790-91. On the other hand, it is unlikely that no army officers subscribed to the *Mercure*. Rather it seems that Mornet has classed nobles only once, as nobles, and has not given their occupations, even if they were noted. This would also help explain the very high proportion of titled nobles among the subscribers to the *Mercure*,[15] though the readership of this paper may well have been aristocratic.

Just over 20 percent of the subscribers to the *Année Littéraire* were titled nobles, a figure that is broadly comparable to that for the *Mercure*. In the case of Royou's paper 13.43 percent of subscribers overall, but 20.81 percent of Parisian subscribers, were titled nobles. Thus the political and intensely royalist *Ami du Roi* appears to have had a somewhat lower proportion of noble subscribers than the literary periodicals of the last decades of the old regime. This suggests that the aristocracy transferred its interest in the literary journals of the old regime to the political dailies of the early Revolution

---

[13] The breakdown for the *Ami du Roi* has been given above. Fourteen of the subscribers to the *Année Littéraire* were classified as belonging to arts and commerce. They include eight booksellers, one *marchand cafetier*, three wholesale merchants (*négociants*) and two bankers. AN T*546¹.

[14] If we bear in mind that these figures are for the entire sample and those in Table 7.1 for subscribers whose occupations are known, the liberal professions seem to provide an element of overall continuity.

[15] Mornet states that "there were not 200 titled nobles" among the subscribers to the *Mercure* ("L'Intérêt historique," 121). By this I take him to mean that there were just under 200, or about 25 percent.

in roughly the same proportions as the rest of the reading public, and not that it suddenly developed an interest in newspapers during the early stages of the Revolution.

After noting that the *Mercure* had 81 female subscribers in Paris and 36 in the provinces (together 15.48 percent of subscribers), Daniel Mornet observed that "The *Mercure* was the women's journal."[16] This statement may have in part reflected the *Mercure*'s reputation for frivolity and a prejudice that therefore caused it to be seen as suitable for women. The thoroughly serious *Année Littéraire*, which after Fréron's death was competently managed by his widow, had nearly 19 percent female subscribers. And though a political daily, the *Ami du Roi* had about the same proportion of female subscribers overall, and 23.39 percent in Paris. This is strong evidence against the frivolity of a female readership and suggests that a significant female presence was an integral part of the readership of the serious periodical press at the end of the old regime and during the early years of the Revolution. To judge by the figures for the Directory, it appears that women played a considerably smaller part in the immediate readership of the periodical press than they had done five or ten years earlier. But if what has already been said about the correlation between female readership and high social standing is correct, then the figures for the Directory may well reflect a less aristocratic readership rather than a decline in women's interest in politics.

The clergy of course played an important role in all aspects of the world of letters at the end of the old regime. During the 1770s, 17.16 percent of the subscribers to the serious *Année Littéraire* were churchmen. Thus the 22.10 percent of clerics among Royou's total subscribers (17.60 percent among his Parisian subscribers) can be seen as the continuation of a pattern established under the old regime rather than the sudden politicization of the clergy. The relatively low figure

---

[16] Mornet, "L'Intérêt historique," 121.

of 6.48 percent clerics among the subscribers to the *Mercure*
may reflect the reluctance of clergymen to take what was
regarded as a frivolous publication.

Certainly in other areas of cultural activity the clergy, and
with them the nobility, maintained their participation at levels
they attained as readers of the periodical press. Of purchasers
of the quarto *Encyclopédie* in Besançon, 15 percent were clerics
and 20-25 percent were noble. Female subscribers, however,
were lacking.[17] At an admittedly more elevated level, we find
that roughly 20 percent of provincial academicians over the
eighteenth century were churchmen, double that number
nobles.[18] It thus appears that the social and professional composition of the subscribers to Royou's *Ami du Roi* is typical of
the readership of literary periodicals of the last decades of
the old regime, and indeed of that part of the enlightened
community about which we are best informed.[19] And if this

---

[17] Darnton, *The Business of Enlightenment*, 290-94. Darnton here bases himself on the
list of subscribers published by John Lough in his *Essays on the Encyclopédie of
Diderot and d'Alembert*, 466-73.

[18] D. Roche, *Le Siècle des lumières en province: Académies et académiciens provinciaux,
1680-1789*.

[19] It is generally true in historical studies, at least up to this century, that we are
better informed about elites than about the masses. It is probably fair to say that
within elite groups more information is available on the wealthier and more
powerful members of the group than on the more modest ones. "Enlightened
community" is a cultural term that designates those who shared an enlightened
outlook (for a discussion of this point, see my *Limits of Reform*, 5-6 and 33). The
most prominent members of this community belonged to social elites, but such
elites did not make up the whole or even the greater part of this community. A
mentality or outlook implies a set of material conditions that support it. Obvious
outward signs of this condition are a measure of economic independence and the
ability to subscribe to periodicals or to purchase sets of the *Encyclopédie*. But if we
restrict our definition of the enlightened community to those who were able to
make financial commitments of this order—that is, those whose involvement in
this community is documented, whether as subscribers to periodicals or purchasers of certain works—we distort it. The enlightened community then appears
both smaller and grander than it was. It is, instead, rather like an iceberg, one-
tenth of which is visible, nine-tenths submerged. We saw above that Delisle de
Sales estimated that for each subscriber to a journal, there were ten readers. It
is no doubt right to insist on the social composition of the subscribers to the
periodical press, but this does not justify ignoring the existence of a broader
readership which came by these same papers at friends' houses, in cafés, in reading
rooms or elsewhere. The problem is identifying the nine-tenths of the enlightened

is so, it raises a question of broad significance, namely, the relationship between the Enlightenment and the Revolution.

C. From Enlightenment to Counter-Revolution

It would be prudent to reformulate the preceding question more precisely. What we are dealing with is several examples of the social basis of the Enlightenment. I have attempted to show that the readership of the *Ami du Roi* was fundamentally similar to that of literary periodicals of the old regime, or, for that matter, of the *Encyclopédie*. I have also tried to show that initially the outlook of the *Ami du Roi* was not altogether hostile to the Revolution. It became so, predictably, with the extension of legislation beyond the fairly moderate reforms acceptable to enlightened opinion, the failure to reach an agreed ecclesiastical settlement, the flight of the king and the threat of continued direct popular action. This was a response not only to vested interests, but also to deeply held convictions.

I have argued elsewhere that while the chief spokesmen of the Enlightenment were secular, progressive and humanitarian in outlook, they were not revolutionary. Rather, they were reformers who sought to work within the existing system.[20] I do not wish to minimize the importance of the legal, administrative and economic reforms that Voltaire, Turgot, Holbach and others advocated or helped to implement, or

---

community that remain submerged, not as a result of the weight of those above them, but simply for the lack of documentary evidence. We do not know how this shadowy 60 to 90 percent of the enlightened community which lies between the elites and the people, or more precisely the upper levels of the artisanat, very well. But failing the discovery and analysis of lists of those who frequented reading rooms or similar evidence, a careful reading of memoirs and autobiographies may yet cast some light on this question. In the meantime, it is unwise to treat the lower levels of the enlightened community as if they did not exist simply because we are inadequately informed about them.

[20] *The Limits of Reform*, 266-70.

the passion with which they fought for them. Yet the sum of these reforms, achieved and projected, was insufficient to transform the society of the old regime. The agenda of practical social and economic thinkers in the eighteenth century was to improve the society of the old regime, and to make it more equitable and comfortable. They sought to improve and reform the existing order, not to overthrow it. There were, to be sure, utopian thinkers at the time who described societies which functioned on radically different principles. But it is questionable whether even these thinkers sought or would have desired the wholesale implementation of their projects.

On the whole, the men and women of the enlightened community, from the great *philosophes* to second- and third-rate writers, purchasers of the *Encyclopédie* and members of the public who paid a few *sous* for entry to a reading room, were devoted to order. In practical terms they accepted the monarchy, the church and society of the old regime, at the same time calling for, or remaining open to, the orderly improvement of some or all of these institutions. They wanted their kings to be enlightened and their societies reformed. But they did not distinguish enlightened monarchs from enlightened despots, and such changes as they desired, they wished to see gradually and carefully effected from above. Probably the limit of mainstream enlightened political opinion was a settlement along the lines of the Glorious Revolution of 1688, a settlement that resulted in a limited constitutional monarchy, but otherwise largely left social, administrative and ecclesiastical structures intact. When it became clear that the changes being made in France went far beyond the constitutional sphere and called the fundamental institutions and structures of the old regime into question, many men and women of the enlightened community withdrew their support or went into opposition.

The response of the *Gazette de Leyde* to the Revolution is a case in point. According to Jeremy Popkin, "The *Gazette de*

Leyde had done much to expose the weakness of the old order and set the Revolution in motion."[21] In its political outlook, the paper was constitutionalist, which is to say that it adhered to the principle of fundamental law and tended to support the parlements against what it perceived as the threat of royal despotism. For the *Gazette de Leyde* the "essential issue" in French politics was "freedom and the right of participation in government."[22] These are views that can fairly be identified with prominent Enlightenment values. Moreover, the paper supported the Americans in their nationalist uprising (as Edmund Burke had done) and welcomed the convocation of the Estates General.[23] Like many Enlightenment figures, the editors of the *Gazette de Leyde* questioned the political competence of the common people and feared popular violence and radicalism. Though relieved at the outcome of the taking of the Bastille, they were concerned by the role of the crowd and the intrusion of popular violence into politics.[24] The *Gazette de Leyde* had opposed radicalism before 1789, and continued to do so thereafter.[25] The political current with which it identified was that of the liberal aristocratic monarchiens (Mounier, Lally-Tollendal, Clermont-Tonnerre) who favored a settlement along the lines of the English model. This is the same political grouping and program initially supported by Royou and the *Ami du Roi*. If, then, the *Gazette de Leyde* can fairly be identified with the Enlightenment, this would call for qualification of the view that "the" Enlightenment directly contributed to, or was a direct cause of, "the" Revolution. The *Gazette de Leyde* was comfortable only with the first stage of the Revolution that lasted through the summer of 1789. However, "By the fall of 1789, when its hero Mounier fled

---

[21] Jeremy Popkin, "The *Gazette de Leyde* under Louis XVI," 76.
[22] Ibid., 90.
[23] Ibid., 79 and 113.
[24] Ibid., 125-26.
[25] Ibid., 79, 86-87 and 124.

the country, the paper was convinced that no good could come of the National Assembly."[26]

I suggested above that the history of the *Ami du Roi* could not well be understood if approached on the assumption that the Revolution was a unified and coherent whole.[27] This proposition is, I think, self-evident if applied to the cultural orientations and interests of the different socioeconomic groups that played a role in the Revolution at different levels and at different stages. Broadly speaking, it seems fair to say that peasants who searched out *terriers* and burned châteaux in the summer of 1789 and artisans and shopkeepers who formed the backbone of the sans-culotte movement had not been introduced to, and did not share, the outlook and values of the Enlightenment. They were, on the whole, concerned with matters of immediate significance, such as the grain supply and taxation, and remained largely unmoved by more general issues such as constitutional reform and personal liberty. By contrast, monarchiens, Feuillants, Girondins and Montagnards can all reasonably be presumed to have had some familiarity with, and indeed to have used, the categories of thought put forward and popularized by the thinkers and publicists of the Enlightenment.

The relationship of the Enlightenment to the Revolution and Counter-Revolution can be examined on a number of levels. One is that of ideology. Another concerns the social bases of these movements. A third addresses itself to methods and agents of the diffusion of ideas. Study of the book trade and of readership has not proceeded far enough to allow us to come to any firm conclusions on this question. Occasionally, however, instances come to light that have some bearing on the issue. We have seen above that the bookseller Bergeret of Bordeaux carried on an extensive correspondence with the offices of the *Ami du Roi*, and that he was a good customer

---

[26] Ibid., 127.
[27] See above, Introduction, 5.

both of the paper and the pamphlets that Madame Fréron and the abbé Royou published. Robert Darnton has found that before 1789 Bergeret was a customer of the Société Typographique of Neuchâtel, and that he ordered from them "hard-core philosophical books" which he required be shipped in concealed form.[28] It is not possible, of course, to generalize from a single case, but it is nevertheless suggestive that the same bookseller was willing to handle books such as *Thérèse Philosophe* and papal briefs. Apparently Bergeret saw no reason why he should not sell both the more daring literature associated with the Enlightenment and conservative political as well as religiously orthodox publications. Perhaps the pursuit of gain is a great leveler, and the businesses of publishing and bookselling should be seen as just that: business. In the case of Bergeret, the channels through which even radical Enlightenment literature moved were also the channels through which publications that can reasonably be associated with the Counter-Revolution found their way.

I do not think it possible on the evidence adduced here to argue conclusively that the Enlightenment led directly to Counter-Revolution. What has been shown is that there was considerable overlap in the social basis of the Enlightenment on the one hand, and the Counter-Revolution on the other. Jeremy Popkin showed some time ago that most right-wing journalists during 1794-97 had been receptive to Enlightenment ideas and values before the Revolution.[29] The implication seems to be that the broad intellectual movement we know as the Enlightenment fed into the counter-revolutionary thought of the earlier phases of the Revolution as much as it contributed to the Revolution. This is a departure from the traditional view that emphasizes the continuity between

---

[28] Robert Darnton, "Philosophy Under the Cloak," in Robert Darnton and Daniel Roche, eds. *Revolution in Print: The Press in France*, 1775-1800 (Berkeley and Los Angeles, 1989), 46. See also ibid, 39.

[29] J. Popkin, *The Right-Wing Press*, chaps. 5 and 6.

the Enlightenment and the Revolution. But the relationship
between these two forces is sufficiently complex, problematic
and important to merit a study in its own right.

Appendix 1: The Contract Founding
the Ami du Roi*

31 Aoust 1790

Dépôt D'acte de Société, Entre Mde. fréron et autres

Aujourd'huy Est Comparu Pardevant les Conseillers du Roy notaires au Chatelet de Paris Soussignes.

M. felix Louis Christoph Ventre Dela touloubre Montjoie, fondateur et Redacteur et Propriétaire du Journal, intitulé L'ami du Roy, demeurant à Paris Rue des postes place de lestrapade paroisse Saint Benoist

Lequel a deposé pour minute a Me. DeCaux L'un des notaires à Paris Soussignés, et L'a Requis de mettre au Rang de Ses minute a la datte de ce jour Le Quintuple d'un acte de Société, fait entre Led. Sieur Montjoie Comparant; De. anne françoise Royou Veuve de Sieur Elie Catherine freron, membre de plusieurs accademies; S. Joseph henry alexandre Poujade de la devize, Prêtre, S. Jean Baptiste Nicolas Crapart imprimeur Libraire à Paris Et S. Pierre Cezar Briand, aussi Libraire à Paris; pour La Redaction d'un nouveau Journal Sous le titre de l ami du Roy, des français, de l'ordre et Surtout de la Verité, avec cette epigraphe, *pro, deo, Rege et Patria*. Le dit acte fait entre les dits Susnommés Sous signature privée Le Dix Sept May mil Sept cent quatrevingt dix. L'original duquel Quintuple d'acte de Société, Controlle à Paris Par Lecau Le trente aoust présent mois est demeuré Cy joint après avoir été dudit Sieur Montjoye Comparant, Certiffié veritable Signé et paraphé en présence desdits notaires Soussignés.

Dont acte Requis, fait et Passé à Paris esEtudes L'an mil Sept cent quatrevingt dix Le trente un Aoust et a ledit Sieur Comparant Signé.

[signed] Montjoy
Le Caux
[illegible]

[Text of Contract]

Les Soussignés anne françoise Royou, veuve du Sieur Elie catherine fréron, membre de plusieurs accademies, joseph hanry alexandre pouyade, de ladeveze et félix louis, christophe ventre de la touloubre montjoye, d'une part

et jean, batiste, nicolas, crapart imprimeur libraire, et pierre cézar, briant, libraire d'autre part

en Conséquance du projet par eux concu de publier un nouveau journal Sous le titre de L'ami du Roy, des françois, de l'ordre et Sur tout de la varité avec cette épigraphe *pro, deo, Rege et patria.* ont arrête ce qui Suit Savoir

primo que la propriété du dit journal Sera divisé en deux part dont l'une appartiendra à madame fréron et aux Sieurs advise et montjoye, et L'autre aux Sieurs crapart et briand.

2° que les dits mde fréron et Sieurs de la devisse et Montjoye serront chargés de la Rédaction du dit journal et répondront personellement de tout ce qui Sera insére dans ici lui portant la Signature de l'un d'eux

3° qu'il Sera payé aux Susnomés Rédacteurs la Somme de sept mille huit cent livres pour la rédaction ainsi qu'il suit: Savoir cinquante livres à mde fréron, même Sommes à mr de ladevissse et même Somme à mr de montjoye par chaques Semaines Sur la quittance de chaqu'un d'eux

4° Que les Sieurs crapart et briant Se chargeront de faire tous les frais nécessaires pour l'impression, papier et exploitation du prospectus, des numéros du dit journal qui paroitera tous les matins aussi que de payer la rédaction Si dessus Sans pouvoir par eux en Cas de non Succès du dit journal prétendre à aucuns remboursements ou indemnité tant pour raison des dit frais de publication que de Ceux de rédaction.

5° Si les frais ci dessus, et notamment Ceux du prospectus rentrés entierement par l'évenement du nombre des Souscripteurs il y a lieu à mi bénéfice quelconque les Sieurs crapart et briand, préleverront Sur yscelui avant tout partage une Somme de Sept mille huit cent livres à eux alloués pour les frais de bureau et dédomagement de leur Soins et avances en suite ce qui restera de bénéfice Se partagera par moitié entre les dit dame fréron et Sieurs de ladvisse et montjoye, et Crapart et briant de l'autre part

6° les dit Sieurs crapart et briant Seront tenus de présenter à chaque trimestre un etat de leur recette et de leur dépense.

7° *dans la dépense* entreront les frais d'impressions de papier, distribution, port, affranchissement et autres choses généralement quelconq nécessaires à l'exploitation.

8° on Suivra pour la manufacture quelconq du dit journal les Cours ordinaires des travaux de chaques espece ou marchandise et le Compte S'en fera Sans discussions d'après les quittances des fabriquants ou fournisseurs même proprietaires

9° il Sera libre a chaquun des cooassociés de Cédér Sa part à La propriété du dit journal ou d'y renoncer ce qui ne pourra avoir lieux qu'a l'expiration de chaque trimestre.

10° le journal sera absolument conforme tant pour la rédaction que pour la partie tipografique et le prix de l'abonement aux Conditions énoncés dans le prospectus qui Sera Signé et parafé par chaqu'un des contractans ci dessus nomès et le quel prospectus aussi Signé et parafé demeurra annexeè au present acte dont chaque contractans aura une Copie.

11° tous les frais résultans de l'échange du présent journal Contre d'autres journaux francois ou étrangers Seront à la charge de la Société

12° chaqu'un des cinq Contractans ci dessus nomès pourra disposer des douze exemplaires aux frais de la Société.

13° le prix des Sept mille huit cent livres pour la rédaction est fixé irrévoquablement à cette Somme et les rédacteurs ne pourront Sous au qu'un prètexte demander une augmentation.

14° les livres et estampes qui Seront adressés pour etre annoncés au dit journal appartiendront aux Susdit rédacteurs

15° dans les cas ou il Surviendrait quelques difficultés Sur le présent acte, les parties S'en rapporteron à des arbitres choisies et agrée par la Société

fait quintuple à paris ce 17 mai 1790

> [signed] Royou fréron
> Crapart
> Briand
> Montjoye
> De Ladeveze

> [signed] Royou fréron

Conqué a paris le 30 aoust 1790
Recu six livres quinze sols

[signed] Lerand

Certiffié veritable Signé et Paraphé en presence des notaires a Paris Soussignés et deposé pour minute a Mr. DeCaux L'un deux par acte de cejourdhuy trente un aoust mil sept cent quatrevignt dix.

[signed] Montjoye
LeCaux
[illegible]

---

*Source: Minutier Central, LXIV[495]. The original orthography and punctuation have been retained.

Appendix 2: Classification of Subscribers to the Ami du Roi as Coded for the Computer

Column	Size Field	Category	Name	Code
1	1	List	AR–Prov.	1
			AR–Paris and prov.	2
			AR–Paris and prov.	3
2–5	4	Subscriber Number		0001
6–7	2	Particle	None	01
			De or D'	22
			De la/Du	44
			Des	66
8–9	2	Gender	Male	11
			Female Unspecified	22
			Mlle.	24
			Mme.	26
			Veuve	28
			Religieuse	32
			Collective	40
			Clubs Literary-Political	41
			Military	42
			National Guard	43
			Municipality	44
			Convent—Male	51
			Convent—Female	52
			Seminary	53
			Collège	54
10–11	2	Geography (Routes)	Amiens	01
			Bordeaux	02
			Bourbonnais	03
			Bourgogne	04
			Bretagne	05
			Châlons-Strasbourg	06
			Chartres	07
			Forbonnais-Vivarais-Dauphiné	08
			Orléans	09
			Provence-Roussillon-Languedoc	10
			Reims	11
			Rouen	12

Column	Size Field	Category	Name	Code
			Saint Quentin	13
			Toulouse	14
			Troyes	15
			Variable	16
			Etranger	17
			Normandy	18
			Champagne	19
			Unknown	22
		Geography	Abbeville	30
		(Towns)	Amiens	32
			Angers	33
			Angoulême	34
			Arles	35
			Arras	36
			Avignon	37
			Besançon	38
			Bordeaux	39
			Bourges	40
			Brest	41
			Caen	42
			Cambrai	43
			Clermont-Ferrand	44
			Dieppe	45
			Dijon	46
			Douai	47
			Dunkerque	48
			Grenoble	49
			La Rochelle	50
			Laval	51
			Le Mans	52
			Lille	53
			Limoges	54
			Lorient	55
			Lyon	56
			Marseille	57
			Metz	58
			Montauban	59
			Montpellier	60
			Nancy	61
			Nantes	62
			Nice	63
			Nîmes	64
			Niort	65
			Orléans	66
			Poitiers	67
			Reims	68
			Rennes	69
			Rouen	70
			Saint Etienne	71
			Saint Omer	72

Column	Size Field	Category	Name	Code
			Strasbourg	73
			Toulon	74
			Toulouse	75
			Tours	76
			Troyes	77
			Valenciennes	78
			à sa terre	86
			en son château	87
			au château de	91
			small town/village	88
			étranger	90
			Versailles	98
			Paris	99
12–14	3	Status, Title	*Clergy*	111
		Institution	Abbé (wfc)	101
			Abbé (title)	102
			Prêtre	103
			Bénéficier	104
			Prébendier	105
			Student—Seminary	106
			Bach./ Theology	107
			Dr./ Theology	108
			Père	113
			Rev. Père	114
			Dom.	115
			Religieux	116
			Religieuse	117
			Chanoine Regulier	118
			Doyen (Head of Chapter)	119
			Nobility (unspecified)	222
			King	201
			Prince	202
			Duke	203
			Marquis	204
			Count	205
			Baron	206
			Chevalier	207
			Ecuyer	208
			Vicomte	209
			Chev. St. Louis	231
			Chev. St. Michel	232
			Chev. St. Esprit	233
			Chev. Ord. Roi	234
			Gentilhomme	240

Column	Size Field	Category	Name	Code
			Seigneur	241
			Noble—Foreign	242
			English	243
			Italian	244
			German	245
			Spanish	246
			German	247
			Russian	248
			American (non-noble)	249
			Douairière	250
			Pensionnaire du Roi	251
			Châtelain	255
			Presumed Noble	322
			Third	
			Undetermined	333
			Bourgeois	301
			Citoyen	302
			Citoyen Actif	303
			Electeur	304
			Notable	305
			Rentier	308
			Pensionnaire	309
			Docteur de la Université	311
			Nationality: Third	
			English	330
			Finance	700
			Taille	750
			Vingtième	751
			Domaine	752
			Monnaie	753
			Régie	754
			Army	755
			Navy	756
			Church	757
			Fermes	760
			Aides	761
			Gabelles	762
			Tabac	763
			Traites	764
			Vivres	765
			Subsistances	766
			Eaux et Forêts	767
			Entrées	768

Column	Size Field	Category	Name	Code
			Consignations	769
			Town	770
			Lottery	771
			Registration	772
			Marque D'Or	773
			Seigneurie	775
			Revolution—unspecified	780
			Douanes Nationales	781
			Département	783
			District	785
			Municipality	790
15–17	3	Function	*Clergy*	111
			Secular-Upper	100
			Cardinal	101
			Archbishop	102
			Bishop	103
			Grand Vicaire (Vicaire Gen)	104
			Archiprêtre	105
			Archidiacre	106
			Chanoine	112
			Chanoine honoraire	124
			Chantre	113
			Chancelier	114
			Ecolatre	115
			(= Capiscol)	116
			Pénitencier	117
			Théologal	118
			Custode	119
			Prévôt Cath.	120
			Chapelain/Aumonier— maison du roi	121
			Chapelain/Aumonier— great house	122
			Chanoine honoraire	124
			Sacristain	125
			Missionaire	127
			Secular—Lower	130
			Doyen (rural)	131
			Curé	132
			Prieur-Curé	133
			Vicaire	134
			Diacre	135
			Aumonier	136

Column	Size Field	Category	Name	Code
			Chapelain	137
			Regular	140
			Augustin	141
			Bénédictin	142
			Capuchin	143
			Carmes	144
			Chartreux	145
			Cordelier	146
			Doctrinaire	147
			Jacobin	148
			Jésuite	149
			Minimes	150
			Oratorien	151
			Recollet	152
			Dominicain	153
			Malte	160
			Carmelite	170
			Saint Cyr	171
			Ursaline	172
			Soeurs de la charité	193
			Abbé	173
			Prieur	174
			Supérieur/Director	175
			Seminary	176
			Convent—Male	177
			Convent—Female	178
			Mission	179
			Charitable Institution	180
			Cellerier	181
			(=Econome)	
			Nonce Apostolique	190
			Nobility	222
			Maison du Roi	201
			Domestic	202
			Bouche	203
			Chambre	204
			Ecurie	205
			Vénerie	206
			Logement	207
			Military	210
			Gardes du Corps	211
			Gendarmes	212
			Chevau Legers	213
			Mousquetaires	214
			Gendarmerie	215
			Gardes Français	216

Column	Size Field	Category	Name	Code
			Other	217
			Army	230
			Bas Officiers	231
			Caporal	232
			Sergent	233
			Maréchal de Logis	234
			Officiers Particuliers	235
			Cornette	236
			Enseigne	237
			Sous Lieutenant	238
			Lieutenant en 2	239
			en 1	240
			Capitaine en 2	241
			en 1	242
			(=chef d'escadron)	
			Off. Supérieurs	243
			Majeur	244
			Lieutenant Colonel	245
			(=Mestre de Camp)	246
			Colonel	247
			(=Chef de Régiment)	
			Officiers Généraux	248
			Lieutenant Général	249
			Capitaine Général	250
			Maréchal	251
			(de Camp)	
			Maréchal Général	252
			Officer and Unit	255
			Chirurgien major	258
			Navy	260
			Admiral	261
			Vice Admiral	262
			Lieutenant Général	263
			Chef d'Escadre	264
			Capitaine/Vais/Roi	265
			Lieutenant/Vais/Roi	266
			Officier de la Marine	267
			Major/Vais/Roi	268
			Paramilitary	270
			Maréchaussée	271

Column	Size Field	Category	Name	Code
			Inspecteur Gen.	272
			Prévôt Gen.	273
			Lieutenant	274
			Sous Lieutenant	275
			Maréchal de Logis	276
			Brigadier	277
			Cavalier	278
			Commandant	279
			Garde Nationale	280
			Commandant	281
			Officier	282
			Sergeant	283
			Military—Administration	290
			Commis des Guerres	291
			Commis des fontes d'artillerie	292
			Commissaire de la Marine	295
			Military Engineer	299
			Third	333
			Capitaine de vaisseaux	301
			Businessman	302
			Homme d'affaires	303
			Homme d'affaires (agent)	304
			Agriculture	311
			Fermier	312
			Laboureur	313
			Métayer	314
			Manouvrier/Journalier	315
			Other	316
			Arts et Métiers, Commerce	340
			Financier	341
			Banquier	342
			Négociant	343
			Marchand en gros	344
			Marchand Fabriquant	345
			Fabriquant	346
			Ouvrier	347

Column	Size Field	Category	Name	Code
			Employé	348
			shop	349
			clerical	359
			Marchand	350
			manufacturing	351
			food	352
			textiles	353
			woodwork	354
			luxuries	555
			metalwork	356
			building	357
			other	358
			Maître	360
			manufacturing	361
			food	362
			textiles	363
			wood	364
			luxuries	365
			metal	366
			building	367
			other	368
			Artisan—independent	370
			manufacturing	371
			food	372
			textiles	373
			wood	374
			luxuries	375
			metal	376
			building	377
			other	378
			Artisan-Comp./Apprent.	380
			manufacturing	381
			food	382
			textiles	383
			wood	384
			luxuries	385
			metal	386
			building	387
			other	388
			Publishing & Bookselling	390
			Libraire	391
			Imprimeur	392
			Imprimeur-Libraire	393
			Hospitality	394
			Aubergiste	395

Column	Size Field	Category	Name	Code
			Cafetier	396
			Limonadier	397
			Marchand de vin	398
			Liquoriste	399
			Liberal Professions	400
			Misc.	401
			Secrétaire	403
			Medicine	410
			Médecin	411
			(= Dr. en med.)	
			Chirurgien	412
			Apothicaire	413
			Me./Pharmacie	414
			Dr./Med. (degree)	415
			Régent	416
			Sage femme	417
			Law	420
			Avocat	421
			Notaire	422
			Notaire Royal	423
			Homme De Loi	424
			Feudiste	425
			Dr. Loix (degree)	426
			Procureur	427
			Procureur Syndic	428
			Commissionaire	429
			Applied Science	430
			Architect	431
			Engineer	432
			Clerical	440
			Greffier	441
			Huissier	442
			Archiviste—private	443
			institution	444
			Bibliothécaire—private	445
			institution	446
			Secrétaire—institution	447
			official	448
			private individual	449
			club	450
			évêché	451
			Bibliothécaire	455
			Journalist	457
			Education	460

Column	Size Field	Category	Name	Code
			University	461
			Recteur	462
			Principal.	463
			Professeur	464
			Administrateur	465
			Collège	471
			Principal	472
			Professeur	473
			Administrateur	475
			Séminaire (professeur)	477
			Maître de Pension	481
			Tutor	482
			Me./Ecole	483
			Régent	484
			Professeur	486
			Ecole Militaire	488
			Student	490
			Law	491
			Medicine	492
			Theology	493
			Collège	494
			Degree Holder	495
			Administration & Justice	500
			Indefinite	501
			Commis	502
			Commissaire	503
			Commissaire du Roi	504
			Conseiller	505
			Conseiller du Roi	506
			Lieutenant	507
			Secrétaire	508
			Secrétaire du Roi	509
			Government	
			Old Regime	510
			National	511
			Minister	512
			Conseiller d'état	513
			Secrétaire d'état	514
			Affaires étrangers	515
			Lieutenant Général de police	516
			Maître des requêtes	517
			Intermediate	520
			Gouverneur	521
			Intendant	523

Column	Size Field	Category	Name	Code
			Subdélegué	524
			Secretary of Intendant	525
			Election	526
			Elu	527
			Président	528
			Lieutenant	529
			Agent/Conseiller	530
			Administrateur	534
			Municipal	540
			Maire	541
			Echevin	542
			Greffier	543
			Huissier	544
			Maire	550
			Revolution	580
			National (député)	581
			Député suppléant	589
			Intermediate	570
			Département	571
			Président	582
			Administrateur	583
			Agent	584
			District	585
			Président	586
			Administrateur	587
			Membre	588
			Municipal	590
			Maire	591
			Agent	592
			Secrétaire/Greffier	593
			Officier	594
			Legal System	600
			Old Regime	
			General	601
			Avocat	602
			Notaire	603
			Prèsident	604
			Procureur	605
			Parlement	606
			Premier Président	607
			Président à Mortier	608
			Conseiller au	609
			Procureur Général	610
			Avocat Général	611
			Avocat en parl.	612
			Avocat au parl.	613
			Notaire	614
			Greffier	615

Column	Size Field	Category	Name	Code
			Huissier	616
			Procureur en parl.	617
			Procureur au parl.	618
			Présidial	620
			Président	621
			Lieutenant	623
			Bailliage/Sénéchaussée	630
			Bailli	631
			Lieutenant du Roi	632
			(=assesseur)	
			Procureur du Roi	633
			Avocat du Roi	634
			Conseiller	635
			Prévôté	640
			Prévôt	641
			Vignier (Provence)	642
			Vicomte	643
			(Normandie)	
			Châtelain	644
			Lieutenant	645
			Seigneurial Court	650
			Président	651
			Procureur Fiscal	652
			Directoire	655
			Special Jurisdictions	660
			Maîtrise Eaux et	661
			Forêts	
			Grueries	662
			Chambre de Trésor	663
			Bureau de Finance	664
			Bureau d' Election	665
			Hôtel des Monnaies	666
			Admiralty	667
			Tribunal Consulaire	668
			Prévôt des	669
			Maréchaux	
			Grand Conseil	670
			Cour des Comptes	671
			Cour des Aides	672
			Cour des Monnaies	673
			Châtelet	675
			Revolution	680
			National	681
			Avoué au Tribunal	682

Column	Size Field	Category	Name	Code
			Département	683
			Greffier	684
			District	685
			Premier Juge	686
			Procureur	687
			Juge	688
			Président	689
			Municipal	690
			Procureur/Com.	691
			Juge de paix	692
			Greffier	693
			General	
			Greffier	696
			Huissier	697
			Finance	700
			Receveur	701
			Receveur Général	702
			Receveur Particulier	703
			Receveur with jurisdiction	705
			Trésorier	706
			Trésorier Général	712
			Trésorier de France	713
			Trésorier with jurisdiction	715
			Fermier Général	717
			Chef	720
			Lieutenant	721
			Commis	722
			Administration	723
			Contrôlleur	724
			Directeur Général	725
			Directeur	726
			Entrepreneur (tabac)	728
			Inspecteur	730
			Preposé	732
			Caissier	733
			Régisseur	734
			Surnuméraire	736
			Quartier Maître	738
			Maître des comptes	745
			Agent de Change	748

Column	Size Field	Category	Name	Code
			Services	800
			Postes	801
			Commis	802
			Diligences	803
			Contrôlleur	804
			Directeur	805
			Facteur	806
			Inspecteur	807
			Receveur	808
			Secrétaire	809
			Maître	810
			Messagerie	820
			Directeur	821
			Navigation	830
			Commis	831
			Contrôlleur	832
			Directeur	833
			Inspecteur	834
			Commandant/port	835
			Ponts & Chaussées	840
			Commis	841
			Contrôlleur	842
			Directeur	843
			Inspecteur	844
			Inspecteur Général	845
			Regulation Industry & Commerce	850
			Commis	851
			Contrôlleur	852
			Directeur	853
			Inspecteur	856
			Other	
			Directeur canal Languedoc	891
			Concierge	892
			Portier	894
			Officier	900
18–19	2	Former	Ancien	01
			Ci-Devant	02
20-21	2	Length Subscription	3 months	03
			6 months	06
			9 months	09
			1 year	12

Column	Size Field	Category	Name	Code
			other	44
			unknown	00
22–23	2	Cost Subscription	9 livres	09
			10 livres	10
			18 livres	18
			33 livres	33
			x livres	x
			free	55
			unknown	00
24–25	2	Former list	yes	11
			no	02
			uncertain	03

BIBLIOGRAPHY

PRIMARY SOURCES

Manuscript Sources

Archives Nationales

D XXlXb dr. 353, pe. 20	report of visit to the offices of the *AR* made 1 August by commissaire of the section Théâtre français
T546	receipts, records and papers of the *AR*
T*546¹	account book of the *Année Littéraire*
T*546²	register of subscribers to *AR*, August–October 1790
T*546³	register of subscribers to *AR*, February 1791
T*546⁴	register of accounts of the *AR*
T*546⁵	alphabetical register of subscribers to *AR*, summer 1791
V¹ 549-552	librairie, 1789

Minutier Central

LXIV⁴⁹⁵	contract founding the *AR*, 17 May 1790

Archives de la Préfecture de Police

AA206, 405-418	report of visit of police to offices of *AR* on 23 July 1791, seizure of papers, interrogation of employees, arrest and interrogation of Madame Fréron; 23 July–17 November 1791

Printed Sources

Delisle de Sales, *Essai sur le journalisme depuis 1735 jusqu'à l'an 1800* (Paris, 1811; Slatkine reprint, Geneva, 1971).

Expilly, J.-J., *Dictionnaire Géographique, Historique et Politique des Gaules et de la France* (Paris, 6 vols., 1762-70; Krauss reprint, 1978).

Greig, J.Y.T., ed., *The Letters of David Hume* (Oxford, 2 vols., 1932).

Marmontel, *Mémoires de Marmontel*, ed. Maurice Tourneux (Paris, 3 vols., 1891; Slatkine reprint, 1967).

Pius VI, *Traduction fidèle et littérale du Bref du Pape à Monseigneur l'Archevêque de Sens* (Paris, 1791), BN Ld[4] .3375.

———, *Bref du Pape Pie VI, à S.E.M. le Cardinal de la Rochefoucault, M. l'Archevêque d'Aix et les autres Archevêques et Evêques de l'Assemblée Nationale au Sujet de la Constitution Civile du Clergé, décrétée par l'Assemblée Nationale* (Paris, 1791), BN 8° Ld[3] 547(17).

———, *Bref du Pape aux Cardinaux, Archevêques, Evêques, au Clergé et au Peuple de France* (Paris, 1791), BN 8° Ld[3] 547(20).

Rivarol, *Le Petit dictionnaire de nos grands hommes* (Paris, 1808; first edition 1788; republished Slatkine, Geneva, 1968).

Royou, M.F., "Avis aux souscripteurs du journal intitulé L'Ami du Roi des françois, de l'ordre et sur-tout de la vérité," BN Lc² 398.

SECONDARY SOURCES

Manuals and Reference Works

Brunot, F., *Histoire de la langue française* (Paris, 13 vols, 1913-1953).

Cabourdin, Guy and Viard, Georges, *Lexique historique de la France d'Ancien Régime* (Paris, 1978).

Caron, Pierre, *Manuel pratique pour l'étude de la Révolution française* (Paris, 1947).

Godechot, Jacques, *Les Institutions de la France sous la Révolution et l'Empire* (Paris, 1968).

———, *Les Révolutions, 1770-1799* (Paris, 1965).

Goubert, P., *The Ancien Régime: French Society, 1600-1750* trans. Steve Cox (New York, 1973).

———, *L'Ancien Régime: Les Pouvoirs* (Paris, 1973).

Jones, C., *The Longman Companion to the French Revolution* (London, 1988).

Labrousse, E., and Léon, P., eds., *Histoire économique et sociale de la France*, vol. II (Paris, 1970).

Lefebvre, Georges, *The French Revolution*, trans. E.M. Evanson, J.H. Stewart and J. Friguglietti (London and New York, 2 vols., 1962-64).

Marion, Marcel, *Dictionnaire des Institutions de la France aux XVIIe et XVIIIe siècles* (Paris, 1923; 1969).

Michaud M., ed., *Biographie Universelle Ancienne et Moderne* (Paris, 45 vols., 1854-65; reprinted Droz, 1966-70).

Mirot, A., *Manuel de géographie historique de la France* (Paris, second ed., 2 vols., 1950).

Mousnier, R., *The Institutions of France under the Absolute Monarchy, 1598-1789*, trans. Brian Pearce and Arthur Goldhammer (Chicago, 2 vols., 1979-84).

Scott, S.F., and Rothaus, B., eds., *Historical Dictionary of the French Revolution* (Westport, 2 vols., 1985).

Soboul, Albert, *La Civilisation et la Révolution française* (Paris, 3 vols., 1970-83).

Tuetey, A., *Répértoire général des sources manuscrites de l'histoire de Paris pendant la Révolution française* (Paris, 11 vols., 1890-1914).

Books and Articles

Aimé-Azam, D., "Le Ministère des Affaires Etrangères à la fin de l'Ancien Régime," *Cahiers de la presse* 1 (1938): 428-38.

Applewhite, H.B., and Levy, D.G., "Women, Democracy and Revolution in Paris, 1789-1794," in S.I. Spencer, ed.,

French Women and the Age of Enlightenment (Bloomington, 1984): 64-79.

———, "Women and Political Revolution in Paris," in R. Bridenthal, C. Koonz and S. Stuard, eds., *Becoming Visible: Women in European History* (Boston, 1987): 279-306.

———, "Ceremonial Dimensions of Citizenship: Women and Oathtaking in Revolutionary Paris," in *Proceedings of the Fifth George Rudé Seminar in French History.* (Wellington, New Zealand, 1986).

Aulard, Alphonse, *The French Revolution: A Political History, 1789-1804,* trans. B. Miall (New York, 4 vols., 1965).

———, *Christianity and the French Revolution,* trans. Lady U. Frazer (Boston, 1927).

Bachman, A., *Censorship in France from 1715 to 1750: Voltaire's Opposition* (New York, Burt Franklin, 1974; 1934).

Balcou, J., *Fréron contre les philosophes* (Geneva, 1975).

Beik, Paul H., *The French Revolution Seen from the Right: Social Theories in Motion, 1789-1799, Transactions of the American Philosophical Society* New Series, Vol. 46, Pt. 1 (1956); reprinted Howard Fertig, New York, 1970.

Belin, J.P., *Le Commerce des livres prohibés à Paris de 1750 à 1789* (New York, Burt Franklin, n.d.; 1913).

Bellanger, C., et al., *Histoire générale de la presse française* (Paris, 5 vols., 1969-76).

Bertaud, J.-P., *Les Amis du Roi: Journaux et journalistes royalistes en France de 1789 à 1792* (Paris, 1984).

Birn, R., *Pierre Rousseau and the Philosophes of Bouillon, VS* 29 (1964).

———, "The Profits of Ideas: *Privilèges en librairie* in Eighteenth-Century France," *Eighteenth-Century Studies,* 4 (1971): 131-68.

Blanc-Rouquette, M.T., *La Presse et l'information à Toulouse des origines à 1789* (Toulouse, 1967).

Bluche, F., and Solnon, J.-F., *La Véritable hiérarchie de l'ancienne France: Le Tarif de la première capitation: 1695* (Geneva, 1983).

Bollème, G., et al., *Livre et société dans la France du XVIIIe siècle* (Paris and La Haye, 2 vols., 1965-70).

Bonnet, J.C., ed., *La Mort de Marat* (Paris, 1986).

Bosher, John F., *French Finances, 1770-1795: From Business to Bureaucracy* (Cambridge, 1970).

Botein, S., Censer, J.R., and Ritvo, H.,"The Periodical Press in Eighteenth-Century English and French Society: A Cross-Cultural Approach," in *Comparative Studies in Society and History* 23 (1981): 464-90.

Burke, Peter, *Popular Culture in Early Modern Europe* (New York, 1981).

Censer, J.R., *Prelude to Power: The Parisian Radical Press, 1789-1791* (Baltimore, 1976).

———, and Popkin, J., eds., *Press and Politics in Pre-Revolutionary France* (Berkeley, 1987).

Cerf, M., "La Censure royale à la fin du XVIIIe siècle," *Communications* 9 (1967): 2-28.

Chartier, R., Compère, M.M., and Julia, D., *L'Education en France du XVIe au XVIIIe siècle* (Paris, 1976).

Chaussinand-Nogaret, G., *The French Nobility in the Eighteenth Century: From Feudalism to Enlightenment*, trans. W. Doyle (Cambridge, 1985; 1976).

Chisick, H., *The Limits of Reform in the Enlightenment: Attitudes toward the Education of the Lower Classes in Eighteenth-Century France* (Princeton, 1981).

———, "School Attendance, Literacy and Acculturation: *Petites écoles* and Popular Education in Eighteenth-Century France," *Europa* 3 (1979-80): 185-220.

Cobban, A., *The Social Interpretation of the French Revolution* (Cambridge, 1964).

Darnton, R., *The Great Cat Massacre and Other Episodes in French Cultural History* (New York, 1984).

———, *The Literary Underground of the Old Regime* (Cambridge, Mass., 1982).

———, *The Business of Enlightenment: A Publishing History of the Encyclopédie* (Cambridge, Mass., 1979).

————, and Roche, D., eds., *Revolution in Print: The Press in France, 1775-1800* (Berkeley, 1989).

Daumard, A., "Une référence pour l'étude des sociétés urbaines en France aux XVIIIe et XIXe siècles: Projet de code socio-professionel," *RHMC* 10 (1963): 185-210.

————, and Furet, F., *Structures et relations sociales à Paris au milieu du XVIIIe siècle. Cahiers des Annales* no. 18 (Paris, 1961).

Dorigny, M., "Honnêtes Gens: L'Expression dans la presse girondine, juin–septembre 1792," in A. Geffroy, J. Guilhaumou, et al., *Dictionnaire des usages socio-politiques (1770-1815)*, fasc. 1, *Désignants socio-politiques* (Paris, 1985).

Ducchini, H., "Regard sur la littérature pamphlétaire en France au XVIIe siècle," *RH* 260 (1978): 113-39.

Duhet, Paule-Marie, *Les Femmes et la Révolution, 1789-94* (Paris, 1977).

Dupaquier, J., "Problèmes de la codification socio-profes-sionnelle," in E. Labrousse, *L'Histoire sociale: sources et méthodes* (Paris, 1967): 157-67.

Echeverria, D., *The Maupeou Revolution: A Study in the History of Libertarianism, France; 1770-1774* (Baton Rouge and London, 1985).

Edelstein, M., *La Feuille villageoise: Communication et moder-nisation dans les régions rurales pendant la Révolution* (Paris, 1977).

————, "Vers une sociologie électorale de la Révolution fran-çaise," *RHMC* 22 (1975): 508-29.

Egret, J., *La Révolution des Notables: Mounier et les Monarchiens, 1789* (Paris, 1950).

Ehrard, J., and Roger, J., "Deux périodiques françaises du 18é siècle: le *Journal des Savants* et les *Mémoires de Trévoux*: Essai d'une étude quantitative," in *Livre et Société* 1: 33-59.

Eisenstein, E., *The Printing Press as an Agent of Cultural Change: Communications and Cultural Transformations in Early-Mod-ern Europe* (Cambridge, 2 vols., 1979).

Fajn, M., *The Journal des hommes libres de tous les pays, 1792-1800* (The Hague and Paris, 1975).

———, "The Circulation of the Press during the French Revolution: the case of R.F. Lebois' *L'Ami du Peuple* and the Royalist *Gazette française*," *English Historical Review* 87 (1972): 100-105.

———, "La Diffusion de la presse révolutionnaire dans le Lot, le Tarn et l'Aveyron, sous la Convention et le Directoire," *Annales du Midi* 82 (1971): 299-314.

Feyel, G., "La Presse provinciale au XVIIIe siècle: géographie d'un réseau," *RH* 272 (1984): 353-74.

———, "Réimpressions et diffusion de la *Gazette* dans les provinces: 1631-1752," in P. Rétat, ed., *Le Journalisme d'Ancien régime*, 69-86.

Fogel, M., "Le Système d'information ritualisée de l'absolutisme français," in *Le Journalisme d'Ancien régime*, 142-50.

Ford, F., *Robe and Sword: The Regrouping of the French Aristocracy after Louis XIV* (Cambridge, Mass., 1953).

Forster, R., *The Nobility of Toulouse in the Eighteenth Century: A Social and Economic Study* (Baltimore, 1960).

———, *The House of Saulx-Tavannes: Versailles and Burgundy, 1700-1830* (Baltimore, 1971).

Furet, F., "La 'Librairie' du royaume de France au 18e siècle," in *Livre et société* 1: 3-32.

———, and Richet, D., *La Révolution française* (Paris, 1973).

Gérard, R., *Un Journal de province sous la Révolution: Le "Journal de Marseille" de Ferréol Beaugeard (1781-1797)* (Paris, 1964).

Gilchrist, J., and Murray, W.J., *The Press in the French Revolution* (London, 1971).

Godechot, J., *The Counter-Revolution, Doctrine and Action: 1789-1804*, trans. Salvator Attanasio (London, 1972).

Gossman, L., *Medievalism and the Ideologies of the Enlightenment: The World and Work of La Curne de Sainte-Palaye* (Baltimore, 1968).

Gough, H., *The Newspaper Press in the French Revolution* (Chicago, 1988).

———, "Les Jacobins et la presse: *Le Journal de la Montagne* (juin 1793–brumaire an II)," in A. Soboul, ed., *Actes du Colloque Girondins et Montagnards (Sorbonne, 14 décembre, 1975)* (Paris, 1980).

Greer, D., *The Incidence of the Terror in the French Revolution: A Statistical Interpretation* (Cambridge, Mass., 1935; Peter Smith, 1966).

———, *The Incidence of the Emigration during the French Revolution* (Cambridge, Mass., 1951; Peter Smith, 1966).

Hatin, E., *Histoire politique et littéraire de la presse en France* (Paris, 8 vols., 1859-61).

Hayden, J.M., "The Uses of Political Pamphlets: The Example of 1614-15 in France," *Canadian Journal of History* 21 (1986): 143-65.

Hermann-Mascard, N., *La Censure des livres à Paris à la fin de l'ancien régime: 1750-1789* (Paris, 1968).

Higonnet, P.L.R., *Class, Ideology and the Rights of Nobles during the French Revolution* (Oxford, 1981).

Hufton, O., *The Poor of Eighteenth-Century France, 1750-1789* (Oxford, 1974).

Hunt, Lynn, *Politics, Culture and Class in the French Revolution* (Berkeley and Los Angeles, 1984).

———, "The Political Geography of Revolutionary France," *Journal of Interdisciplinary History* 14 (1984): 535-59.

Jouhaud, C., *Mazarinades—La Fronde des mots* (Paris, 1985).

Kates, G., *The Cercle Social, the Girondins and the French Revolution* (Princeton, 1985).

Kennedy, M.L., "The Jacobin Clubs and the Press: Phase Two," *FHS* 13 (1984): 474-99.

———, *The Jacobin Clubs in the French Revolution: The First Years* (Princeton, 1982).

Klaits, J., *Printed Propaganda Under Louis XIV: Absolute Monarchy and Public Opinion* (Princeton, 1976).

Labrosse, C., and Rétat, P., *L'Instrument périodique: La fonction de la presse au XVIIIe siècle* (Lyon, 1985).

Langlois, C., and Tackett, T., "A l'Epreuve de la Révolution

(1770-1830)," in F. Lebrun, ed., *Histoire des Catholiques en France du XVe siècle à nos jours* (Toulouse, 1980).

Latreille, A., *L'Eglise catholique et la Révolution française* (Paris, 2 vols., 1970).

Le Goff, T.J.A., and Sutherland, D.M.G., "The Social Origins of Counter-Revolution in Western France," in *P & P* 99 (1982): 65-87.

——, "The Revolution and the Rural Community in Eighteenth-Century Brittany," in D. Johnson, ed., *French Society and the Revolution* (Cambridge, 1976): 29-52.

Le Mée, R., "Population agglomérée, population éparse au début du XIXe siècle," *Annales de démographie historique* (1971): 455-509.

Levy, Darlene Gay, *The Ideas and Careers of Simon-Nicolas-Henri Linguet: A Study in Eighteenth-Century French Politics* (Urbana, 1980).

Lough, J., *Writer and Public in France from the Middle Ages to the Present Day* (Oxford, 1978).

——, *Essays on the Encyclopédie of Diderot and d'Alembert* (London, 1968).

——, *An Introduction to Eighteenth-Century France* (London, 1960).

McManners, J., *The French Revolution and the Church* (London, 1969).

Martin, H.-J., and Chartier, R., eds., *Histoire de l'édition française*, vol. II, *Le Livre triomphant: 1660-1830* (Paris, 1984).

Maspero-Clerc, H., *Un Journaliste contre-révolutionnaire: Jean-Gabriel Peltier (1760-1825)* (Paris, 1973).

Mathiez, A., *The French Revolution*, trans. C. A. Phillips (London, n.d.).

——, "La Presse subventionnée de l'an II," *Annales Révolutionnaires*, 1918: 112-13.

Maza, S., *Servants and Masters in Eighteenth-Century France: The Uses of Loyalty* (Princeton, 1983).

Mitchell, H., "The Vendée and Counterrevolution: A Review Essay," *FHS* 5 (1968): 405-429.

——, *The Underground War Against Revolutionary France: the Missions of William Wickham, 1794-1800* (Oxford, 1965).

——, "Resistance to the Revolution in Western France," in *French Society and the Revolution*: 248-87.

Moreau, C., *Bibliographie des Mazarinades* (Paris, 3 vols., 1850-51).

Mornet, D., *Les Origines intellectuelles de la Révolution française* (Paris, 6th edition, 1967).

——, "L'Intérêt historique des journaux littéraires et la diffusion du *Mercure de France*," *Bulletin de la Société d'histoire moderne* 22 (April 1910): 119-22.

Moulinas, R., *L'Imprimerie, la librairie et la presse à Avignon au XVIIIe siècle* (Grenoble, 1974).

——, "Les Journaux publiés à Avignon et leur diffusion en France jusqu'en 1768," *Provence Historique* 18 (1968): 121-38.

——, "Du Rôle de la poste royale comme moyen de contrôle financier sur la diffusion des gazettes en France au XVIIIe siècle," in L. Bescond et al., *Modèles et moyens de la réflexion politique au XVIIIe siècle. Actes du Colloque organisé par l'Université lilloise des Lettres, Sciences Humaines et Arts, du 16 au 19 octobre 1973* (Lille, 3 vols., 1977-79), I: 383-96.

Mousnier, R., *La Stratification sociale à Paris aux XVIIe et XVIIIe siècles: L'Echantillon de 1634, 1635, 1636* (Paris, 1975).

Murray, W.J., *The Right-Wing Press in the French Revolution: 1789-1792* (Exeter, 1986).

O'Keefe, C.B., *Contemporary Reactions to the Enlightenment (1728-1762): A Study of Three Critical Journals: The Jesuit Journal de Trévoux, the Jansenist Nouvelles Ecclésiastiques and the Secular Journal des Savants* (Geneva and Paris, 1974).

Ozouf, Mona, *La Fête révolutionnaire: 1789-1799* (Paris, 1976).

Pappas, J.N., *Berthier, the Journal de Trévoux and the Philosophes* VS 3 (1957).

Payne, H.C., *The Philosophes and the People* (Yale, 1976).

Popkin, J., *The Right-Wing Press in France, 1792-1800* (Chapel Hill, 1980).

————, "Les Abonnés des journaux nantais en 1807," *Annales de Bretagne* 91 (1984): 385-91.

————, "The *Gazette de Leyde* under Louis XVI," in *Press and Politics in Pre-Revolutionary France* (see Censer, J.R.).

Pottinger, D.T., *The French Book Trade in the Ancien Régime, 1500-1791* (Harvard, 1951).

Rétat, Pierre, "Forme et discours d'un journal révolution-naire: *Les Révolutions de Paris* en 1789," in Labrosse and Rétat, *L'Instrument périodique.*

————, ed., *L'Attentat de Damiens: Le discours sur l'événement* (Paris and Lyon, 1979).

————, ed. *Le journalisme d'Ancien régime: Questions et propositions* (Lyon, 1982).

————, and Sgard, J., eds., *Presse et histoire au XVIIIe siècle: L'année 1734* (Paris, 1978).

Roberts, J.M., *The French Revolution* (Oxford, 1978).

Roche, D., *Le siècle des lumières en province: Académies et académiciens provinciaux, 1680-1789* (Paris and La Haye, Mouton, 2 vols., 1978).

Rose, R.B., *The Enragés: Socialists of the French Revolution?* (Melbourne, 1965).

Rudé, G., *The Crowd in the French Revolution* (Oxford, 1967).

————, "Prices, Wages and the Popular Movement in Paris during the French Revolution," in *Paris and London in the Eighteenth Century: Studies in Popular Protest* (Bungay, 1970).

Salvemini, G., *The French Revolution*, trans. I.M. Rawson (London, 1954).

Seguin, J.P., *L'Information en France avant la périodique: 517 canards imprimés entre 1529 et 1631* (Paris, 1964).

————, *L'Information en France de Louis XII à Henri II* (Geneva, 1961).

Sgard, J., ed., *Dictionnaire des journalistes* (Grenoble, 1976).

————, *Bibliographie de la presse classique: 1600-1789* (Geneva, Slatkine, 1984).

Shapiro, G., Markoff, J., and Weitman, S.R., "Quantitative

Studies of the French Revolution," *History and Theory* 12 (1973): 163-91.

Siebert, F.S., *Freedom of the Press in England 1476-1776: The Rise and Decline of Government Control* (Urbana, 1952).

Soboul, A., "Personnel sectionnaire et personnel babouviste," in M. Dommanget et al., *Babeuf et les problèmes du babouvisme: Colloque international de Stockholm, 21 août 1960* (Paris, 1963): 107-31.

Solomon, H.M., *Public Welfare, Science and Propaganda in Seventeenth Century France: The Innovations of Théophraste Renaudot* (Princeton, 1972).

Stone L., "Literacy and Education in England, 1640–1900," *P & P* 42 (1969): 69-139.

Sydenham, M.J., *The French Revolution* (London, 1965).

Thompson, J.M., *The French Revolution* (Oxford, 1947).

Thompson, L.S., *A Bibliography of French Revolutionary Pamphlets in Microfiche* (New York, 1974).

Thore, P.H., "Essai de classification des catégories sociales à l' intérieur du tiers état de Toulouse," in the *Actes du 78e Congrès national des Sociétés Savantes: Toulouse 1953* (Paris, 1954): 149-65.

Trevedy, J., *Fréron et sa famille* (Saint Brieuc, 1889).

Tucoo-Chala, Suzanne, *Charles-Joseph Panckoucke et la librairie française, 1736-1789*, (Pau and Paris, 1977).

Vaillé, E., *Histoire générale des postes françaises* (Paris, 6 vols., 1947-53).

Vovelle, Michel, *La Chute de la monarchie: 1787-1792* (Paris, 1972).

Wade, I.O., *The Clandestine Organization and Diffusion of Philosophic Ideas in France from 1700 to 1750* (Princeton, 1938).

Walsh, J.E., ed., *Mazarinades: A Catalogue of the Collection of Seventeenth-Century French Civil War Tracts in the Houghton Library Harvard University* (Boston, 1976).

Wartelle, F., "Honnêtes gens: La Dénomination comme enjeu des luttes politiques (1795-1797)," in Geffroy, Guilhaumou, et al., *Dictionnaire des usages socio-politiques (1770-1815)*.

Wilson, A., *Diderot* (Oxford, 1972).

Index

www.ingramcontent.com/pod-product-compliance
Lightning Source LLC
Chambersburg PA
CBHW030810100426
42814CB00002B/68